Mircea A. Tamas

THE QUEST FOR THE CENTER

ROSE-CROSS BOOKS

2016

www.rose-crossbooks.com

This first edition is published by **Rose-Cross Books**
TORONTO

Cover design by *Imre Szekely*

Tamas, Mircea A. (Mircea Alexandru), 1949-, author
    The quest for the center : René Guénon and the
traditional spirit / Mircea A. Tamas.

ISBN 978-0-9865872-6-9 (paperback)

    1. Guénon, René. 2. Metaphysics. 3. Symbolism.
4. Civilization, Subterranean. 5. Geographical myths.
I. Title.

B2430.G84T338 2016   194   C2016-901138-0

TABLE OF CONTENTS

I

THE CENTER AND THE QUEST

The first Crusade was considered a *peregrinatio* and its partakers *peregrini*,[1] because as any pilgrimage it was a quest for the center.[2] But not all the pilgrims were fully conscious about the meaning of their enterprise and even though apparently they were all energized by the love for God, in fact a few of them could tame or ignore the human factor and worldly distraction. Dante stated: "Some pilgrims were passing along a road, which runs almost through the center of the city where that most gracious lady was born, lived and died. These pilgrims, it seemed to me, were very pensive as they went their way; and so, thinking about them, I said to myself: 'These people seem to be journeying from far away, and I do not think that they have ever even heard about my lady; they know nothing about her, indeed their thoughts are on quite other things than those that

---

[1] The appellation *crucesignatus*, "signed by the cross," started to be used only in the 12th Century, coexisting with that of *peregrinus*. "For Suger's generation, pilgrimages and crusades were no longer distinct" (Otto von Simson, *The Gothic Cathedral*, Harper Torchbooks, 1956, p. 79).

[2] In accord with some traditional data, the first pilgrims were the Three Kings or Magi, the center being Christ; the Three Magi were painted as pilgrims on special vessels (*ampulla*, diminutive for *amphora*), which were sold to the pilgrims at the holy places; but Christ himself was represented as a pilgrim with the shell and the pouch. Pseudo-Turpin (*Historia Karoli Magni et Rotholandi*) describes Charlemagne as the first pilgrim; and there is a tradition meant to establish St.-Denis as a secondary center connected to Jerusalem, in which Charlemagne brought to St.-Denis relics from his pilgrimage to Jerusalem (Simson 84-85). Unfortunately, today, St.-Denis is a bazaar, France rejecting with suspicious enthusiasm the sacred symbolism of St.-Denis.

are around them here; perhaps they are thinking of their friends at home."'[1] Dante's "gracious lady" was not so much Beatrice, but *Madonna Intelligenza*, the target of the initiatory pilgrimage. The fact that the pilgrims passed along the sacred road, without knowing or thinking of her, referred to "the many" who followed the ritual of this holy journey without getting profoundly involved, but offering just a superficial participation.[2] In fairy tales and other initiatory writings, if the neophyte looks back and remembers his family (the world), he is lost and fails initiation. Dante suggested that many pilgrims thought not of the *Madonna*, but of home and friends, therefore dooming themselves to failure.

Sure, even in the times of the Crusades, the medieval society was not an "ideal" one, yet it allowed a development of spirituality and, more importantly, it presented the needed support for the initiatory process, illustrated by the multiple pilgrimages, the Crusades, the Troubadours' literature, the building of the cathedrals, etc.

The Latin word *peregrinus*, from which *pilgrim* derived, Guénon wrote,[3] signifies at the same time "traveler" and "stranger," both having initiatory meanings and being used in *Compagnonage*: the pilgrim, like the *companion*, was a "stranger" embarked on a spiritual journey, and Masonry (even the modern one) used the name "journey" for the symbolic initiatory trials. However, in various traditions, the initiatory degrees were often described as parts of a journey (on land or sea) and the voyage sometimes became a warlike one (the Crusades, the Trojan war); in religious terms, even terrestrial life was a journey, a pilgrimage aiming at the Earthly Paradise.

---

[1] *Vita Nuova*, Penguin Books, 1969, XL, p. 96.

[2] Any rite in which the individual does not participate with his entire being is a wasted one. Moreover, an initiatory realization implies a theoretical training and an indispensable theoretical knowledge (see René Guénon's letter of 1918, L'Age D'Or, *René Guénon*, Pardès, 1987, p. 99). In the case of the exoteric rites, the training is more "moral" and sometimes not even so.

[3] René Guénon, *Études sur la Franc-Maçonnerie et la Compagnonnage*, Éd. Traditionnelles, 1980, I, pp. 52 ff.

The initiates are "noble voyagers," hiding in the crowd of common travelers. The initiates' pilgrimage, Guénon showed, has to be related to the "royal art" and the "royal caste" (*Kshatriya*), and to Hermeticism, with Saint John corresponding to metaphysics and pure intellectuality and Saint Jacob to the "traditional sciences"; everything that was transmitted using the pilgrimage belonged to this "intermediary" domain. It is interesting that the pilgrims' insignias were the staff and the shell, corresponding to *Purusha* and *Prakriti* of the Hindu tradition represented by *vajra* (lightning, scepter) and *shankha* (shell, in the Tibetan tradition the shell being replaced by the ritual bell, *dilbu*).[1] The pilgrim is a traveler through the Cosmos; he is the Mediator, the Man who reunites Heaven and Earth due to this spiritual voyage. All the pilgrims who went to Compostela, following "Saint Jacob's way," carried the shell, illustrating, among other meanings, the pilgrim's status of vassalage with respect to God.[2]

Ananda K. Coomaraswamy specified that *diksha*, though it is a word with not many derivations, has one which means "a long time initiate" (in pali, *chira-dikkhita*), an expression equivalent to *chira-pabbâjita*, "a long time consecrated pilgrim"; the primal meaning of *pabbajati* (in Sanskrit, *pravrajati*) is "to go into exile," "to become a stranger," signifying the abandonment

---

[1] A lama has the *vajra* in his right hand and the *dilbu* in his left hand. The bell, like the shell, hides the primordial sound. The Tarot contains the pair staff – cup.

[2] Vassalage in medieval times had a much deeper significance than the one the historians suggest, who considered it a humiliating state of servitude. Regarding the pilgrims, we would like to quote here the description given by Strassburg in his *Tristan*: "They [two pilgrims] were of godly aspect, advanced in days and years, hairy and bearded, as God's true children and pilgrims often are. Those wayfarers wore cloaks of linen and such other clothing as is appropriate to pilgrims, and on the outside of their clothes there were sewn-on sea-shells and many other tokens from distant lands. Each bore a staff in his hand. Their head and leg-covering was well suited to their kind. These servants of God wore round their thighs linen hose trussed close to the leg and reaching down within a hand's breadth of their ankles. Feet and ankles were bare to the obstacles under foot" (Gottfried von Strassburg, *Tristan*, Penguin Books, 1967, p. 75).

of the domestic life to become a "pilgrim" without a roof, reaching the state of "strangeness."[1] There is at the same time the state of "travelling" attached to *peregrinus*, and the initiates were called, in Antiquity and Middle Ages, "noble travelers."[2] As Guénon affirmed, it seems that "noble" referred not to any type of initiation but to one regarding *Kshatriya*, that is, a royal initiation or what we could call "royal art."[3] And to this Art belong the various vestiges transmitted to the present days, like the fairy tales, the legends, the *chansons de geste*, the epopees, and the stories of the Holy Grail, where an important role is played by the state of servitude.[4]

---

[1] Originally, the pilgrimage meant "to be exiled into the wilderness" (*peregrinatio ascetia*), like in the case of Râma, but afterwards it became a *peregrinatio ad loca sancta*.

[2] Guénon, *Franc-Maçonnerie*, I, pp. 52, 57.

[3] Guénon, *Franc-Maçonnerie*, I, p. 59.

[4] The word *geste* comes from the Latin *gero*, meaning initially "to bear" (hence gestation, "to carry an embryo"); from *gero* derived the Latin words *gesta* and *gestus*. The English *gesture* and the archaic *geste* (signifying "a heroic deed") are close related and they must be, since both belong to what René Guénon called a "theory of the gesture" (René Guénon, *Aperçus sur l'initiation*, Éd. Traditionnelles, 1992, p. 116). This theory has nothing to do with the modern "gesticulation," but illustrates the overwhelming importance of the gesture in the initiatory process. As Guénon said, the essential elements of any initiation are the traditional (sacred) rites and the symbols; both have a "non-human" origin and are "vehicles" for the spiritual influences. A rite contains an assembly of symbols, but these symbols are "in action" or "activated," which explains the importance of the gesture (*ibid.* pp. 115, 119). In the Hindu tradition, the gestures used in various rites are called *mudrâs*, and they constitute, Guénon said, a genuine language of movements and attitudes; similarly, the *grips*, used by the initiatory organizations, are a particular case of the *mudrâs* (*ibid.* p. 119). Moreover, we could accept a "gesture of chanting" (sacred formulas, *mantras*) and "kissing" (in both cases the *prâna*, as support of the spiritual influence, is transmitted) (also, the Christian gesture of "kissing the cross" is only superficially a sign of adoration, because, in fact, represents an Act of Truth); a "gesture of drawing," where we should include not only the *yantras* and *mandalas*, the *tracing board* and the *pentagram* (as an uninterrupted line), but also the sacred calligraphy; and a "gesture of inhaling," to which the theory of the perfumes is related (*ibid.* pp. 116-118).

Ibn 'Arabî wrote: "During the pilgrimage, the servant is dominated by the station of servitude, *Maqâm al'-ubûdiyya*, obeying all the restrictions through which the wisdom escapes the rational. It is, somehow, a work of pure adoration, which cannot be accomplished but with the qualifications of a vassal." And: "Allâh calls the pilgrims only to test them and to make them see the one faithful to the status of vassalage. Therefore most of the pilgrimage's rules are related to worshiping, without a rational cause or meaning."[1]

Mohyiddin Ibn 'Arabî's words indicate the significance of pilgrimage in Islam. At least theoretically, every Muslim should complete the pilgrimage's rites, which makes it an exoteric ritual, even though it is a reflection of an initiatory process, representing a voyage to the Center of the World, a voyage that each one, proportional to his capability, assimilated and was transformed by accordingly. In the same way, during the pilgrimage of the medieval voyagers to Compostela or to Jerusalem, besides the exoteric crowd, there were the chosen ones for whom the journey was a "materialization" of an inner, spiritual voyage. For the Islamic tradition the first pilgrim was Adam who completed forty times the pilgrimage from India to Mecca.[2] The Islamic pilgrimage, the *hajj*, has two parts: *umra* or "the lesser pilgrimage," which could be completed anytime and contains: the initial consecration (*ihrâm*), the rite of circumambulation around the Kaaba (*tawâf*), followed by a prayer at Abraham's station (*Maqâm Ibrâhîm*) and the *sa'y* (the race between the two rocks Safâ and Marwa)[3]; the greater pilgrimage, the *hajj*, occurs at a specific time of the year, in places different from Mecca, and is composed of *wuqûf* ("the halt" of the pilgrims at the foot of the merciful mountain, Jabal

---

[1] For Ibn 'Arabî, among the natural kingdoms, the mineral is the one which possesses the greatest knowledge through Allâh and the greatest servitude to Allâh, and we have here another essential reason for the importance of the black stone and of the Rock.

[2] Michel Vâlsan, *Inde et Arabie*, Études Traditionnelles, no. 396-397, 1966.

[3] Each of these rites corresponds to initiatory rites from various traditions and has an esoteric significance, which deserves total attention.

ar-Rahma, on the plateau Arafa),[1] and *ifâda* ("the overflowing," when the pilgrims descend to Minâ and then to Mecca), with two stages: the nocturnal *wuqûf* at Muzdalifa and the rites at Minâ (*ramî* or the lapidation of the devil, when seven stones are thrown to three pillars, *nahr*, the sacrifice of animals, and *halq*, the shaving of the hair). Having arrived at Mecca, the pilgrims carry out the *tawâf* around the Kaaba, and then they spend the night at Minâ (*layalat al-qarr*, "the stabilization night"). Yet, Ibn 'Arabî stressed, even if it is the greater pilgrimage, the *hajj* is limited by the fixed date when it has to take place, while the *umra* does not depend on the time, which suggests that only the target is beyond any kind of limitations, the ways being forced to obey more or less important determinations. The pilgrimage to Mecca means to leave the "outside darkness," to penetrate the Cosmos surrounded by the Great Wall, covered by the circular mountain, and for this reason Ibn 'Arabî dedicated a large part of the chapter concerning the pilgrimage to the "state of holiness" through which the pilgrims reach the harmonious concordance with the primeval state symbolized by the sacred area (*haram*) that surrounds Mecca.[2]

Any authentic pilgrimage achieves such a "state of holiness." Each stage, marked by a holy place, allows the pilgrim to leave the profane standpoint and step inside the sacred domain. And we don't have in view only the initiatory aspect.[3] The exponents of the exoteric domain also have the

---

[1] We note that the Islamic pilgrimage does not mean only the journey to Mecca; the Prophet Muhammad said: *al-Hajj 'Arafa*, that is, "the pilgrimage is Arafa."

[2] The *haram* is Adam's heritage, since Allâh ordered the angels to guard Adam's Tent; the angels composed a circular barrier, with their backs to the "outside darkness," to stop the demons and the *djinns* from entering the sacred land.

[3] Of course, the common pilgrims, like the ones who went to Jerusalem or, on their knees, followed the labyrinth traced on the tiled floor of the cathedral, were not conscious of the initiatory meaning, yet they knew that, accomplishing the pilgrimage, at least once in a lifetime, they could reach "sainthood," that is, they could share the blessings of the visited places. It was also obvious that, for those with a callous heart, and for those who

possibility of enjoying this "state of holiness"; it is an important fact, which should be better understood by those who want at any price to consider the Christian religion an eso-exotericism, fearing that Christianity is at a lower level than other traditions or religions. Only those, who Dante described in such a gentle manner as we saw above, will remain in the "outside darkness." Only those, who, instead of having the heart full of love for God, visit the sacred places full of wrath and anger, those who are more interested in other people's business, thinking of themselves as little gods, only those will have no part of the "state of holiness."

However, there is a strong connection between the pilgrimage and the holy war, since the Prophet had to conquer Mecca and after eight years Omar had to fight to capture Jerusalem. This form of pilgrimage, aiming not only at reaching a holy place, but also at conquering or liberating it, unveils even better its *Kshatriya* quality and its appurtenance to the Royal Art. We notice here a secret significance, profound and initiatory, similar to that found in fairy tales and myths. The belligerent pilgrimage, aspiring to liberate a holy place, like Jerusalem for example, has as archetype the initiatory process of the "solar hero" whose goal is the Center of the World where is kept the divine Knowledge under the aspect of the Maiden abducted by the dragon. We must understand that, as the Islamic tradition underscored so well, the external war to conquer a fortress is only a pallid reflection of the inner war; that, in fact, the battle takes place against the devils inside us and the liberation of the Maiden or of the city symbolizes the Liberation of the Self. Meister Eckhart has explained the Evangelic episode about the cleansing of the Temple as being our inner purification, absolutely necessary, before the descent of the divine influence

---

completed the pilgrimage just superficially, for the eyes of the others, or waiting for a reward, the result was proportional. On the other hand, for the initiates, that is, for those who were conscious of the sacred journey's meaning, the pilgrimage represented an initiatory operative rite, which allowed them at each church, temple, or shrine to receive the divine influence and support for their personal spiritual efforts.

in our heart. The conquest of the city, either Troy, Jerusalem, or Mecca, the massacre, the expulsion, or the conversion to the true religion of the inhabitants, symbolize this purification of the heart and the eradication of the demons; if we do not recognize this significance, it will be impossible to see the cruelties of the Crusaders or of the Saracens after the conquest as anything else but human evilness.

When Omar conquered Jerusalem, he first visited, accompanied by the patriarch Sophronius, the Temple of Solomon,[1] since his conquest represented a setting in the center. When such an initiatory motivation did not exist, the conquering army appeared as a horde of Gog and Magog with a dissolving function, and that is what happened two decades earlier, in 614, when the Persians conquered Jerusalem. The Christians were slaughtered without discrimination and the Jews participated beside the Persians in this massacre.[2] As a result, the first Christian crusade was born, in 622, when the Byzantine emperor, Heraclius, dedicated his army to God and reconquered Jerusalem. Taking into account the prophecy that the Jews would ruin the empire, Heraclius ordered all Jews to be baptized, an order, of course, impossible to fulfill, and so the Christians, in their turn, massacred the Jews.[3]

Later, in 1071, the Byzantine army suffered a terrible defeat against the Turks of Alp Arslan, at Manzikert, and in the same year Atsiz ibn Abaq captured Jerusalem. At that time, Otto of Lagery was 29 years old; in 1078, Pope Gregory VII appointed him bishop of Ostia; in 1088, he became pope under the name of Urban II. In November 1095, at the Council of Clermont, Pope Urban II started to preach the Great Pilgrimage, that is, the Crusade. In July 1099, Jerusalem was liberated by the Western Christians and all day and night, the soldiers slew without discrimination Muslims and Jews, men, women, and children,[4] a deed that, even if from an external viewpoint seems

---

[1] Steven Runciman, *A History of the Crusades*, The Folio Society, 1994, I, p. 3.

[2] Runciman, *A History of the Crusades*, I, p. 9.

[3] Runciman, *A History of the Crusades*, I, p. 10.

[4] Runciman, *A History of the Crusades*, I, pp. 237-238.

horrible, only followed the sacred archetype previously mentioned.

For the Christian knights, the liberation of Helen of Troy was also a model kept in mind permanently, since the battle for Troy belongs to a *Kshatriya* type of initiatory process.[1] Crossing on knees the Cathedral's labyrinth represented only superficially the pilgrimage to Jerusalem, symbolizing in fact a spiritual realization towards Heavenly Jerusalem, so the Crusades only externally meant the liberation of Palestinian Jerusalem. "The Pilgrimage to Jerusalem" was an initiatory rite, and therefore, in an esoteric sense, it was equivalent to the "quest of the Lost Word" or to the "quest of the Holy Grail,"[2] a quest that only apparently was represented by the "lesser war" when, in fact, it was an inner spiritual realization, the "greater war." The *chansons de geste*, the "romance" of Tristan, the quest of the Holy Grail, the innumerable fairy tales, Dante's *Divine Comedy*, and the famous epopees are, no doubt, descriptions of an inner initiatory process, which does not mean that all the other various meanings are less present, including the most apparent and peripheral ones such as the historical aspect[3]; but, it would be a serious error to forget even for an instant that all these sacred narratives are, first and foremost, "supports" and "parts" of the Royal Art and Royal Initiation.[4] They belong to the royal

---

[1] It was not necessary for all the Crusaders to be aware of the esoteric significance of their deeds. It was enough that the inspirational people behind the Crusades, together with members of the sacerdotal authority and temporal power, in full accord, had the secret conscience of the true and essential meaning of the center.

[2] René Guénon, *Aperçus sur l'ésotérisme chrétien*, Éditions Traditionnelles, 1983, p. 49.

[3] The essence of the initiatory scenario is immutable, but, of course, it was dressed in various garments in accord with the historical period in which it was designed to serve. For the same reason, in the Christian religious paintings, the individuals were dressed in contemporary clothing, regardless of the epoch when they were supposed to have lived.

[4] See René Guénon, *Autorité spirituelle et pouvoir temporel*, Véga, Paris, 1976, pp. 32-36, where Guénon underlined the difference between the Sacerdotal Art and the Royal Art, the former belonging to the *Brâhmanas*, the latter to the *Kshatriyas*. Also, see Guénon, *Études sur l'hindouisme*, Éditions Traditionnelles,

initiatory rites and are, in a way, a spiritual *aide-memoire*, which in the Hindu tradition is called *Smriti*.[1]

In this sense are to be understood the words of Maximus the Confessor, unveiling the symbolism of Abraham's journey to the Center: "The one who is still satisfying the passionate appetites of the flesh dwells as a maker and worshiper of idols in the land of the Chaldeans. But after some reflection on this matter he becomes aware of behaviour which is more proper to nature, leaves the land of the Chaldeans, and goes to Harran in Mesopotamia, that is, the frontier state between virtue and vice which is not yet purified of the deception of the senses. This is what the word Harran means. But if one looks even beyond the understanding of the good which is suitable to the senses, he will press on to the good land, that is, to the state which is free from all vice and ignorance which a faithful God points out and professes to give as a reward of virtue to those who love him."[2] As Philo of Alexandria stressed, we must shift from the "macro-city" (macrocosm) to the "micro-city" (microcosm, that is, the self-knowledge, *gnōthi seauton*), which is represented precisely by "Abraham's migration": the emigration from Chaldea to Harran signifies the abandonment of idols (the

---

Paris, 1979, pp. 13, 18, where the characteristics of the *Brâhmanas* and of the *Kshatriyas* are defined.

[1] The two *Itihâsas*, the *Râmâyana* and the *Mahâbhârata*, belong to *Smriti*, which makes them, René Guénon said, traditional writings and, therefore, they are something totally different than just "epic poems"; the *Bhagavad-Gîtâ*, which is a part of the *Mahâbhârata*, is mainly intended to the *Kshatriyas* (Guénon, *Études sur l'hindouisme*, pp. 9, 11). However, Guénon cautioned, they are not the actual rituals as some people could think (René Guénon, *Symboles fondamentaux de la Science sacrée*, Gallimard, Paris, 1980, p. 58, where Guénon was referring to the Grail stories in particular); on the other hand, in Masonry, the "legends" are "set in action" and they cannot be separated from the rites, being incorporated in these rites (*Aperçus sur l'initiation*, p. 121).

[2] Maximus Confessor, *Selected Writings*, Paulist Press, 1985, p. 153. Besides its spiritual inner meaning, the pilgrimage has also a cosmologic significance: Adam's pilgrimage with his change of stature, his attitudes and his "stations" are "symbolical representations of a biological and spiritual process concerning not a particular individual but humankind in its phases of cyclical development" (Vâlsan, *Inde et Arabie*).

stars) in favour of self-knowledge, which in a first phase is the knowledge of the ego, of the individual being. "Abraham's migration" is a journey of the intellect when this one renounces the consideration of the world being God, and starts to acknowledge its ego, with the body and the senses; and then, in a higher phase the intellect concentrates on itself, leaving Harran and discovering the one and only God; and Abram becomes Abraham.[1]

Likewise in all the traditional tales, the inner spiritual realization involves the existence of numerous "centers," with the quest being represented by a route connecting various places, which are all images of the Center, namely, these centers, even though presented as "explication" and along a string, are in fact (as "complication") one and the same center. In the case of Abraham, Ur and Harran were "lunar" centers: Ur was a Sumerian city with a great ziggurat for the moon deity Nanna; Harran was a Mesopotamian center of the moon god Sin.[2] However, as we know, Abraham himself established, guided by God, spiritual centers.[3]

"Abraham's migration" is a spiritual voyage that was repeated cyclically: From Ur, Abraham ascends to Harran (the most Nordic point), then descends to Egypt and returns to Canaan; Jacob ascends to Harran then returns to Canaan, where he sees God; Joseph and his brothers descend to Egypt and then the Jews return with Moses to Canaan. Yet, there is also a

---

[1] In his "migration," Abraham was accompanied by the *Shekinah* (*Zohar*, I, 49b).

[2] The importance of moon for the nomadic peoples, and also in Islam, is well known. It is said that Adam and Eve settled in Harran after they were banished from Eden.

[3] "And he removed from thence unto a mountain on the east of Bethel, and pitched his tent, having Bethel on the west and Hai on the east: and there he built an altar unto the Lord, and called upon the name of the Lord" (*Genesis* 12:7-8). "Then Abram removed his tent, and came and dwelt in the plain of Mamre, which is in Hebron, and built there an altar unto the Lord" (*Genesis* 13:18). "And they came to the place which God had told him of; and Abraham built an altar there, and laid the wood in order, and bound Isaac his son, and laid him on the altar upon the wood" (*Genesis* 22:9).

meaning related to Ibn 'Arabî's sayings regarding the "return": a spiritual voyage is a quest aiming at the "farthest" center, followed by a return to the initial center. This theme is to be found in the majority of fairy tales, but also in the *Iliad*, where the "farthest" center is Troy, or in the *Râmâyana*, where this center is Râvana's island.

Even though Troy was conquered and destroyed, it was no doubt a spiritual center. As Guénon said, the foundation of a city could symbolize the institution of a doctrine or of a traditional form, and in the case of Troy the Tradition was symbolized by the *palladium*,[1] and later by Helen herself.[2] We should not forget that Poseidon, the architect of Atlantis, also built the walls of Troy, and Apollo, the god of spiritual wisdom, helped him.[3] In fact, during the Trojan War, we see the gods supporting both sides: Apollo, Aphrodite, and Ares were helping the Trojans; Pallas-Athena, Hera, and Artemis were assisting the Greeks, which suggests that the "inner" or "greater" war is not just a war against demons, but is, in fact, a complex spiritual process of overcoming a multitude of trials governed by God Himself.[4] Apollo's main function in the Trojan War was to produce initiatory trials, and his arrow killing Achilles, for example, represents the hero's "liberation." Each conquered inner level was populated by *yin* and *yang*

---

[1] The *palladium* was a wooden statue of Pallas-Athena, which descended from heaven in answer to the prayer of Ilus, son of Tros, the founder of Troy.

[2] The symbol of Leda's twins, Castor and Pollux, is well known from Greek mythology. Pollux is immortal, the sacred kernel, his father being Zeus; Castor is mortal, the profane skin. It is less known that Leda also gave birth to a pair of twin girls, Helen and Clytemnestra, Helen being the immortal one, with Zeus as father. Regardless of her terrestrial life, she remains the everlasting, divine maid, the Virgin.

[3] Later, Poseidon punished Laomedon, the son of Ilus, for his ungratefulness.

[4] The Trojan War is this spiritual war, which, from Man's point of view, takes place within us, the stake being the Kingdom of Heaven (*Luke* 17:21). We can trace this symbolism in any tradition; this Kingdom as fortress is also Troy. In the Middle Ages, Troy became the archetype of the Center as fortress to be conquered; also the maze was called "Troy-Town," and the maze is a symbol of the Center.

influences fulfilling the divine plan, and Râvana's center is the best illustration of this.

However, the initiatory process is always accompanied by a cosmic one, and any traditional and sacred story will contain a triple significance related to Cosmos (the cosmogonic process), Year (the cosmic cycles) and Man (the initiatory process), which is expected to be found in the Trojan War tale too. *Fiat Lux* creates the Cosmos by manifesting the divine light, and the super-luminous Principle is the real owner of the World. It becomes obvious then, that taking back the light or the waters symbolizes the death of our world, the end of our cycle of manifestation and, by transposition, the end of the entire Cosmos (the "Three Worlds"), which from a human point of view means the biggest abduction ever. When the Dragon steals the light or the cows or the rivers, the Cosmos dies; also, the divine kernel is stolen, the spiritual knowledge is hidden from us and the darkness of ignorance covers the dying world, as well as our heart and eyes. In the sacred writings, a symbol for absolute, divine Knowledge is the Virgin, where *Madonna Intelligenza* for Dante, *Shakti* for the Hindu tradition, and Helen of Troy are exactly this "virgin," symbolizing the spiritual light. Thus, the abduction of Helen illustrates the end of a cosmic cycle, the end of a world, the end of the sacred wisdom, when the Dragon steals and hides the spiritual sun, the celestial rivers, i. e., life and knowledge.

The Greeks started an implacable war to bring back the light, and it is not very difficult to understand the significance of this war: to begin a new cycle, to produce a new Cosmos, to resurrect the worlds and the beings, means to liberate the abducted sun, the stolen cows or rivers, to rescue the Virgin, Helen of Troy,[1] which does not make Troy an infernal city, even though usually in these "myths" the dragon (often considered a Titan or *Asura*) is the abductor; metaphysically, Troy is the super-luminous center, the non-manifestation. This

---

[1] This deed is anticipated by Odysseus abducting the *palladium*.

ambiguity, related to the symbolism of the two nights,[1] allows us to consider such a center both a "demoniac" city and the Hindu *Brahmapura*, Meister Eckhart's castle,[2] "the City of God"[3] where *Âtmâ*, the Universal Spirit, dwells.[4] As René Guénon affirmed,[5] the spiritual obscuration that occurred, due to the cyclical laws, in the evolvement of human history, caused the loss of the primordial state (that is, the loss of the Center) and of the tradition that is, in its essence, identical to this state. The Holy Grail symbolizes both the Center or the primordial state and the Tradition,[6] and the Quest of the Grail illustrates precisely the spiritual process of recovering the lost Center and the lost Tradition, which means, from a cosmic perspective, that by accomplishing the Quest, a new cycle or a new world is born.[7] Similarly, Helen of Troy's retrieval represents the beginning of a new cycle, of a new Troy, since it took ten years of war to conquer Troy: the nine plus one years of war are, like all the other spans of time in sacred writings, symbolical and usually represent the duration of a more or less extensive cycle.[8]

---

[1] As Guénon explained, the two *tenebrae*, the superior and inferior (or supernal and infernal, as Coomaraswamy would say), are in the Islamic tradition the two nights represented by *laylatul-qadr* (the night – identified by Ibn 'Arabî with the Prophet's "body" – when the *Qur'an* descended) and *laylatul-mi'râj* (the nocturnal ascension of the Prophet, that is, the return to the Principle) (René Guénon, *Initiation et réalisation spirituelle*, Éditions Traditionnelles, Paris, 1980, pp. 239-250).

[2] *Intravit Iesus in quoddam castellum*, *Luke* 10:38. See Maître Eckhart, *Sermons*, Éd. du Seuil, 1974, I, p. 50.

[3] Ananda K. Coomaraswamy, *What is Civilisation?*, Lindisfarne Press, 1989, p. 2.

[4] Therefore Troy was considered the traditional origin of other centers (like Rome for example).

[5] *Franc-Maçonnerie*, II, pp. 26-27.

[6] René Guénon, *Le Roi du Monde*, Gallimard, Paris, 1981, p. 44.

[7] See Guénon, *Franc-Maçonnerie*, II, p. 33.

[8] The ten years of the Trojan War symbolize a complete development of a cosmic cycle, including its end. Actually, the symbolism of ten, as nine plus One, is so important to Homer that he mentions it, at the beginning of the *Iliad*, not once but twice. The epic commences with Apollo punishing the Greeks. Nine days in a row Apollo has sent his deadly arrows upon the

Greek army; on the tenth day the Greeks ask for mercy. This first episode of the epic is a synthesis of the entire poem. Agamemnon, the leader of the Greeks, has abducted a virgin, the daughter of Apollo's priest, Chryses. The virgin Chryseis is, of course, an *alter ego* of Helen. In Greek, the names Chryses and Chryseis mean "the golden one" that is directly related to the spiritual Sun (in the *Râmâyana*, there are also names referring to "gold": Hiranyâksha and Hiranyakashipu). Apollo starts the "war" against the Greeks, and Agamemnon on the tenth day accepts defeat and returns the girl. Chryseis' home city is Thebes, near Troy. Thebes, as we know, is a symbolic name for the Center of the World. "The circle, with its central point, symbol of the number ten, is at the same time the symbol of the cyclical perfection, namely of the integral realization of the possibilities involved in a state of existence (world)," Guénon tells us (*Le symbolisme de la croix*, Guy Trédaniel / Véga, Paris, 1989, p. 46, *La Grande Triade*, Gallimard, 1980, p. 188).

II

RÂMA'S QUEST

In the *Râmâyana*,[1] we notice one more time the triple story: the cosmogonic process, the evolvement of the cycle, and the spiritual realization, all related to the birth of an *avatâra*, who, paradigmatically, starts an invisible war from the beginning of the cycle (the nine and a half years of the Trojan War), a war that in the end becomes a total conflagration that will destroy the old center, will regenerate the world, will recover the Tradition (Sîtâ) and will re-establish the Center (the return to Ayodhyâ). It needs divine "inspiration" to describe all these elements in a tale, but usually we find them in any traditional myth or fairy tale, where the various participants are images of the same One, where what is simultaneous is presented in succession, where the hero starts his work of regenerating the world from the beginning of the new cycle and in accord with the work of the dragon that tirelessly facilitates the decay of the world.

In the *Râmâyana*, the starting point is the well known center, Ayodhyâ, described as "inaccessible to all," and where "once reigned king Dasharatha like Indra, the Ruler of Heaven ... All men and women were of excellent character ... The Kshatriyas obeyed the Brâhmanas, the Vaishyas were respectful towards the Kshatriyas, and all were served by the Shûdras."[2] This

---

[1] Even today you can witness, on the bank of Gangâ, *sannyasins* ritually chanting the *Râmâyana* as support for a spiritual realization.

[2] See *The Râmâyana of Valmiki*, tr. Makhan Lal Sen, Munshiram Manoharlal Publishers, 2003, which we use only for orientation.

depiction shows us the center at the beginning of the cycle, in opposition to the *Kali-yuga*, when, the Hindu tradition affirms, reign deceit, falseness, inertia, greed and depravity; the *Brâhmanas* become addicted to luxury, the servants quit their masters, and the *Shûdras* take the power; the whole world is filled with perverted people, and the strongest among the *Brâhmanas, Kshatriyas, Vaishyas* or *Shûdras* will become kings; the kings will behave like villains; the castes will be all like *Shûdra*.[1]

René Guénon said: "Agarttha … has received, as Saint-Yves indicated, the heritage of the antique 'solar dynasty' (*Sûrya-vansha*) that resided once at Ayodhyâ,[2] and which originated with Vaivaswata, the Manu of the present cycle."[3] Undoubtedly, Ayodhyâ was an important spiritual center and, symbolically, Agarttha was its successor, which brings us to the question: why then should spiritual realization be illustrated by a Quest aiming at Râvana's island? As we suggested, Râvana's city also represents the Center, but in this case there is a more complex meaning, this "farthest" place symbolizing at the same time the "end" of the cycle, the "other world," both as infernal

---

[1] Obeying the hierarchy and order is what characterizes the "righteous man," while "revolt" is what induces decay, confusion and disorder, as illustrated in the doctrine of the *avatâras* (see Guénon, *Études sur l'hindouisme*, p. 20, about the disorder triumphing in our modern world). In the Judaic tradition, Abraham is a model for the "righteous man," since he was ready to sacrifice his son. In the Hindu tradition, Râma is the perfect *Kshatriya*, who will obey with joy the command to go into exile; even better is this sacred obedience described in the case of Parashu Râma, who was asked by his father Jamadagni to behead his mother Renukâ and he did it without hesitation (while his four brothers refused the command and were burned to ashes by Jamadagni).

[2] However, Râma from the solar dynasty is called *Râma-chandra*, "Râma-moon," and the solar Krishna has as father a king from the lunar dynasty. There were two traditional dynasties in India: the solar one, descended directly from Manu of the present cycle, and the lunar one to which belonged the legendary emperor Bharata, son of the famous Sakuntala (who was the fruit of king Vishwâmitra's failure to accomplish the *tapas* leading to the *brâhma-rishi* station).

[3] And Guénon compared Ayodhyâ to the "solar citadel" of the Rose-Cross and to Campanella's "city of the sun." See *Le Roi*, p. 14.

and supernal night, and *Brahmapura*, the heart of the integral
being[1]; at the end of his Quest, Râma returns to Ayodhyâ,
which becomes now the *Brahmapura* of the new being, of the
new king, and of the new world, while the "farthest" center
becomes the "closest."[2]

Râvana's center is, actually, a center inside a center inside a
center inside a center, and so on (this progression should be
understood oriented from the corporeal domain to the spiritual
one, and only symbolically referring to the corporeal world).
The center is an island in the middle of the ocean; it is a
mountain in the center of the island; it is the city in top of the
mountain,[3] which, like Agarttha, is inaccessible.[4] And this city
is not demonic but heavenly, built by the Great Architect of the
Universe: "Across the ocean there is my capital Lankâ like
Amaravati – the heavenly city," similar to the Heavenly
Paradise: "it is surrounded by a white wall. The city gates are
made of lapis lazuli gems, and its rooms are made of gold."
"The glorious Hanumân neared the city of Lankâ ruled by
Râvana, and saw the city which looked like the city of Gods in
heaven. He then saw the city of Lankâ with beautiful white

---

[1] With respect to the theory of the three *gunas*, the wedding of Râma and Sîtâ
corresponds to *rajas*, the abduction of Sîtâ relates to *tamas*, and Râma's war to
liberate Sîtâ corresponds to *sattwa*.

[2] Ayodhyâ was described as a quadrangle, similar to a chess table, having
eight squares on each side, with the center marked by *Brahmapura* or
Brahmâsthana (the "station" of Brahma) (Titus Burckhardt, *Principes et méthodes
de l'art sacré*, Dervy, 1976, p. 44, *Symboles*, Archè, 1980, p. 22; see also Pierre
Grison, ET, no. 356, 1959, p. 274). The game of chess is also an element of
the Holy Grail stories, since it is a game for *Kshatriyas*, the chess table being
the "battle field" (*kshêtra*) (Guénon, *Le symbolisme de la croix*, p. 57).

[3] "Nestled on a mountaintop, my great city known as Lankâ is there in the
midst of an ocean and all over encompassed by an ocean" (*Râmâyana*, p. 202).

[4] "It is impossible to assail this Lankâ even for Indra with all of the gods and
demons, as an ocean roundly enshrouds this Lankâ which is hundred-*yojanas*
widthwise. I behold none matchable to my vitality is existent among gods;
among Yakshas – no; among Gandharvas – no; among sages – no, nor
anyone in any world" (*Râmâyana*, p. 209). Evidently, this Lankâ is not the
physical island of Ceylon, but concerns the subtle modalities and even the
super-individual states of the being.

buildings situated on the top of a mountain like a city located in the sky. He saw that city of Lankâ ruled by Râvana the king of Râkshasas, constructed by Vishwakarma, and which looked as though it were floating in the sky."[1] The center of the city is Râvana's palace,[2] and "Hanumân entered the inner city of Râvana which was filled with gold, which had a golden court-yard, with a central area decorated by pearls and diamonds of great value and sprinkled daily with

[1] *Râmâyana*, p. 314. "That gorgeous city is completely walled in with compound walls that are adorned with whitish silver, and its palace-chambers are golden, and its archways are fully jewelled with lapis jewels. It is encumbered with elephants, horses and chariots, well sounded by the sounds of trumpets, and with trees which yield fruits that fulfill all the savours, and it is bedecked with chirrupy pleasure-gardens." "There is a lavish city in the oceanic island afar a hundred *yojanas* all in all from here, which Vishwakarma, the Divine-Architect, has built, and it is called Lankâ. Its multi-storied buildings are built very symmetrically and they will be in golden tinge with completely golden doors. The golden podia of verandas are amazing. That city is securely enclosed in a gigantic rampart that will be dazzling in the colour of sun." The city, "built very symmetrically," is a square like Ayodhyâ, like the Heavenly Jerusalem, like the Paradise of *Vaikuntha*: "Lankâ is situated on the other side of the ocean, which is difficult of access, Oh Râma! It offers no passage for vehicles either and there is no proper communication from all sides. That city of Lankâ, resembling the city of Gods, is built on a mountain peak and is inaccessible. Hundreds of thousands of Râkshasas ... are positioned at the eastern gate. Millions of Râkshasas ... are positioned at the southern gate of the city. Ten millions of Râkshasas ... are positioned at the western gate. Hundreds of millions of Râkshasas ... are positioned there at the northern gate" (*Râmâyana*, p. 396). The geometrically increasing numbers 1-10-100-1000 indicate a *pradakshina* of the evolvement of the cycle.

[2] "That paradisiacal mansion house of Decahedral Râvana is congestive with innumerable cupolaed skyscrapers, adored with thousands of females, frequented by diverse bevies of birds [symbolizing the "angels"], and it comprised of numerous gemstones. The pillars are amazingly gilded with engraving of ivory, gilt, quartz, silvery linocuts, and they are even embossed with diamonds and with lapis gems, which are heart-pleasing for a look. The drumbeats of divine drums are echoing in entire palace, and its archways are adorned with the gildings of pure gold." "The son of Vâyu, Hanumân, saw Râvana's palace like heaven thrown upon earth, effulgent with glory, embedded with variety of diamonds covered by flowers of various trees, like the summit of a mountain covered by pollen" (*Râmâyana*, pp. 209, 318, 320).

water containing superb algallocum and sandal-wood"; when inside, Hanumân exclaimed: "This is heaven! This is indeed the abode of Dêvas! This is a city of Indra. This might be the result of a great austerity (*tapas*). ... This building shines by the light of lamps and the brilliance of Râvana and also due to the radiance of jewellery." Its center is the flying [subtle] *Pushpaka Ratha*,[1] yet the inner-most center is Râvana's bed.[2] The bed as a symbol of the inner center is to be found also in the *Odyssey*, where it constitutes the so-called "initiatory secret." Ulysses built the conjugal bed from an olive tree, having the tree as a post, and ornamented the bed with gold and silver and ivory, like the Heavenly Jerusalem.[3] The olive tree represents the *Axis Mundi* and the chamber that Ulysses built around this tree is the Cosmos; the "one-footed" bed, is the Center of the World. Revealing the "secret" about the bed, Ulysses proves to his divine wife that he has reached the supreme Knowledge, that he is the "worthy" husband, the immortal one, the second

---

[1] "That Hanumân, the courageous one, the son of Lord Vâyu, saw the great Pushpaka Ratha [Brahmâ's vehicle] standing in the middle of that building with a surprising hue, due to diamonds, and gems decorated by series of refined gold. That plane shone like symbol for solar path standing in the aerial path obtaining the sky. Manufactured by Vishwakarma himself and praised by him as one without comparison in beauty. ... One that has been obtained by [Râvana's] austerities (*tapasya*) and by prowess, one that moves about by thoughts of concentrated mind [beyond the corporeal modality], made from various significant parts, collected from here and there from all over the world. Obtaining a special construction as a special object, like a mountain with wonderful peaks adorned by many peaks, attractive to soul, calm like an autumnal moon, like the peak of a mountain with other wonderful small peaks." "Hanumân saw another house in the middle of that house ... wonderful flying vehicle by the name of Pushpaka, decorated with all kinds of precious stones, made by Vishwakarma in heaven for lord Brahmâ (and resembling Fire and Sun in splendour)."
[2] "Hanumân saw in a part of that room an umbrella white in colour decorated with best flower garlands and resembling moon – the lord of stars. Hanumân saw an excellent couch made of gold with radiance equalling that of fire, spread by garlands of Ashoka flowers." In the Grail tradition, the bed plays an important role, as a symbol of the center.
[3] *Odyssey* XXIII.190-200.

Adam, and thus, Ulysses gets his reward, Penelope (an equivalent of Sîtâ), and the second wedding takes place.

Yet, beyond this center in a center in a center, there is the supreme center where Sîtâ was hidden, symbolized by the Ashoka forest or garden: "Let this Maithilî be taken to the center of Ashoka gardens, where you all shall blockade and guard her stealthily"[1]; "That Ashoka garden shone by Santanaka creepers, Santana trees with heavenly aroma and juice, well decorated in all directions equalling the garden of Nandana [Indra's garden]." The garden is a well known symbol of the center, but also the forest represents a central place, even though usually the forest is the labyrinth or the outside darkness, or just the world of multiplicity, and conceals the center.

Râma's Quest, from Man's perspective, is a spiritual journey from the first Adam (the first center Ayodhyâ) to the second Adam (the new center Ayodhyâ),[2] from the primordial state before the "fall" to the primordial state after the "redemption," from the virtual Universal Man to the effectively realized Universal Man.[3] From the Year's viewpoint, the evolvement of the cycle is illustrated in more than one way, like, for example, considering Sîtâ and Râma's wedding as the start of a new cycle

---

[1] *Râmâyana*, pp. 210, 329. The name Maithilî is derived from the word Mithila, the kingdom of Janaka, Sîtâ's father.

[2] "And so it is written, The first man Adam was made a living soul; the second Adam was made a life-giving spirit" (*1 Corinthians*, 15:45). The first Adam corresponds to the Earthly Paradise and the second Adam to the Heavenly Jerusalem (Guénon, *L'ésotérisme de Dante*, Gallimard, 1957, p. 68).

[3] See Guénon, *Le symbolisme de la croix*, p. 23. A divine principle must reside, at least "virtually," in the center of the being, because otherwise the existence of this being would be more than an illusion; it would be nothingness. This divine principle is the "intellectual intuition," symbolized by the eye of the heart, or what the Judaic tradition calls *Shekinah*. The Hindu tradition represents the divine principle as a grain, a seed (*dhâtu*), or a germ (*bhija*), because it resides only virtually in the being, until the "Union" is effectively realized; only when the "neophyte" (as a "new plant") becomes aware of this divine presence, he passes from virtual to real and reaches the center, not only his center but the supreme center (Guénon, *Symboles fondamentaux*, pp. 377, 409, 438, 447).

with a perfect state, when the Regent, residing in the center, possesses the wisdom and the traditional knowledge, symbolized by Sîtâ herself[1]; then, with the descent of the cycle, the tradition is lost, which means the abduction of Sîtâ, of Helen of Troy, and the loss of the Holy Grail, which becomes hidden,[2] and a initiatory journey, a spiritual war is necessary to regain the Lost Word. However, this perfect state corresponds to the first Adam, but Râma is not the actual King and it is essential for him to accomplish a spiritual realization, through which he recovers the Tradition (Sîtâ), and Râma would be invested King, as a second Adam, and a second wedding (the real wedding) would take place.[3]

On the other hand, even though Ayodhyâ is presented as a Paradise, the story suggests at the same time the end of the cycle, since King Dasharatha is barren, without sons, which illustrates the agonizing world when the fertile Garden becomes a wasteland, when the king presents dragonic characteristics.[4] And later, when Râma and Sîtâ go into the initiatory "exile," the signs of the end are even more powerful: Vasishtha the *brâhmana* says: "Then this deserted city [Ayodhyâ] will turn into a dreary forest where even the necessities of life will not be available"; "The whole Ayodhyâ looked like a starless night."[5]

---

[1] "Verily, there exists here no purifier equal to Wisdom (Knowledge). He who is perfected by Yoga finds it in time in himself by himself" (*Bhagavad-Gîtâ*, IV, 38).

[2] Guénon, *Le Roi*, p. 42.

[3] Even today, there is the custom in some countries to "abduct the bride," a reflection of the initiatory abduction; we see two weddings, parted by the "abduction of the bride."

[4] *Ab intra*, in non-manifestation, the dragon is sterile, blind, without feet. The old king is the dying world; he is now the dragon, the same dragon he beheaded as solar hero at the beginning of the cycle. The dragon Vritra tells Indra, the solar hero: "You are now what I was before" (*Panchavimsha Brâhmana*, XXV.15.4). In the Judaic tradition, Abraham and Sarah are old and they don't have a child. God says to Abraham: "your wife Sarah shall bear you a son whom you are to name Isaac" (*Genesis* 17:19), but Sarah laughs, since she is old and infertile.

[5] *Râmâyana*, pp. 95, 101. The king Dasharatha says to Kaikeyî: "It is the duty of the woman to act according to the wishes of her husband. You are bent

As a conclusion, Dasharatha dies, apparently of bitterness, but, in fact, the old king dies with the cycle, and Râma is in "exile," which represents precisely the obscure period between two cycles described in the tale in this manner: "Where there is no king, the clouds do not rain there, seeds are not sown, the son does not obey the father, nor wife the husband. ... Brâhmanas cease to perform their sacrifices, and all rites end there. ... A kingdom without a king is in fact a river without water. ... The king is the eye of the people."[1] However, since for the human mind there must be a beginning and an end, the *Ragnarök* is transferred to the "farthest" center; Vibhîshana, Râvana's youngest brother, says to Indrajît (Râvana's son): "These faults which destroy one's life and lordship killing great sages terribly, waging war against all celestials, arrogance, becoming angry very easily, quarrelsomeness, ill-will have concealed the good qualities of my elder brother, as the clouds conceal the view of mountains."[2] Râvana, like Dasharatha, is the "old" king, the Dragon, the sum of the lowest and last possibilities of manifestation.

In a way, Râvana represents what René Guénon called the "counter-initiation." Guénon wrote: "The 'counter-initiation' appears through degeneracy... which is more profound than that of a deviated tradition or of an incomplete tradition reduced to its inferior part. There is also here something that is more than in the case of those lost traditions that were abandoned by the spiritual influence (in which case their residues can be used by the 'counter-initiation' for its own purpose). Logically, this leads us to think that the degeneracy had to go back into the past; and, as obscure as its origin is, we

---

upon to alter the time-honoured law of succession to the throne. How pious men will live in this kingdom?" (p. 93); Bharata also says: "the city appears to me like a forest today. ... Leaves are falling off from every roadside tree, and the sweet notes of birds ["angels," spiritual influences] are no more to be heard" (p. 118).

[1] *Râmâyana*, p. 115. We should not forget that this *Itihâsa* is meant to teach the *Kshatriyas*.

[2] *Râmâyana*, p. 511.

may admit as credible that it is attached to some distortion of an ancient civilization that disappeared in a cataclysm of the present Manvantara. ... 'Counter-initiation,' we must say, cannot be considered a purely human invention, which would be no different from 'pseudo-initiation.' In fact, it is more than that, and to be so effectively, it must, in a specific mode, and with regard to its origin, derive from the unique source to which every initiation is attached, and, generally speaking, everything that manifests in our world a 'non-human' element."[1] In a similar way, "the *Dêvas* or 'Angels' and the *Asuras* or 'Titans,' that is, the powers of Light and the powers of Darkness in the *Rig-Vêda*, even though opposed in their actions, are of a same essence ... the two appellations could be applied to a same and one entity, function of its mode of operation."[2]

Through a monkey-like projection, imitating the projection of *Âtmâ* as *jivâtmâ*, it is possible to envisage a sort of

---

[1] *Le règne de la quantité et les signes des temps*, Gallimard, 1970, pp. 351-352. Such "degeneracy" took place at the end of the "Age of Silver" (*Trêtâ-yuga*), when Vishnu had to descend as Parashu Râma, his sixth *avatâra*, and punish the revolted *Kshatriyas*, ending this Age. Râma-chandra is Vishnu's seventh *avatâra* and Râvana appears as a heretic *Kshatriya*, since the abduction of Sîtâ was considered a terrible deed and against the *Kshatriya*'s rules.

[2] Guénon, *Études sur l'hindouisme*, p. 133. Coomaraswamy has stressed that *Asuras* and *Dêvas*, the Titans and the Angels, are *ab intra* identical, in accordance with the Supreme Identity (*tad êkam, sadasat*), expressed as *Sarpyâ vâ âdityâh*, "the serpents are the suns"; *ab extra* the serpents represent the anterior states (the former gods, parents of the present gods), the dark, tenebrous states, while the suns are the superior, luminous states (the gods). The passing from darkness to light occurs due to a sacrifice consumed in different ritual modes, either by beheading the serpent, or by throwing away the serpent skin, or by endowing the "dragon" with feet, in essence, *Fiat Lux*, the genesis of the world, signifying the passing from the anterior dark cycle to the new luminous one; the former emperor, who became at the end a dragon, was sacrificed and transformed into the new emperor – the sun rising from the cave where the dragon concealed it (*ab intra* the sun being the dragon). The Titan is a potential Angel, the Angel a Titan made actual, since the darkness *in actu* is light, and the cycle that dies contains *in potentia* the seed of the new cycle (Ananda K. Coomaraswamy, *La doctrine du sacrifice*, Dervy, 1978, pp. 23-24).

anti-*Anima*, beyond the *Corpus*, that is, "infra-human," which represents the counter-tradition. For this reason it is said that the devils have our souls as abode; and therefore, *Corpus* is not the counter-initiatory obstacle, but our soul, our sentiments and desires, our mind and our thoughts. At the end of the cycle, when *Anima* breaks up with *Spiritus*, the counter-initiation becomes fully active and imposes its own projection, *Anima* receiving the reflection of the anti-*Anima*. From an initiatory point of view, Râvana is the anti-*Anima* that invaded the "ego," the *jîvâtmâ*; therefore, only the man will be able to destroy him, and by beheading Râvana the *jîvâ* disappears and *Âtmâ* will be fully unveiled.

Nonetheless, Râvana is much more than that. We have to remember that the "counter-initiatory" forces have no access to the angelic states and to the *Greater Mysteries*, but Râvana is, in a way, the *principial* and universal root of the "counter-initiation," and he could be compared to Lucifer.[1] Râvana is even more than Lucifer: he "oppresses" all the Three Worlds and the angels address Vishnu thus: "The preposterous Râkshasa Râvana with his invigorated doggedness is torturing gods along with eminent saints, Gandharvas, and siddhas. This furious one with his insolence is knocking down sages from their celestial abodes, and like that he is knocking down the celestial Gandharvas and Apsaras too from the heavenly gardens Nandana, where they will be taking delight. We the celestial

---

[1] "Thy pomp is brought down to the grave, and the noise of thy viols: the worm is spread under thee, and the worms cover thee. How art thou fallen from heaven, O Lucifer, son of the morning! how art thou cut down to the ground, which didst weaken the nations! For thou hast said in thine heart, I will ascend into heaven, I will exalt my throne above the stars of God: I will sit also upon the mount of the congregation, in the sides of the north: I will ascend above the heights of the clouds; I will be like the Most High. Yet thou shalt be brought down to hell, to the sides of the pit" (*Isaiah* 14:11-15). The symbolism of the "fall of the angels," Guénon said, could be analogically applied to the human order (*Le règne*, p. 352); therefore, as for the fallen angels the gates of heaven became closed, so for the "counter-initiation" of our world the super-individual states are inaccessible. But Râvana's symbolism is exceptionally complex.

beings like siddhas, Gandharvas, and Yakshas along with sages have actually come for his elimination, and thereby we seek shelter in you."

Râvana is also a sage,[1] and from the Cosmos' viewpoint he is an image of the Principle as Prajâpati, or more as Vritra, his sacrifice producing the new world, with his head becoming the new Sun.[2] Since Râvana also illustrates the transformation of the Hero into Dragon, of the "Golden Age" into the *Kali Yuga*, he deserves a Luciferian description, as suggested by Hanumân's admonition: "It is not proper for you to lose your exceptional longevity and that fortune which is an outcome of your virtue, both of which have been acquired by you through the practice of austerities. ... The fruit of righteousness does not exist together with the result of unrighteousness. Righteousness in abundance destroys unrighteousness."[3]

---

[1] "Formerly, this dreadful Râvana practised great austerities and penance and thereby received boon from Brahmâ" (*Râmâyana*, p. 18).

[2] "Râvana was endowed with a great splendour and shone with a glittering and precious diadem of gold as also encircled with strings of pearls. That Râvana was adorned with bright-coloured gold ornaments, inlaid with diamonds and decorated with worthy gems, which appeared as though they were prepared with the mind. Râvana was attired in very costly silk and his body was smeared with red-sandal paste and well painted with various brightly coloured designs. Râvana looked strange with his ten heads" (*Râmâyana* p. 371). Râvana appears as the divine Sun, and the ten heads should be compared with the ten suns of the Far-Eastern tradition; see our work *About the Yi Jing* (Rose-Cross Books, 2006, pp. 97-98): "The Chinese tradition describes here the Dragon with ten heads as supreme Principle, as the Light of the superior Darkness, a light that cannot exist in manifestation, because the manifestation cannot exist under such an omnipotent and pure light. This light has to be crippled, to become a mutilated and a lame light, which means that the dragon has to be beheaded, and the last head will become the sun, the one sun to shine on the sky." The ten heads are equivalent to the ten years of the Trojan War. Lancelot has to fight ten knights to reach the center.

[3] *Râmâyana*, p. 373. Hanumân's words follow another description: "Seeing the glittering Râvana, the king of Râkshasas, Hanumân was bewildered by his splendour and thought in his mind as follows: 'What figure, what courage, what strength, what splendour and what amalgam of auspicious marks, alas, this king of Râkshasas has! Had this lord of Râkshasas perhaps not strong in

This admonition concerns the abduction of Sîtâ, but obviously, what from the cosmic point of view appears as an unrighteous deed,[1] from the Principle's perspective, reabsorbing the manifestation is a necessary act, and Râvana is exercising his function as an aspect of the Principle itself. It is interesting to note that, even though the world is at its end, some sages have the responsibility of striving to keep it alive, since, by definition, a sage will act along *sattwa*, the upward *guna*[2]; on the other hand, from an initiatory viewpoint, when *Râkshasa* Mârîcha advises Râvana not to abduct Sîtâ and, so, not to provoke Râma, it is the "voice of reason" that tries to keep the *status quo* of the *ego*.[3]

---

unrighteousness, he would have been a protector of even the world of celestials together with Indra the lord of celestials. By his cruel and violent acts despised by the world, all people including gods and demons indeed remain frightened of him. If enraged, he is indeed capable to turn the entire world into a single ocean" (p. 371). Shiva also is seen as the "destroyer," yet he is in fact the "transformer" who ends a world to facilitate the birth of the new one.

[1] As we already mentioned, at the end of the world there are no more "righteous men." The world laments Sîtâ's abduction, which announces its own end: "The lakes with lotuses as their faces, and fishes as their eyes, and with the other facial adornments like the swimming, sweeping and sailing water-moving beings like tortoises, waterfowls and the like are unenthused, for a similar girlfriend of theirs, the lotus-faced, fish-eyed, lotus-modeled Sîtâ is beleaguered, and thus they are sorrowing for such a selfsame Maithilî. All lions, tigers, animals and birds have then gathered in herds from all-over and ran rancorously and pursuantly shadowing the shadow of Sîtâ. The mountains appeared bewailing with their waterfalls as shedding tears and with their peaks as upraised arms, while Sîtâ is thus being abducted" (*Râmâyana*, p. 206).

[2] For example, Jatâyû, the king of birds, tries to stop Râvana from abducting Sîtâ, telling him that it will have as consequence the death of the Râkshasa race, but Râvana will cut off his wings (*Râmâyana*, pp. 203, 205). Cutting off the wings illustrates the solidification of the world, but also the interruption of the connection with the supernal states (the angelic states). It is true that other sages have the function of keeping under cover the seeds of the Tradition and they will disappear underground.

[3] Similarly, in the Christian tradition, Peter is the "voice of reason": "And He [Jesus] began to teach them, that the Son of Man must suffer many things, and be rejected by the elders, and by the chief priests, and scribes, and to be

Even Râvana's youngest brother, Vibhîshana,[1] is against the abduction, but he is a "prophet," not the "voice of reason," and he describes Sîtâ to Râvana as the dragon that will end the cycle: "Before the City of Lankâ is shattered by arrows, let Sîtâ be given away to him. Not so long as the huge army of monkeys which is very dangerous and unconquerable attacks our Lankâ, let Sîtâ be given away. If the beloved wife of Râma is not given away of your own accord, the city of Lankâ will indeed perish. ... By whom, O, king, has been wrapped around your neck this great serpent of gigantic body called Sîtâ, with heap of expended hoods as her bosom, having poison as her anxiety and with sharp fangs as her sweet smile and with five hoods as her five fingers. Even before the monkeys with their body size as mountain peaks, having their teeth and nails as weapons, rush full upon the city of Lankâ, give back Sîtâ to Râma."[2] Sîtâ is compared to a dragon, to a gigantic serpent, and, besides her apocalyptic aspect, she could be viewed as a *Nâgî*, as the theme of Garuda (the eagle symbolizing the Sun) abducting a *Nâgî* (the dragon, the serpent) is well known.[3] Vibhîshana is similar to the prophets from the Judaic tradition, but he is also, as the "youngest" brother,[4] the seed of the new cycle, the one who will be kept in Noah's Ark to become the

---

put to death, and after three days to rise again. And He spake that saying openly. And Peter took Him, and began to remonstrate with Him. But when He had turned about and looked on His disciples, He rebuked Peter, saying, Get thee behind me, Satan [*vade retro Satana*]: for thou savourest not the things that be of God, but the things that be of men" (*Mark* 8:31-33).

[1] For the comparison of Vibhîshana with Krishna see Coomaraswamy, *La doctrine du sacrifice*, p. 83. Both *Asuras* will help the production of a new cycle.

[2] *Râmâyana*, p. 406.

[3] See Coomaraswamy, *The Rape of a Nâgî*, in *Traditional Art*, p. 331. The initiatory meaning of this abduction is, of course, the "liberation" from the earthly ties, the change of the serpent (the *ego*) into the Sun (the Self), and we have here suggested a different viewpoint, where the abduction of Sîtâ is a paradigm of a spiritual realization with Râvana as solar God; the purification of Sîtâ with fire, at the end, stresses this aspect. During the initiatory process, that is, during the battle against Râvana, terrible snakes have bound Râma and Lakshmana, and Garuda will "liberate" them (*Râmâyana*, pp. 448-449).

[4] In fairy tales, the youngest brother is the *avatâra*.

king of the new world, and from this perspective he is an *alter ego* of Râma himself.[1] Sîtâ, like other characters of the *Râmâyana*, and like the characters of any initiatory tale, presents numerous symbolic facets. She is a *Nâgî*, but she is also the spiritual Sun hidden in the non-manifestation. She is *Shakti, Natura naturans*, the divine Maiden, Sophia, and *Madonna Intelligenza*; but she is also *Prakriti, Natura naturata*,[2] since King Janaka found her one day while ploughing the field, and her name means "furrow." She is, therefore, a miraculously-born child, and it is said that Sîtâ is Lakshmî's *avatâra*. Yet the main *avatâra* is Râma himself, and it is interesting to observe how this fundamental event, namely the Divinity's manifestation as *avatâra*, is symbolized in this sacred tale. Similar to other sacred stories, the birth of an *avatâra* (principal or secondary) is described as "miraculous," since the mother is a virgin, or the parents are very old and barren, or the child is born from a flower, a pepper seed, etc. In Râma's case, King Dasharatha is old and barren, and to make the miracle happen the essential royal ritual *Ashwamedha* was performed.[3] This sacrifice on earth, in which all the castes participated, had its response in heaven, where the gods said to Brahmâ: "O Lord! A Râkshasa named Râvana grown mighty by your boon oppresses us all and we cannot resist him by any means. This wicked-minded one is tyrannizing over the Three Worlds and is envious of others' prosperity. Blinded by power and by your boon, he is now thinking of conquering Indra, the king of gods, and is continually harassing the saints, the Yakshas, the Gandharvas, the Brâhmanas and the Asuras." We

---

[1] On the other hand, in the Grail stories, Vibhîshana's function is played by the father. Meleagant abducted Queen Guinevere, and his father, Bademagu, upset with this wicked deed, becomes Lancelot's adviser. Bademagu's kingdom is a symbol of the Center, of the "other world," which makes Bademagu the King of Peace; his son is, on the contrary, the "dragon," the "fallen angel" (Chrétien de Troyes, *Arthurian Romances*, J. M. Dent & Sons Ltd., 1982, pp. 308-313).

[2] Guénon, *Études sur l'hindouisme*, p. 102.

[3] *Râmâyana*, pp. 10, 14-15.

see the accord between Heaven and Earth, and we may notice the critical moment, that is, the end of a cycle, when an *avatâra* is destined to come down and start a new cycle. Usually, in fairy tales and other stories, this heavenly response is not explicitly presented, nor is the reason given why the *avatâra* is manifested as man. In the *Râmâyana*, the man is the only one that can destroy Râvana: "Then the lotus-born Brahmâ after some thought replied, 'I have found out the means of his destruction. At the time of asking the boon from me, he asked that he might not be slain by any god, Gandharva, Yaksha and Râkshasa. And I agreed to it but in disdain he did not mention the name of Man.'"[1] Only secondarily is this exceptional role due to man's central position with regard to his state of existence[2]; the main reason is related to what Ibn 'Arabî said about the "return": a complete spiritual realization means not only taking possession of the super-individual or angelic states, nor even reaching the non-manifestation, "beyond the Sun," but also integrating the formal (mortal) manifestation in "its-Self," and only then is the complete Universal Man realized, and the dualities like immortal and mortal, non-manifestation and manifestation become extinct in the Supreme Identity.

The Angels or *Dêvas* correspond to the informal manifestation, and, due to their high level of spiritual (initiatory) Knowledge, they took immediately possession of the super-individual states of the being, following *dêva-yâna* without accomplishing the whole initiatory process (like the descent to Hell), which implies a significant difference, since the integral initiatory process encompasses the Three Worlds and even the non-manifestation, while the Angels are limited by the conditions of their informal degree (state), and therefore Ibn 'Arabî considers Adam as Universal Man, above the Angels.

---

[1] For Râvana, the "man" is Achilles' heel.

[2] See also Guénon, *Initiation et réalisation spirituelle*, p. 80, about the advantage regarding the man's central position.

'Abd al-Karîm al-Jîlî defined the Universal Man (*al-Insân al-Kâmîl*) as "the synthesis of the Existence's all essential realities (*haqâiq*)" and added: "the Universal Man is the Pole around which the spheres of Existence evolve, from the first to the last one; he is Unique ... but is dressed in various forms and unveils himself through different traditional forms, having numerous names. ... The Names of the Essence and the divine Qualities belong to the Universal Man, as well as the universal kingdom ... He is to God what the mirror is to a person who looks in the mirror ... because God imposed to Himself not to contemplate His own Names and Qualities but in the Universal Man. This is also the meaning of the saying: 'Lo! We offered the faith [pact[1]] unto the heavens and the earth and the hills, but they shrank from bearing it and were afraid of it. And man assumed it. Lo! He hath proved unjust to himself and foolish [ignorant].'[2] It means that he was unjust to his own soul by lowering it from such a high rank; and he is ignorant of his own capacity, because he is the place of the divine pact and he does not know."[3] The Angels, the Heaven, the Earth, etc. preferred to perform their tasks and fulfill their functions for which they were created, but did not dare to undertake the fulfillment of the divine pact, while the man accepted to become a *Muslim* and so he became a universal symbol; moreover, the man has a "central" position in his world, encompassing all the other kingdoms and species, which makes him a "unique prototype" (*al-Unmûdhaj al-farîd*) and the *summa* of the essences of the Universal Existence.

As a "central" being in his domain of existence and with regard to the other beings of the same domain, the individual man is the most complete expression of this individual state, which makes him at the beginning of the cycle and in the primordial or Edenic state, possess, at least virtually, the state of the Universal Man, controlling all the possibilities of the

---

[1] Obedience to the divine law.

[2] *Qur'an* 33:72.

[3] 'Abd al-Karîm al-Jîlî, *De L'Homme Universel*, tr. Titus Burckhardt, Dervy-Livres, 1975, pp. 27-29.

individual domain and being indeed a *panton metron*. "And Adam gave names to all cattle, and to the fowl of the air and to every beast of the field,"[1] the name (Sanskr. *nâma*), as the essential principle of the individuality,[2] given by Adam to each being, representing a "measure" through which man, as a "central" being, determines, produces, and explicates the world that he sheltered in himself in a state of complication. God, Ibn 'Arabî narrated, has created the whole world as something amorphous first, like an unfinished mirror[3]; then, with the mirror polished and the amorphous thing shaped as a "form," Adam became the clarity of this mirror and the spirit of this "form" of the world, called the Great Man (*al-insân al-kabîr*), while the Angels represented only some of its faculties, they being for the Man what the mental and physical faculties are for the human organism. Therefore it is said: "And again, when he bringeth in the firstbegotten into the world, he saith, And let all the angels of God worship him"[4] and "For unto the angels hath he not put in subjection the world to come, whereof we speak."[5]

In the Hindu tradition, *Mârttânda* is the prototype of Man.[6] As Christ unites the divine and human natures, as Râma unites in himself the immortal and mortal, as the fairy tales' hero unites the water of life and water of death,[7] so *Mârttânda*, born

---

[1] *Genesis* 2:20.

[2] Guénon, *Études sur l'hindouisme*, p. 95.

[3] In the Hindu tradition, *Mârttânda* was born unformed (not deformed) and his brothers, the *Adityas*, shaped him into a sun.

[4] *Hebrews* 1:6.

[5] *Hebrews* 2:5. "He said: Surely I know that which ye know not. And He taught Adam all the names, then showed them to the angels, saying: Inform Me of the names of these, if ye are truthful. They said: Be glorified! We have no knowledge saving that which Thou hast taught us. Lo! Thou, only Thou, art the Knower, the Wise. He said: O Adam! Inform them of their names, and when he had informed them of their names, He said: Did I not tell you that I know the secret of the heavens and the earth? And I know that which ye disclose and which ye hide. And when We said unto the angels: Prostrate yourselves before Adam, they fell prostrate, all save Iblis" (*Qur'an* 2:30-34).

[6] For what follows see *About the Yi Jing*, pp. 94-95, 122-123.

[7] See *Folk Tales from Roumania*, Routledge and Kegan Paul, 1952, p. 56.

in accordance to a "reversed thinking" (*pratyakcêtanâ*), from the main oblation (and not from the remains, as it happened with his brothers), is the synthesis Aditi – Diti, and therefore he is indeed superior to the other *Adityas*; he is the midnight Sun, the Sun of initiatory realization, he is the real golden embryo, the integral seed, the primordial *Avatâra* and man's prototype.[1] Twashtri, "the carpenter," was in the Hindu tradition the Great Architect of the Universe. He decided to marry off his celestial daughter Sharanyû or Sanjnâna,[2] and he gave her *Mârttânda* (or Vivaswat) for a husband: it was the sacred wedding of the Sun and the Dawn. "Sanjnâ, Twashtri's daughter, was the Sun's wife. She gave him children, called Manu, Yama and Yamî"; "Twashtri's noble daughter, named Sanjnâ, was Mârttânda's wife, and she gave birth to Manu, who, as Vivaswat's son, was called Vaivaswata. Sanjnâ used to close her eyes when the Sun was looking at her. Her husband cursed her and she gave birth to Yama, a son, and to the changeable river Yamunâ, a daughter."[3] Aditi has either twelve suns as offspring,[4] or eight.[5] eight.[5] We must note that Aditi's children are pairs of twins, because, as it usually happens in the case of all sacred tales, the hidden symbolism is manifold and a synthesis of innumerable meanings and aspects.[6] The last pair of twins is special: one

[1] The name *Mârttânda* meant initially "born from an egg," and we could advance the supposition that he has a bird's form, and so he is "the sun-bird" or "the fire-bird" (that is, the *phoenix*), or that he has a serpent's form (both the bird and the serpent are born of eggs, which consolidates the idea of a feathered serpent), all this having precise equivalences in the Far-Eastern tradition.

[2] For this story, we follow *Rig-Vêda*, *Vishnu-Purâna* and *Mârkandeya-Purâna*.

[3] In Sanskrit, *yama* means "twin," and Yama – Yamî, the primordial pair, are literally The Twins. *Mârttânda* established the solar dynasty, *sûrya-vansha*. Ikshvaku was his grandson, hence the name *Ikshvaku-vansha* for Râma's family. Not only the Hindu tradition, but also Shah Jahan considered Yamunâ a holy river.

[4] "Who are Adityas? They are the twelve months of the Year" – *Brhadâranyaka Up.*, III.9.5.

[5] See *Maitrâyanî Samhitâ*, 1.6.

[6] The *Yi Jing*'s hexagrams perfectly illustrate the twins' doctrine; this doctrine doctrine is not just a theory, but it is fully and actually realized during the

became Indra and just having been born he launched himself upwards; the other one fell down, a "dead egg." This "dead egg" is *Mârttânda*, to whom the sons of men belong; he became Aditya Vivaswat, the ancestor of Manu and Yama Vaivaswata.[1]

The falling down-here of *Mârttânda* is, in fact, as the Islamic tradition specifies, a descent, an *avatarana*, and this is also how Râma was born.

---

initiatory process. We stress that two of Râma's brothers were twins: Lakshmana and Shatrughna.

[1] "Eight are the suns of Aditi who from her body sprang to life. With seven she went to meet the gods: she cast Mârttânda far away. So with her seven sons Aditi went forth to meet the earlier age. She brought Mârttânda thitherward to spring to life and die again" (*Rig-Vêda*, 10.72).

III

RÂMA-CHANDRA

Very strong symbolism accompanies Vishnu's manifestation as *Râma-chandra avatâra.* The *Dêvas* ask Vishnu to manifest as Dasharatha's sons, and the king receives from a divine messenger a large golden cup containing the celestial *Pâyasa.* "Then, from the sacrificial Fire of Dasharatha's Altar emerged a greatly vigorous and energetic Divine Being with an unparalleled resplendence, called yajna purusha." We see the importance of the sacrifice, which assures communication between Heaven and Earth, and establishes a center (the Altar) where the divine being "sent by Prajâpati," with a height "like a mountain peak," can emerge.[1] "That great Ritual Being personally brought a big golden vessel carrying it with both of his hands as if he would personally handle his own wife, which vessel is made from the molten gold and covered with a silver lid, and which appeared to be crafted out of a divine illusion, since it is dazzling like sun and glowing like the tongues of flame, and that vessel is full with the celestial Pâyasa." The vessel is doubtless similar to the Holy Grail and represents the Tradition of the new cycle, the manifested Center, and the spiritual influences (the celestial nourishment) that will nurture the world to come; yet, in this particular case, it symbolizes first of all the *avatarana*, since the king will split the *Pâyasa* in four

---

[1] Obviously, this divine messenger should be compared to the Archangel Gabriel, who was similarly implicated in the "miraculous" birth of John the Baptist (whose parents were very old) and of Jesus Christ (whose mother was a virgin), and in the descent of the *Qur'an.* We should note that the "divine being" is likened to a lion and a tiger.

parts and give it to his three queens[1]: Dasharatha gave one half
to Kaushalyâ, half of what remained to Sumitrâ, and the other
half to Kaikeyî, who gave half of it to Sumitrâ, and therefore
from three queens were born four brothers, Râma (Kaushalyâ's
son), Bharata (Kaikeyî's son), and the twins Lakshmana and
Shatrughna (Sumitrâ's sons),[2] who are all manifestations of
Vishnu and only apparently "parts" of him.[3] Since Vishnu is
indivisible,[4] his partition into four is just an illusion, and this
illusion is related, we saw, to the golden vessel, "which appeared
to be crafted out of a divine illusion," and is associated with
Râvana too, since his main wife, Mandodari, is Mayasura's
daughter.

The word "illusion" is defined today as "an erroneous
perception of reality," and derives from the Latin *illudere* (*in* +
ludo), "to play," yet, from a traditional perspective, this
"illusion," which, basically, is identical to the universal
manifestation, is very real, even though this reality is relative
and, in comparison to the Principle, is "non-permanent,"
"changeable," and therefore "illusory." As Coomaraswamy was
saying, "there is but One Hero,"[5] who plays all the characters of
this universal "play,"[6] and the divine manifestation and activity

---

[1] In any traditional writing there is this association 3 – 4.

[2] The symbolism of the twins is well known and important in any genesis of a
new world. We could also relate the splitting of *Pâyasa* to the doctrine of the
cosmic cycles, keeping in mind that the 3 – 4 association will alter the
traditional proportions; Râma represents 4/8, the twins 3/8, and Bharata 1/8;
on the other hand, the four brothers could illustrate the four castes. These
proportions suggest how the castes, but not only, were based on the
difference of the individual's nature (see Guénon, *Autorité spirituelle*, pp. 16-17).

[3] *Râmâyana*, p. 20.

[4] "The foolish regard Me as the unmanifested coming in manifestation,
knowing not My higher, immutable, unsurpassed nature. I am not manifest to
all, veiled as I am by Yoga-Mâyâ. This deluded world knows not Me, unborn
and imperishable" (*Bhagavad-Gîtâ*, VII, 24-25).

[5] *Metaphysics*, Princeton, 1977, p. 137.

[6] "It is by His magic powers (*mâyâbhih*) that He proceeds in a plurality of
aspects" (Coomaraswamy, *Metaphysics*, p. 184), where *mâyâbhih* is the "power
of illusion," yet, as we'll see, this power is the Art. "The Absolute plays in
many ways: as Ishwara, as the gods, as man, and as the universe" (Ananda K.
Coomaraswamy, *The Bugbear of Literacy*, Perennial Books, 1979, pp. 111-112).

are considered as *lîlâ*, a "sport," "playing," or "dalliance,"[1] which is the meaning of the Latin word "illusion."[2] *Brahma nirguna*, the supreme Principle, one and only, produces the worlds "simply by way of sport," as pastime.[3] Playful, the Principle unveils one of its many faces and manifests the Cosmos; playful, the Principle unveils another face and "falls" as a Dragon, together with the World; and, revealing another face, the Principle comes down as the solar Hero to save the decaying Cosmos and behead the Dragon. At the same time, the Principle remains immutable, infinite, without parts, unchanged in Itself. *Brahma* is, therefore, the Creator, the Saviour and the Devil all-together, the same as his *Shakti* is the one-and-only, yet has many faces. The Principle is the supernal Sun, super-luminous, absolute and unmovable; yet it "comes down" as *Oriens (Sol Invictus*, the Saviour) and also "falls" as a lamed, "mortal" sun to produce and maintain the Existence. This last one, evolving with the decaying cycle, appears as Dragon or Devil, the solar essence being eventually forgotten. The Saviour doesn't belong to the world: "You are from below," says Jesus; "I am from above. You are of this world; I am not of this world"[4]; instead, the Devil is *princeps hujus mundi*, belonging to this world, and the world belongs to him.

The traditional Hindu epic *Mahâbhârata* offers an excellent exemplification. The virgin Kuntî, the sacred poem tells, uses Shiva's spell and asks the Sun to come down and be her husband, and the Sun obeys and comes down to her: "By his wizardry he had split himself in two, and thus came there and

---

[1] *Metaphysics*, p. 148.

[2] "This Vedantic *mâyâ-vâda* doctrine must not be understood to mean that the world is a 'delusion,' but that it is a *phenomenal* world and as such a theophany and epiphany by which we are deluded if we are concerned with nothing but the wonders themselves, and do not ask 'Of what?' all these things are a phenomenon" (Coomaraswamy, *Traditional Art and Symbolism*, Princeton, 1977, p. 538).

[3] *Brahma Samhitâ* XVII.

[4] *John* 8:23.

went on shining in the sky."[1] This is a very important statement, describing how the Sun, emblem of the supreme Principle, sacrifices himself and operates the "cutting": it is the scission of Heaven and Earth; the two halves of the Sun are the twins, the immortal and the mortal one.[2] But the truth is that the Principle is without parts and will never split; the supernal Sun will be forever, infinite, immutable, and unchangeable, and only for the benefit of the world it seems that the Sun splits in two. The "mortal" sun comes down and will be the father of a solar hero, Karna.[3]

The "mortal" solar half, which comes down, has two faces: its first aspect is the *avatâra*, the second one is the fallen angel, the dragon. The miraculous birth of Karna (similar to Christ's birth) illustrates the first aspect: Karna is the "manifestation" of the "coming down" sun, and only seems to be "mortal"; essentially, he belongs to the "immortal" solar half that "went on shining in the sky." At the same time, the fact that, like in other spiritual tales, the child is left in an ark floating on the waters suggests the existence of a dragon; that represents the opposite face of the solar half, the "fallen" sun, which is the real "mortal" one.[4]

Aditi, the solar, infinite mother, gives birth to eight suns; she throws away the eighth sun, *Mârttânda*, the mortal one, which falls into "this world,"[5] and similarly, Hera drops Hephaestus, abandoning her child, because he is lame and deformed.[6] Therefore, *Mârttânda* and Hephaestus, both connected to celestial light and presented as fallen gods, could symbolize the Devil as Râvana or Lucifer, the fallen angel, whose name means

---

[1] *The Mahâbhârata*, Univ. of Chicago Press, 1981, tr. and ed. by J. A. B. van Buitenen, III.290.

[2] *Rig Vêda* I.164.38.

[3] Note that Kuntî will remain a virgin and she, afraid of her family, will set the child in a basket and throw him into the river (*Mahâbhârata* I.104, III.292).

[4] At the end, Karna himself becomes the dragon. Arjuna's arrow will behead Karna and his head will become the new sun.

[5] *Rig Vêda* X.72.8. See Coomaraswamy, *La doctrine du sacrifice*, p. 82.

[6] *Iliad* XVIII.394.

"light giver." Kuntî also abandoned Karna; Karna could symbolize accordingly both the *avatâra* and the fallen angel.[1] We encounter some very complicated symbolism.[2] The solar god, who was asked by Kuntî to come down, is the *avatâra*, yet an *avatâra* is also her son, Karna, the abandoned child, who could play the role of the fallen angel, the same as his father, the mortal solar half, can.[3] In this last case, the fallen sun is the king-dragon of the old cycle trying to suppress the newborn, and we know the sacred scenario: the "fall" of the cycle brings the change of the solar king into a dragon; the new solar king will behead the dragon. In fact, the solar heroes and the dragons are just the effects of the Principle's pastime, and the Vêdic statement *sarpyâ vâ âdityâh*, "the serpents are the suns," illustrates their common origin and essence.[4]

Mandodari and Sîtâ, Râma and Râvana, Vishnu's *avatâras*, and so on, are all parts of this divine playing, of this "illusion," which we have to comprehend if we want to see beyond the "irrationality" and even the "absurdity" of some elements in fairy tales, sacred stories, and initiatory epics.[5] Mandodari is an

---

[1] Eventually, the solar brothers brought Mârttânda back into Heaven and the gods also accepted Hephaestus into Olympus, events describing the alchemical "rectification." Alchemical *vitriol* illustrates, by using its letters as initials, the operative sentence, *Visita Interiora Terrae, Rectificando Invenies Occultum Lapidem*, "Visit the Bowels of the Earth, in Order that You May Come Up the Hidden Stone by Rectification" (M. Caron and S. Hutin, *The Alchemists*, Grove Press, 1961, p. 137). The "rectification" is a spiritual recovery, following the "fall," and is similar to *Kundalinî's* awakening and ascension from *chakra* to *chakra* (Guénon, *Symboles fondamentaux*, p. 229). The emblem of alchemical *vitriol* is the "green lion"; note that green, which is the colour of the stone the Holy Grail was made of, is the colour of regeneration ("rectification") and indicates the absolute Truth (Latin *viridis*, "green," and *veritas*, "truth," are very close phonetically).

[2] The same intricate symbolism appears in Jesus' statement, "It was the stone rejected by the builders that became the keystone" (*Luke* 20:17).

[3] "The Father is in me and I am in the Father" (*John* 10:38).

[4] "There were two classes of Prajâpati's sons, the Dêvas and the Asuras" (*Brhadâranyaka Up.* I.3.1).

[5] "Verily this Divine Illusion of Mine, made up of gunas, is hard to surmount. Those who seek Me alone, only they cross over this Illusion." "The Lord

equivalent or an aspect of Sîtâ,[1] but she is also, some traditional data say, Sîtâ's mother, an affirmation that makes explicit what should be a self-evident even though hidden truth[2]; moreover, the "illusory" characteristic is openly unveiled by calling Mandodari "the golden-skinned Daughter of Illusion"[3] and introducing Mayasura into the story.

Mayasura is the king of the *Asuras, Daityas* and *Râkshasas*, representing the past cycles, the races that revolted,[4] and the counter-initiatory forces, which makes his symbolism intricate, since he appears also as the single parent of Mandodari[5] and as the Lord of Tripura, the center of the Three Worlds (whose architect Mayasura is)[6]; but most of all, he symbolizes the "illusion." Yet here this "illusion" is aggressive and deceptive, belonging to the counter-initiation, as attested by the *Râmâyana* episode of the "black cave," when Hanumân and the *Vânaras*, in quest for Sîtâ, entered a dark cave in the Vindhya mountains

---

dwells in the hearts of all beings, O Arjuna, whirling by Mâyâ all beings like wooden dolls mounted on a machine" (*Bhagavad-Gîtâ*, VII, 14, XVIII, 61).

[1] When Hanumân enters Râvana's center, he mistakes Mandodari for Sîtâ (*Râmâyana*, p. 324).

[2] Mandodari, it is said, abandoned her daughter in the field where King Janaka was ploughing; it was also suggested that the name Mandodari means "a stomach like earth," which symbolically makes her an image of *Mâyâ-Prakriti*. However, this "illusion" is not singular; for example: "Daksha was born of Aditi, and Aditi was Daksha's child" (*Rig-Vêda*, 10.72); Sûrya, the sun, is both Aditi's husband and son; "O most noble and most excellent heart which is intent upon the spouse of the Emperor of the heavens – and not the spouse only, but sister and daughter best beloved!" (Dante, *The Banquet*, Anma Libri, 1989, p. 110); and also: "Virgin mother, daughter of your Son" (*Paradiso*, XXXIII, 1).

[3] *Râmâyana*, retold by William Buck, Mentor, 1978, p. 25.

[4] To revolt against the normal hierarchy means to create disorder ("anti-Cosmos") and confusion (Guénon, *Autorité spirituelle*, p. 17). Normally, the *Dêvas* are associated with the "truth" (*satyam*) and the *Asuras* with "falsehood" and "disorder" (*anritam*) (Coomaraswamy, *La doctrine du sacrifice*, p. 169).

[5] He is the "widower."

[6] In this case, Mayasura is comparable to Râvana, being described at the end of the cycle, when the unrighteousness reigned in Tripura and Shiva had to destroy the triple center. Nowadays in India, the capital-city of the small province Tripura is Agartala.

and discovered a paradisiacal-like center built by Mayasura.[1] It is a deceiving center,[2] which tempts the hero of the quest away from the straight route, like the many other temptations present in various initiatory stories[3]; it is an "illusory" center, but at the same time, from a higher perspective and obeying the *lîlâ* of *Brahma*, it appears like a subterranean, hidden, and inaccessible center, similar to Agarttha,[4] which is protected by a thick curtain of darkness,[5] and where Mayasura kept Hema captive.[6]

When Mayasura met Râvana, he declared: "I am Maya, a poor artist struggling to survive. She is my daughter Mandodari[7]; Hema the Apsara is her mother. I lived happily in love with Hema for a thousand years, but then just after Mandodari's birth her mother left us"[8]; and then he said about himself: "Maya, the Master of all Arts and Skill"; or, as Swayamprabha told Hanumân, "Maya is known as

---

[1] *Râmâyana*, pp. 295-300. "Here the monkeys beheld choicest mansions everywhere made out of gold and silver, some with golden and some with silver domes, while some with golden and some with silver multi-stories, but all are studded with lapis gems with golden windows covered with laceworks of pearls. They have also seen everywhere flowered and fruited trees that are similar in shine to red corals and rubies, and golden honeybees, as well as honeys."

[2] In the Grail stories, this paradise-like center is the initiatory starting point, and illustrates the adage that the "Paradise is a prison." This paradise-like center was born at the same time with the need for initiation.

[3] The *Vânaras* decide to give up the quest and remain in the cave (*Râmâyana*, p. 299), which, as in the Grail stories, suggests how the "Paradise is a prison."

[4] At the beginning of the cycle, the spiritual center was situated in the top of the mountain; at the end, it hid in the cave (Guénon, *Symboles fondamentaux*, p. 223).

[5] This tenebrous curtain could be penetrated only because Hanumân chanted Râma's name as a *mantra*.

[6] We see the similarity with Râvana, who abducted Sîtâ; Hema is here the daughter of Mount *Mêru*. On the other hand, the same Hema was Mayasura's beloved wife (not a captive) and Mandodari's mother.

[7] Another daughter was Somaprabhâ. See Coomaraswamy, *Trad. Art*, p. 538, and *The Bugbear of Literacy*, p. 111, where Coomaraswamy also presents another "carpenter," Râjydhara (the "royal power"), who lives in a golden palace of a Golden City (that is, in the center of the center) and is comparable to the Rich King of the Grail Castle (pp. 100-101).

[8] *Râmâyana*, retold by Buck, p. 24.

Vishwakarma ("the universal craftsman") amongst the Danavas."[1] Indeed, Mayasura is the Great Architect, comparable to Vishwakarma and considered his rival, who rebuilt Râvana's center (built initially by Vishwakarma) after its destruction,[2] but his work, in comparison to that of the divine architect Vishwakarma, is explicitly related to the idea of "illusion."[3]

In fact, Mayasura discloses another metaphysical truth: Illusion is actually Art, and therefore he is the Master of all Arts and comparable to Twashtri (the Divine Carpenter).[4] Coomaraswamy said: "Mâyâ, the 'Art' or 'Power' of creation and transformation, is an essentially divine property and can be rendered by 'Magic' only in Jacob Boehme's sense … The creation is always conceived in these terms, viz. as mâyâ-maya, a 'product of art.'"[5] René Guénon wrote an article in 1947 entitled Mâyâ, in which, commenting on Coomaraswamy, he agrees that it is much better, from a principial viewpoint, to translate mâyâ as "art" than "illusion," because the One who produces the manifestation by his "art" is the Divine Architect, and therefore the world is neither more nor less illusory (not real) than the works of art, and everything manifested is not an illusion but has its relative reality.[6]

---

[1] Râmâyana, p. 297. Danavas were the grandsons of Daksha ("the skilful one") who revolted against the Dêvas.

[2] Râvana's center presents two facets: the "illusory" Paradise (built by Mayasura, in an epoch when the initiatory process became necessary), and the real Paradise (built by Vishwakarma, and lost).

[3] Coomaraswamy said: "In connection with the Titan Maya, Mâyâ must be identified with his wife Lîlâvati, who can be called 'Illusion' only in the literal and etymological sense of the word, as being the 'means' of the divine Lîlâ" (Trad. Art, p. 538). Lîlâvati was also the name of the saintly wife of Hiranyakashipu, mother of the holy Prahlada.

[4] See our About the Yi Jing, p. 122. "Twashtri knew each magic art (mâyâ vet)" (Rig-Vêda, 10.53.9). Coomaraswamy identifies Mayasura with Twashtri (Trad. Art, p. 538).

[5] Trad. Art, p. 538. We see the deepest significance of the Mason. There is no surprise that mâyâ is derived from mâ, to "measure" (Trad. Art, p. 151, Metaphysics, p. 207).

[6] Études sur l'hindouisme, p. 101.

Mâyâ, Guénon acknowledged, is the maternal "power" (*Shakti*) and the Divine Activity; *Mâyâ-Shakti* is the superior aspect of the Virgin, woman and mother within the Principle, while *Mâyâ-Prakriti* is the inferior aspect, woman and mother within the world. *Mâyâ*, because it is the divine "art" residing in the Principle (and *a fortiori* in the Center), is identical to "Wisdom" (*Sophia*), and therefore she is the mother of the *Avatâra*.[1] As we suggested previously, the doctrine of the *avatâras* is as well part of the *mâyâ*, since there is only one eternal *Avatâra*, the principle of all the particular *avatâras* manifested during the various cycles and situated in the Center.[2] One of Vishnu's *avatâras*, Krishna, said: "Though I am unborn, of imperishable nature, and though I am the Lord of all beings, yet ruling over My own nature, I am born by My own Mâyâ. Whenever there is a decay of Tradition, O Bharata, and an ascendancy of profane, then I manifest Myself."[3] If the first *sûtra* refers to *Mâyâ-Shakti*, mother of the eternal *Avatâra*,[4] the second one indicates how any new cycle, more or less important, has its particular *avatâra* assigned to restore the Tradition.[5]

The ten *avatâras* of Vishnu, for example, are related to the four *yugas*: Matsya, Kûrma, Varâha and Narasimha *avatâras* correspond to the *Satya-yuga*, Vâmana, Parashu Râma and Râma-chandra to the *Trêtâ-yuga*, Krishna to the *Dwâpara-yuga*, while Buddha covers the end of the *Dwâpara-yuga* and the last Age, the *Kali-yuga*, which will end with *Kalki-avatâra*.

Vishnu's first divine manifestation, the *Matsya-avatâra*, refers to the passing from the previous *Manvantara* to the present one: the end of the preceding world is marked by a final cataclysm

---

[1] Guénon, *Études sur l'hindouisme*, p. 102, *La Grande Triade*, p. 22.
[2] Guénon, *Aperçus sur l'initiation*, p. 300.
[3] *Bhagavad-Gîtâ*, IV, 6-7. See also Guénon, *Études sur l'hindouisme*, p. 246.
[4] Guénon quoted this first part with regard to the *Avatâra* (*Études sur l'hindouisme*, p. 102).
[5] The doctrine of the *avatâras* or of the "divine manifestations," Guénon wrote, is closely related to the conception of the cosmic cycles (*Introduction générale à l'étude des doctrines hindoues*, Guy Trédaniel, 1987, p. 203). Vishnu's ten *avatâras* could be as well correlated to the "precession of the equinoxes."

(governed by the element water), and Vishnu as fish (in accord with the water element) will advise Manu to build an Ark (the container of the seeds necessary to commence the new cycle) and then he will be a guide and save the Ark[1]; moreover, the *Matsya-avatâra* will bring the Tradition (the *Vêda*) from the waters, the Tradition which is indispensable for the new *Manvantara*.[2] As we said with other occasions, from the very beginning of the cycle the eternal *Avatâra* is present, and so is the Dragon, which will fulfill its mission to weaken the world more and more, to produce the "fall" of the cycle, proving the ephemeral characteristic of manifestation.[3] Indeed, this is *Mâyâ* at work: even though her son, the *Avatâra*, is eternal, his projections along the cycle will be less and less durable, in accord with the duration of the four *yugas*. Therefore, not far from the starting point of the *Manvantara*, the first significant "fall" occurs when the *Dêvas* lose their power and immortality, and, again, Vishnu is the saviour and the restorer of the cycle: first, he advises the gods to drink the *amrita* (the "nectar of immortality") to regain their lost status, for which purpose the famous churning of the milky ocean (*samudra manthan*) takes place[4]; second, Vishnu manifests as a turtle, the *Kûrma-avatâra*, to stabilize Mount Mandara (the *Axis Mundi*), which is used in the churning process.[5] In the Far-Eastern tradition, the turtle has the same function: to support and stabilize the world[6]; "In

---

[1] We see the similitude between Manu and Noah, yet the Biblical flood corresponds to a secondary cycle (Guénon, *Symboles fondamentaux*, p. 173).

[2] See Guénon, *Symboles fondamentaux*, pp. 167-169.

[3] "But there was a giant from the kingdom of the dragon, who came to the place of the five mountains in no more than a few strides. In one throw he hooked six of the turtles in a bunch. (…) Therefore two of the mountains drifted to the far North and sank in the great sea" (*Lie-zi*, *The Questions of Tang*, 2).

[4] As a curiosity, we note that even today it is possible to witness in the villages of India the "churning of the milk," imitating with exactitude the divine archetype.

[5] Guénon, *La Grande Triade*, p. 51.

[6] In the Far-Eastern tradition, the turtle is a symbol of the universal manifestation: the carapace corresponds to Heaven, the plastron to Earth, and, so, the whole shell represents the Universe; in between the upper and

ancient times, Niu Wa smelted stones of all the five colours to patch up the flaws, and cut off the feet of the turtle to support the four corners."[1] The next crisis symbolizing the cycle's decline is generated by the king of the *Asuras*, Hiranyâksha,[2] who, like Râvana later, obtained from Brahmâ (due to his intense *tapas*) a boon that made him invincible; yet, he used the boon to revolt against the normal order, and battled and defeated the *Dêvas*, defeated Varuna too, and he became the Lord of the Three Worlds, with Varuna's palace under the ocean as his residence, which made him hurl the Earth into the depth of the waters. What we have here, no doubt, is the description of the end of the previous cycle, when the manifestation was retracted into the Universal Possibility and the Earth returned to its *principial* and embryonic stage, which corresponds to *Hiranyagarbha* – the "Golden Embryo"; we should recall what René Guénon said: "the Hindu tradition designates the spiritual 'embryo' in the macrocosmic order as *Hiranyagarbha*; and this 'embryo,' with regard to the world in the center of which it situates itself, is precisely the primordial *Avatâra*."[3] Hiranyâksha represents the "old king" who fell from hero to dragon, but his name, which means the "golden eye" or the "golden axis," suggests as well a direct relation with *Hiranyagarbha* and the *Avatâra*. However, Vishnu, in the form of a boar (*Varâha-avatâra*), killed the "usurper" Hiranyâksha and brought back the Earth with its tusks.

As René Guénon reported, there is an analogy (not sameness) between the cycles,[4] which with the evolvement of the *Manvantara* becomes more explicit; for this reason the following secondary cycle has Hiranyâksha's brother,

---

lower shell the turtle itself represents Man as the median term of the Great Triad (*La Grande Triade*, p. 124). In the Amerindian traditions, the turtle is the Ancestor (the *Avatâra*); in Greek mythology, the turtle was one of Hermes' symbols (his lyre was made of a turtle's shell).
[1] *Lie-zi, The Questions of Tang*, 1. The Mongols too thought the turtle supported the central mountain.
[2] He was Diti's son.
[3] *Aperçus sur l'initiation*, p. 300.
[4] Guénon, *Formes traditionnelles et cycles cosmiques*, Gallimard, Paris, 1980, p. 49.

Hiranyakashipu ("Golden Hair") as the main character. It is said that originally the two brothers were the guardians of *Vaikuntha*, the Paradise of Vishnu, yet, due to a curse, they had to manifest on Earth as Hiranyâksha and Hiranyakashipu, and then, in a later cycle, as Râvana and Kumbhakarna, and lastly, during the *Dwâpara-yuga*, as Shishupâla and Dantavakra, who were both killed by Krishna, Vishnu's eighth *avatâra*.[1] Hiranyakashipu, as well as Hiranyâksha and Râvana, spent years in meditation and great austerity (*tapas*), inducing Brahmâ to promise him that all his wishes will be fulfilled.[2] And again we see the same *Kshatriya* wish: Hiranyakashipu asked that nobody (god, human or demon) should be able to kill him, nobody should be able to defeat him in battle, and his powers, obtained by *tapas* and *yoga*, should never be lost; once more it is described how, at the end of the cycle, arrogance and revolt against God replace the normal hierarchy and order, because the decayed Hiranyakashipu wanted his son Prahlada, who became a disciple of Vishnu, to acknowledge his and not Vishnu's supremacy as the Lord of the Three Worlds. The cycle ends with Hiranyakashipu breaking in two the *Axis Mundi* (a crystal pillar)[3] and Vishnu, emerging from this very *Axis* as *Narasimha-avatâra*,

---

[1] We see once more *Mâyâ*'s activity.

[2] The theme of the wishes is common in fairy tales. Brahmâ's boon granted to Râvana, Hiranyâksha, or Hiranyakashipu is an indirect way of saying that everything is controlled by the Principle, that everything is his Art, his *Mâyâ*.

[3] At the beginning of the cycle, Hiranyakashipu himself became the Axis Mundi, because for his *tapas* he stood, for many years, recluded in the loneliness of Mount Mandara, on the toe of his right foot, with his arms raised straight up and his eyes looking up at the sky (in Hatha-yoga, this is the *Sûrya Namaskar asana*); for the symbolism of the *ekapâda* (one-footed) see our *The Everlasting Sacred Kernel.* The theme of the central pillar is common to the stories of the Holy Grail; we mention here the "great iron column" that Peredur found in the Grail Castle and which represented an initiatory trial for him: he had to "smite the iron column" three times with a sword; each time the column and the sword were smote in two pieces (*The Mabinogion*, Everyman, 1994, p. 159). We may also note the Masonic expression *The Builder is Smitten.*

kills the Dragon,[1] since he took the form of a creature that was half lion and half man, which was not part of Brahmâ's boon.

The reason why we decided to present, in some detail, the first *avatâras* of Vishnu is that these four "divine manifestations" all belong to the *Satya-yuga*, which could be puzzling for some people, since by definition the "Golden Age" is a paradisiacal era and we could expect no convulsions or battles, but only peace and harmony; yet, as we have already suggested with other occasions, the decline of the *Manvantara* starts with the cycle itself, at the very moment when the wheel commences to turn, and four *avatâras* are needed to restore this *yuga* again and again,[2] each time on a lower level[3] or on a more external circle.[4] We also notice that the "revolt" already begins in the *Satya-yuga*,[5] after the second *avatâra*, but here this "revolt" is rather a universal one and at the *principial* level, regarding the passing from non-manifestation to manifestation and not so much the humankind.

With the evolvement of the cycle, the "revolt" becomes more and more explicit and "anthropomorphic": there is first an intermediary stage when Valî, Prahlada's grandson, battled and defeated the *Dêvas*, and Vishnu as a dwarf, the *Vâmana-avatâra*, recovered the Three Worlds; then Vishnu as *Parashu Râma-avatâra* destroyed twenty-one times the *Kshatriyas* of the world who revolted.[6]

---

[1] Hiranyakashipu, the "old king," became a dragon in the end.

[2] We can assume that the secondary cycles composing the "Golden Age" are more numerous and so are the *avatâras*.

[3] In this case the Principle is transcendent – the "Most High."

[4] Here the Principle is immanent – the Center.

[5] In fact, this "revolt" had its archetype in the gods' realm. Guénon reported in a review Coomaraswamy's sayings with respect to the revolt of the *Kshatriyas* against the *Brâhmanas*, a revolt that the Jainism and Buddhism reflected, but which was prefigured, as possibility, by Indra's "Luciferian" aspect (Guénon, *Études sur l'hindouisme*, p. 228).

[6] Even the *avatâra*'s name "Râma with the Axe" indicates the dominance of the *Kshatriya* mentality. Guénon considered that *Parashu Râma-avatâra* destroyed the *Kshatriyas* who revolted when the Hindus' ancestors still lived in a Nordic region (*Autorité spirituelle*, p. 20). In the same work, Guénon specified that the attitude of the revolted *Kshatriyas* could be characterized as

Later, *Râma-chandra-avatâra* reinstated the righteous world of the *Kshatriyas*.[1]

The gradual, intensified "explication" that accompanies the evolvement of the *Manvantara* represents the journey from Center to circumference, from the principial state to that of full manifestation, and it is illustrated by the series of the ten *avatâras*: fish, turtle, boar, half lion – half human, human dwarf, and then humans. We see here a "ladder of beings" representing a gradual "humanization" in accordance with the decline of the cycle: if, at the commencement of the present *Manvantara*, the fish, a very simple being, that is, a synthetic and non-explicit symbol,[2] representing the Divine Activity and the actualization of the Universal Possibility, was intellectually understood by Manu, later, at the end of the cycle, Vishnu had to manifest as man to be comprehended; the modern "evolution chain," imitating the ten *avatâras*, is a ridiculous and absurd caricature.

If we take, for example, the first four *avatâras*, corresponding to the "Golden Age," we can trace a similitude between them and the Judeo-Christian *Genesis* with the "creation" of the Earth,[3] and we can uncover here a gradual *Genesis* that starts

---

"Luciferianism"; the "Luciferianism" is the refusal to accept a higher authority, while the "Satanism" is the reversal of the normal order and hierarchy (*ibid.* p. 46).

[1] To the *Brâhmanas* belong the super-natural or super-individual domain, and the *Greater Mysteries*; to the *Kshatriyas* belong the individual or the natural domain, and the *Lesser Mysteries*; at the same time, with the revolt of the *Kshatriyas*, the "individualism" and "naturalism" developed and became today parts of the antitradition (Guénon, *Autorité spirituelle*, p. 74, *Aperçus sur l'initiation*, p. 257).

[2] The use of animals as symbols is nothing extraordinary, and Guénon wrote an article discussing the symbolism of the boar and the bear (*Symboles fondamentaux*, p. 177). See also our *The Everlasting Sacred Kernel*, p. 52, where we showed the connection between the boar (*varâha*) and the wolf (*vrka*). The animal, since it is much less complex a being when compared to man and from the human viewpoint, is preferred to symbolize various specific functions and spiritual elements. On the other hand, for the whole manifestation, man is a better symbol, hence the doctrine of the Universal Man.

[3] "And God said, Let the waters under the heaven be gathered together unto one place, and let the dry land appear: and it was so" (*Genesis* 1:9).

with the Waters and ends with the emergence of the Earth.[1] Yet, what could be called "evolution" from a profane point of view is, in fact, an "actualization" of the possibilities of manifestation from a *prakritian* viewpoint, and decadence or "fall" from a *purushan* perspective; indeed, following the four *avatâras* we witness *Genesis* presented as a series of "falls," which could not be otherwise, since to produce the manifestation means not "to be Light," but to cripple the absolute, superluminous and eternal Light of the Principle, as recorded by many traditional data.[2] After the *Matsya-avatâra* saved the "seeds" of the new cycle, the *Dêvas* lost their powers and immortality: it illustrates the act of weakening and crippling the Principle (of course, as *Mâyâ*'s activity) in order to produce the universal manifestation and, to be even more specific, in order to produce the "duality," since the Universal Existence cannot exist without duality.[3] For this very reason the churning of the milky ocean takes place, where the two opposite forces, the *Asuras* and the *Dêvas*, are unveiled as the fundamental (yet *illusory*) "duality," suggesting why in all the cycles we have to

---

[1] "This vibration is the *Fiat Lux* that illuminates the chaos and is the necessary departing point for all the further developments" (Guénon, *Aperçus sur l'initiation*, p. 34).

[2] See for details our *About the Yi Jing*, pp. 95-99. "From the celestial point of view, the Principle is absolute Light, so powerful, so burning, that the worlds cannot survive or exist. This Light is the light of the ten suns [of the Far-Eastern tradition] shining simultaneously. Producing the universal manifestation is in this case not *Fiat Lux*; on the contrary, it is *Fiat Umbra*, the shadowing of Light. Killing the nine suns means to cripple, to veil the power of the devastating Light. We find here a second symbolism of the Trojan War. The nine years of war take place *ab intra*, in the night of non-manifestation, between two cycles, each year representing the death of a sun. In the tenth year, the Light is lame enough to show 'one foot' (Helen of Troy) without burning the World and bringing it to existence" (*The Everlasting Sacred Kernel*, p. 9).

[3] On the other hand, from the Year's specific viewpoint, the Hindu tradition stresses the implacable decay of any cycle, and therefore "in Rig-Vêda, the Angels (*dêvah*), though incorruptible (*ajara, ajurya, amrita, amartya*) during their entire 'aeviternity' (*amritatva*), are subjects to degradation at the end of a cycle (*yuga*), and to resurrection at the beginning of another one" (Coomaraswamy, *La doctrine du sacrifice*, p. 80).

have a Râma and a Râvana, while the battle between these two
forces is always a symbol of the Greater War aimed at
destroying the "illusion" of duality, at recovering the reality of
One and only, and at unveiling that "crippled" is in fact "one-
footed."[1]

The churning of the milky ocean[2] implies also
"solidification" and "multiplicity," since now the *Axis* is
stabilized by the *Kûrma-avatâra*, and evidently the "duality" will
produce "multiplicity" (yet initially it was a spiritual or *principial*
"multiplicity"); therefore, it is said that the churning brought to
light the following *principial* items: Surabhi, the cow of
abundance[3]; Vârunî, the goddess of initiatory wine (*amrita*); the
tree Pârijâta; the Apsaras; the Moon; the poison Kâlakuta; the
primeval physician Dhanvantari, an *avatâra* of Vishnu; Lakshmî;
the solar horse with the seven heads (suns); the three-headed
elephant Airâvata[4]; and the precious stone Kaustubha. As a
logical consequence, the Earth is brought up by the *Varâha-
avatâra*, but again, this cosmic event did not mean "progress": it
was another step in *Manvantara*'s (or *Maha-yuga*'s) decline,[5] since
we could say that the *avatâras* illustrate as a whole the
development from the informal manifestation to subtle
manifestation (*Vâmana*, the dwarf[6]) to corporeal manifestation.

---

[1] It is said in the Hermetic tradition: "It is a holy and divine road; but it is hard
for the soul to travel on that road while it is in the body. For the soul must
begin warring against itself, and stirring up within itself a mighty feud; and the
one part of the soul must win victory over the others, which are more in
number. It is a feud of one against two, the one part struggling to mount
upward, and the two dragging it down" (*Hermetica*, Shambhala, 1993, p. 393).
[2] See *The Mahâbhârata*, I, 16.1, The Univ. of Chicago Press, 1973, trans. A. B.
van Buitenen, I, p. 73, *Râmâyana*, p. 35.
[3] It is also called Kâmadhenu or Shabalâ.
[4] See Heinrich Zimmer, *Myths and Symbols in Indian Art and Civilization*, Harper
& Row, 1962, p. 104.
[5] It was marked by the revolt of Hiranyâksha. Indeed, any degree of making
the manifestation more explicit and more estranged from its origin is
essentially a "revolt" against Unity, against the non-manifestation, and only
the Greater War could defeat this "revolt."
[6] See Guénon, *Le règne*, pp. 210-211.

However, we are aware that, from a different standpoint, the series of the ten *avatâras* could allude to the "central" position of man with respect to his state of existence and to all the other beings belonging to this state, the man who is somehow the "seal" and the synthesis of all the elements and kingdoms existing in his world. As the Universal Man is the result and the mediator between the two Poles (Heaven and Earth), yet, at the same time, he is the synthesis and principle of the universal manifestation, so the individual man is the result and the finality of the world's "making," but he is also the central being who integrates in his primordial state all the possibilities of his state of existence, and in him the Self is most manifest.[1]

In the primordial state, the man had the benefit of peace and harmony, of what Islamic esotericism calls the Great Peace (*Es-Sakînah*) and the Rose-Cross *Pax Profunda*.[2] He enjoyed the state of immortality of the first Adam, before the "fall," and René Guénon related this state to Zhuang Zi's description: "But (the perfect man) attains to be (as it were) without form, and beyond the capability of being transformed. Now when one attains to this and carries it out to the highest degree, how can other things come into his way to stop him? He will occupy the place assigned to him without going beyond it, and lie concealed in the clue which has no end. He will study with delight the process which gives their beginning and ending to all things. By gathering his nature into a unity, by nourishing his vital power, by concentrating his virtue, he will penetrate to the making of things. In this condition, with his heavenly constitution kept entire, and with no crevice in his spirit, how can things enter

---

[1] See Guénon, *Le symbolisme de la croix*, p. 22, Coomaraswamy, *What is Civilisation?*, p. 76, Titus Burckhardt, *Mirror of the Intellect*, State Univ. of New York Press, 1987, p. 42, Guénon, *La Grande Triade*, p. 31, Guénon, *L'Erreur spirite*, Éd. Traditionnelles, 1984, p. 216.

[2] Guénon, *Le symbolisme de la croix*, p. 51. In the Far-Eastern tradition, the center, called the City of the Willows, was the House of the Great Peace (Guénon, *La Grande Triade*, p. 202).

(and disturb his serenity)?"[1] This means that nobody can damage the primordial man and, we remember, this is the main boon Hiranyakashipu requested from Brahmâ: to be immune to death, that nobody (god, human or demon) should be able to kill him, nobody should be able to defeat him in battle, and his powers obtained by *tapas* and *yoga* should never be lost.

Therefore, if we have to consider the Greater War, this is only because "we are no longer in the primordial epoch, when all men were normally and spontaneously in possession of a state that today is related to a high degree of initiation; and even the word initiation, in that epoch, did not have any sense ... Another [initiatory] condition is effort,[2] which men of the primordial ages did not need, because the spiritual development was realized in them as naturally as the corporeal development."[3] Consequently, the man's "central" position becomes crucial for the initiatory process, for the Greater War, for the "development towards a perfect Self-awareness,"[4] and if at the end of the "Golden Age" it was enough to be "half man" to defeat Hiranyakashipu, later, to defeat Râvana, a "full" man was needed (in fact, four men). "For all beings a human birth is difficult to obtain ... rarer than that is Brâhmanahood; rarer still is the attachment to the part of Vedic tradition; higher than this is knowledge of the scriptures; discrimination between the Self and not-Self, Realization, and continuing in a state of identity with Brahma – these come next in order ... These are three things which are rare indeed and are due to the grace of God – namely a human birth, the longing for liberation, and the

---

[1] *The Texts of Taoism*, Dover, 1962, tr. James Legge, II, p. 13, Guénon, *Le symbolisme de la croix*, p. 54, Léon Wieger, *Les pères du système taoïste*, Les Belles Lettres, 1983, p. 357 (*Tchoang-tseu*, chap. 19, B).

[2] Today, this effort is indispensable; it is a personal or an individual effort, which cannot be granted or accomplished by somebody else, and it defines the Greater War. This effort follows the "second birth," namely a "regeneration" that "re-establishes the being in the prerogatives that were only natural and normal in the primeval ages of humanity" (Guénon, *Aperçus sur l'initiation*, p. 35).

[3] Guénon, *Aperçus sur l'initiation*, pp. 31-32.

[4] Coomaraswamy, *What is Civilisation?*, p. 77.

protecting care of a perfect sage ... What greater fool is there than the man who having obtained a rare human body ... neglects to achieve the real end of this life?"[1] And the *Râmâyana*, although it was specifically intended for the *Kshatriyas*, contains a famous example of a *Kshatriya* reaching *Brâhmanahood*, namely Vishwâmitra, who is paradigmatic in his efforts to win the Greater War[2]; and it is no coincidence that Râma's first *guru* would be the same Vishwâmitra. While Parashu Râma is considered a *Brâhmana-Kshatriya*,[3] Râma is a

---

[1] Shri Shankarâchârya, *Vivekachûdâmani*, 2-5.

[2] See *Râmâyana*, pp. 38 ff. (*Bâla Kânda*, sarga 51 ff.). Vishwâmitra's "initiation" (*initium* = "entrance, beginning," Guénon, *Aperçus sur l'initiation*, p. 31) is described as a terrible war against the maharishi Vasishtha, which appears as a "revolt" of the *Kshatriyas* against the *Brâhmanas*; Vishwâmitra wanted to abduct *Brâhmana*'s holy cow Shabalâ (born from the churning of the milky ocean), a cow that could be compared to the Holy Grail. *Brâhmana* Vasishtha plays the role of the hidden *guru*, since externally he battles and defeats the *Kshatriya* king, while internally he provokes him to accomplish a series of very severe *tapas*; at the end, Vasishtha is the one who grants him *Brâhmanahood*. In a way, we could compare Vishwâmitra with Râvana: while the former cannot abduct Shabalâ (the Knowledge, the Tradition), but is forced to accomplish a difficult spiritual realization to take possession of this Knowledge (similar to Dante who could not reach the Paradise directly), the latter abducts Sîtâ, but fails miserably. We should as well mention the controversial last chapter of the *Râmâyana*, *Uttarâkânda*, in which is described the battle between Râvana and Haihaya king Kârtavîrya Arjuna (see *Râmâyana*, p. 585) and the humiliating defeat of the former (moreover, the *Vâyu Purâna* describes how Kârtavîrya conquered Lankâ and took Râvana prisoner). This *Kshatriya* Kârtavîrya Arjuna tried to abduct from Jamadagni the same divine cow, Kâmadhenu; Jamadagni was, like Vasishtha and Vishwâmitra, one of the *saptarishi* (the seven sages). Parashu Râma, Jamadagni's son, killed Kârtavîrya and his army, but later the king's sons beheaded Jamadagni, and therefore Parashu Râma exterminated all the *Kshatriyas*. We saw the difference between Vishwâmitra and Râvana, and, again, there is an essential distinction between Vishwâmitra and Kârtavîrya, since, even though both are *Kshatriya* and both try to abduct the holy cow, the first will replace his "revolt" with a sincere and relentless spiritual realization, recognizing the superiority of the *Brâhmanas*, while the second (and his partisans) symbolize the temporal power that will usurp the spiritual authority and will illusorily think that the Knowledge received from the *Brâhmanas* belongs rightly to the *Kshatriyas* (Guénon, *Autorité spirituelle*, p. 34).

[3] His mother, Renukâ, was from a *Kshatriya* family; like in fairy tales (which contain initiatory lore for the royal caste), Parashu Râma was the "youngest"

pure *Kshatriya,* where "pure" defines not only that he is entirely
from the royal caste, but also that he is a perfect *Kshatriya.*[1]

---

son (see *The Everlasting Sacred Kernel,* p. 43) and he got his name ("Râma with
the Axe") because of his *Kshatriya* behaviour.

[1] "Râma was beautiful in form, a hero of valour and without envy. That Râma
was always peaceful in mind and spoke softly. He did not react to the hard
words spoken by others. Râma was a wise man. His speech was
compassionate. He was valorous. But he was not arrogant of his mighty
valour. He did not speak untruth. He was all knowing. He used to be receptive
and worshipful to the elders. People used to love him and he used to love the
people. He had always self-control. That Râma, having an attitude suitable for
his social rank, giving due respect to righteousness of warrior-class, believed
that by following the righteousness he would attain great fame and through it
the fruit of heaven. Râma knew the theory and practice of sciences. He
understood the differences among men. He could judiciously discriminate
whom to protect and whom to punish. He was efficient in riding and taming
of elephants and horses. Râma was the best of persons knowing the science of
archery in the world; and was well appreciated by the champions of archery.
He attained skills in marshalling the army. He faced and killed the enemies in
battle" (*Râmâyana,* pp. 53, 55). "Bravery, boldness, fortitude, promptness, not
flying from battle, generosity and lordliness are the duties of the Kshatriyas,
born of nature" (*Bhagavad-Gîtâ,* XVIII, 43).

IV

THE GREATER WAR

The commencement of Râma's Greater War is a typical one, since the position corresponding to the "first Adam" is comfortable, even though somehow "illusory" because of the descent of the *Manvantara*,[1] and when Vishwâmitra had asked King Dasharatha to approve Râma's departure in order to fight the *Râkshasas*, the father first refused the demand,[2] yet later agreed when he understood that it was about Râma's initiation (and, consequently, the redemption of the world); the great sage Vasishtha explained to Dasharatha: "Râma is Justice manifestated on earth. He is the wisest and mightiest of all; he is the protector of all sacred rites and is skilled in weapons.[3] And the great sage [Vishwâmitra] you see before you is not less

---

[1] It is a paradise-like position.

[2] *Râmâyana*, p. 22. Likewise, Ulysses and Achilles tried to avoid participating in the Trojan War.

[3] He is the perfect *Kshatriya*. It is interesting to quote Râma's traditional view about death: "Man is not able to do what he wills. What rises, ends in a fall. Union ends in separation. Life ends in death. How a ripe fruit does not fear for anything other than its falling, so also a man once born, does not fear for anything other than his death. As a house that is solidly constructed ultimately falls into decay, human being too is subject to age and death. You grieve for yourself. Why do you grieve for another? Even while you stay at home, or departed to another place, your life-span gets shortened. Death walks just with us (as we walk) and sits with us (as we sit). Having traveled a very long distance (with us), death returns along with us (as we return). As pieces of drift-wood floating on the ocean come together for a span, so wives, children, kinsmen, wealth and property come together for a while and part with us. Here, no being can escape its destiny (in the form of birth and death)" (*Râmâyana*, pp. 146-147).

mighty; the past, the present, and the future are known to him. Therefore, do not hesitate for a moment to send Râma with him. Vishwâmitra himself can destroy those Râkshasas; it is for the benefit of Râma that he wants him."[1] In fact, this first "war" of Râma is just a "summary" of the real War, and would end with his "first" wedding, after Râma successfully passed the initiatory trial of the Great Bow; like in fairy tales,[2] in the Râmâyana, King Janaka vowed to marry his daughter, Sîtâ, to the man who could put string to the divine bow,[3] a trial that is also found in the Odyssey, but where it concerns Ulysses' "second wedding" (that is, his Greater War and the end of his initiatory "return").[4] There is no direct suggestion in the Râmâyana about the "two weddings," yet, symbolically, each of these "weddings" is also a "coronation" and we see in the sacred tale how Râma's initiatory journey occurs between two "coronations": the first one initiates the spiritual realization, in accord with the divine plan,[5] while the second one seals the "return," namely the descending realization as part of the integral spiritual process.[6]

---

[1] Râmâyana, p. 23.
[2] It is well known that in fairy tales the emperor promises to marry his daughter to the hero who will accomplish the initiatory trials.
[3] Râmâyana, pp. 29, 44-45.
[4] See The Everlasting Sacred Kernel, p. 17. This initiatory trial is common to fairy tales, but we will find it also in the Romance of Tristan and Iseult, where the king of Ireland promises to give his daughter Iseult to whoever would kill the dragon (see Gottfried von Strassburg, Tristan, Penguin Books, 1967, p. 159, Joseph Bédier, The Romance of Tristan and Iseult, Vintage Book, 1965, p. 23).
[5] In this case, Râma's brother, Bharata, reigns as Râma's substitute. His mother, Kaikeyî, apparently provokes Râma's initiation, when she hears that Dasharatha wants to enthrone Râma; Kaikeyî, the "step-mother," has well known counterparts in fairy tales.
[6] Râmâyana, pp. 54, 62, 63, 67. We observe that Râma's "way," as in Jesus Christ's case, is primary an archetypal itinerary through which not only a new tradition and cycle are established (meaning, in Christian words, salvation for all), but also the initiatory process. Râma is Vishnu's avatâra, which means that he already realized the "return" when Vishnu descended (avatarana) and manifested as Râma (this descent Guénon illustrated by explaining how a Bodhisattwa becomes a Buddha by a descendant realization). With this descent, an avatâra brings the spiritual influences to the new world (the Tabula

As the knights of the Holy Grail prefer to wander into the forest and leave their families, so Râma for fourteen years[1] is doomed to leave his family, throne and wealth, and go into exile, accompanied by Sîtâ and Lakshmana[2]; like the Grail Knights, Râma, on his way to Dândaka forest,[3] will meander from hermitage to hermitage, completing his spiritual journey from center to center, from the sage Bharadwâja to Vâlmiki and next to the paradisiacal hill Chitrakûta, where Râma said: "I feel great delight in this beautiful hill abounding in fruits and flowers and in tuneful birds. ... My forefathers have assigned forest-life as best suited for the attainment of liberation. ... So I feel myself immensely happy."[4]

The next center is the hermitage of the sage Sharabhanga, in the Dândaka forest,[5] and Râma's spiritual adviser is now the terrible *Râkshasa* Virâdh that, mortally wounded by Râma, would show him the way; in fact, by killing Virâdh, Râma helps him to obtain "salvation," liberating him from a curse, which is the real significance of a sacrifice. Similarly, the sage Sharabhanga shows Râma the way and then tells him: "I shall cast off this infirm body in your presence, as a snake cast off its slough," illustrating a well known symbolism regarding spiritual liberation, when the "old skin" or the "snake skin"[6] is thrown

---

Smaragdina said: "taking unto itself thereby the power of the Above and the Below") (Guénon, *La Grande Triade*, pp. 195-196).

[1] The number 14 could allude to the 14 *Manvantaras*.

[2] Similarly, Tristan, Iseult and Governal have to leave the world and find shelter in the forest (Bédier 66, Beroul, *The Romance of Tristan*, Penguin, 1982, p. 75). For Grison, the forest where Tristan and Iseult live is a figure of the Earthly Paradise (Jean-Louis Grison, *Notes sur les œuvres de Chrétien de Troyes*, Études Traditionnelles, 1973, no. 437-438, p. 168).

[3] The dark "forest," Coomaraswamy said, is equivalent to the "cave," which is Vritra's belly and "Brahma's womb," from where all things were produced at the beginning (*La doctrine du sacrifice*, p. 112). For Gottfried von Strassburg, the dark forest where Tristan and Iseult will hide is in fact the "cave of lovers" (p. 261).

[4] *Râmâyana*, pp. 133-4.

[5] "On entering the mighty forest of Dândaka, Râma saw hermitages surrounded by a halo of spiritual glory" (*Râmâyana*, pp. 158, 160-161).

[6] See Coomaraswamy, *La doctrine du sacrifice*, p. 62.

away to let the glorious solar Self shine.[1] Râma continues his
journey and, after meeting the sage Sutîkshna and then the sage
Agastya, finds residence in the Panchavati forest, another
center: "Râma lived happily for some time in that forest like a
god in the heavenly region."[2]

We must repeat that Râma's "journey" has to be seen
primarily as an inner spiritual realization, and each phase means
that the center of the corresponding level of the being has been
taken into possession, which includes assimilating a higher
knowledge, purifying and discarding the "old skin," and
reaching a superior center of conscience.

Râma begins his Greater War by going into exile, together
with his wife, and, even though there are numerous initiatory
steps in this War, we can discern two main phases separated by
Sîtâ's abduction, something similar to the *Lesser Mysteries* and
Greater Mysteries.[3] The trials of the first phase prepare the

---

[1] It is worth noticing how the same initiatory station contains a *Râkshasa* and a
sage; they both reach liberation, yet this symbolizes in fact Râma's own
spiritual advancement.

[2] *Râmâyana*, p. 170.

[3] Commenting on Dante's work, René Guénon stressed that normally the
Lesser Mysteries, with the Earthly Paradise as target, are the appanage of the
Kshatriyas, and the *Greater Mysteries*, aiming at the Heavenly Paradise, are for the
Brâhmanas. Dante specified that the first goal is accomplished using the
"philosophy" and the second using the "Revelation." The "philosophy,"
Guénon explained, must be understood in its primary sense (found at the
Pythagoreans) of "love for wisdom," and this way is just a preparation for the
real *Sophia*, as Earthly Paradise is for Heavenly Paradise. However, Dante's
"philosophy" indicates that, to reach Earthly Paradise, the being needs all the
individual faculties (that Dante comprised them in one, the mind) but nothing
beyond. To reach Heavenly Paradise, a "jump" is needed (Dante said *sallire alle
stelle*), like Lancelot's jump, famous in the Grail stories; this "jump" means that
the individual faculties are now powerless, and the "Revelation" is needed,
which represents a direct "communication" with the super-individual states
(heavenly or angelic), based on transcendent faculties with regard to the
individual, called either "intellectual intuition" or "inspiration" (this
"inspiration" was witnessed in the Christian tradition when the Holy Spirit
descended upon the Apostles). This "communication" is first of all (as the
words "revelation" and "inspiration" prove) a "teaching" from above
downward, along the Solar Ray (which is, in the Hindu tradition, *Buddhi*, the
pure intellect, of a universal and not individual order); it is the "teaching"

neophyte for the Quest and disrupt the illusory peace and happiness of this substitute center which is Dândaka forest, a center where Râma lived in a very similar way as he did at home, namely without making any special effort to try to advance on his initiatory voyage.[1] The purpose of this first phase is to activate Râma's initiatory possibilities, and God uses the best instruments available, which are Râvana's sister and brother, though these two are unaware of their role.[2]

"At one time when Râma is sitting in the hermitage and heartily absorbed in telling narratives some *Râkshasi* arrived at that place, fortuitously.[3] She is but the sister of ten-faced demon Râvana, Shûrpanakhâ by her name, and she has seen

---

Krishna (representing the "Self," *Âtmâ*) gave to Arjuna (the "me," *jîvâtmâ*), illustrating from an inner point of view, as Guénon said, how the "Self" reveals and communicates itself to the "me" through the supra-rational, intellectual intuition (which is, in fact, this "teaching"); however, for this communication to become effective a "qualified" and prepared "me" is absolutely necessary (actually, a "sacrifice" occurs with its essential function of establishing the communication with the superior states; see Guénon, *Études sur l'hindouisme*, p. 11, *L'homme et son devenir selon le Vêdanta*, Éditions Traditionnelles, Paris, 1991, p. 180). The achievement of this "communication" means that *jîvâtmâ* gets undressed of *jîva* and realizes that it is not different from *Âtmâ*. Also, in the Hindu tradition, the distinction between "Revelation" and "philosophy" is the difference between *Shruti* and *Smriti*. The *Shruti* is the direct inspiration, the direct light, the pure intelligence, and corresponds to the *Greater Mysteries* and to the *Brâhmanas*; the *Smriti* is the reflected light, and corresponds to the *Lesser Mysteries* and to the *Kshatriyas* (Guénon, *Autorité spirituelle*, pp. 99-102; see as well *L'homme et son devenir*, pp. 20-21, and *Introduction générale*, pp. 189-190). We also should remark the association between the initiatory process and the cosmogony. In the Hindu tradition, the "activation" of the three *gunas* follows the sequence: *tamas, rajas, sattwa*; also, the Three Worlds are produced in this order: *Bhu, Bhuvar, Swar*. The initiatory process goes from *Corpus* to *Anima*, and then to *Spiritus*, and this is also the way the Masons built a cathedral, where the last element was the keystone.

[1] We should not forget that Râma was born in the *Trêtâ-yuga*, when the initiation became a necessity, and the starting point only imitates the primordial state.

[2] As Guénon said, it is a mistake to confuse the "terrible" gods with diabolic entities (*Études sur l'hindouisme*, p. 205).

[3] Of course, nothing is "fortuitously."

him on reaching the paradisiacal being like Râma. He whose face is radiant, arms lengthy, eyes large like lotus petals, stride like that of an elephant, wearing bunches of hair-tufts, delicate yet greatly vigorous, possessor of all kingly aspects, complexion deep-blue like blue lotus, similar to Love-god in brilliance and in simile to Indra, the demoness has seen such a Râma and became lovesick."[1]

Shûrpanakhâ is, essentially, Sîtâ's *alter ego* or her "opposite visage," and that is why Râvana's sister describes Sîtâ as hideous: "I am endowed with such preponderances and I can operate with my independent might, as such you become my everlasting husband ... by the way, what can you bring off with Sîtâ. Unlovely and unhappily is this one, such as she is, this Sîtâ is unworthy to be your wife, and I am the lone one worthy to be your wife, hence treat me as your wife. ... Shall I eat up this disfigured, dishonest, diabolical human female with a hallow stomach along with him, that brother of yours, to make you free." Ananda K. Coomaraswamy covered *in extenso* the symbolism of the *Hideous Bride* (the *Loathly Lady*),[2] who, from an initiatory viewpoint, represents the Self and the absolute Knowledge that the neophyte has to unveil and uncover (discover) at the end of his Quest, which implies kissing or beheading the Dragon-Lady, or just killing the Dragon that abducted the Lady.[3] In Râma's case, since the end of the Greater War is not the transformation of Shûrpanakhâ, but of Sîtâ herself, Lakshmana (Râma's substitute) will just chop the

---

[1] *Râmâyana*, p. 172.

[2] See *La doctrine du sacrifice*, pp. 139 ff.

[3] Often, the symbolism is presented in a more explicit form, and therefore the Maiden becomes associated with the Dragon against her will, even though, in fact, the Maiden and the Dragon are one and the same. As the hero at the end of the cycle becomes the dragon, so the maiden becomes the hideous wife, and another hero is needed to disenchant the dragon-lady; the transformation of Cinderella at the end of the tale or the "taming of the shrew" is nothing else but this disenchanting. The story of the Holy Grail includes, as expected, this symbolism (see for example Sir Gawain's wedding).

nose and ear of the *Loathly Lady*,[1] as an anticipation of the final act.[2]

To avenge his sister, Khara, Râvana's brother, attacks Râma with a large army of *Râkshasas*, but Râma will start an "all-destructive cosmic-dance," exterminating them all, a deed symbolizing the annihilation or the reintegration of multiplicity[3] and the anticipation of the final war against the revolt and heterodoxy at the end of the cycle. Râma said: "You are atrocious in conduct because you countervail against Vêdas, debased by conscience because you counteract to Vêdic rituals, and you are countermanding Vêdic procedures because you have always been bothersome to Brâhmanas, and those Brâhmanas becoming sceptical of your deeds of hindrance, they are hesitatingly consigning oblations into Ritual-Fire, which are to be swiftly dropped into fire to the chants of hymns and even on time, hence you are countervailing against Vêdas and counteracting to their rituals, and countermanding their procedures."[4]

There is in the *Râmâyana* a visible application of the initiatory method that gradually leads the neophyte to liberation (*Arundhati-darshananyâya*): at first, Râma considered Dândaka forest and his exile as a goal in itself; then, he regarded the extermination of Khara and his army as a conclusion to the war, but, in fact, this was only a small step of his spiritual ladder and the Greater War was still to come; indeed, Râvana will force *Râkshasa* Mâricha to take the form of a golden deer and lure

---

[1] *Râmâyana*, p. 173.

[2] In the final act, Sîtâ is "purified" in fire, which means that she loses the "serpent skin," unveiling her splendour and brilliancy. See Coomaraswamy, *La doctrine du sacrifice*, pp. 91, 93-95, 110-111.

[3] The *Râkshasas* asked Râma: "what capability do you have as a lone one to stand against many of us?" (*Râmâyana*, pp. 175, 178).

[4] On the other hand, Khara's death is a spiritual advancement for Râma; Râma said to Khara: "In boasting you are knavish, in character roguish, and in behaviour ghoulish, such a demon as you are, I will take your life away as the divine eagle Garuda took away *soma*."

Râma away from Sîtâ, which allows Râvana to abduct her,[1] and consequently initiates the Quest.

The Quest commences with two encounters, contradictory in appearance, since one is with a *Râkshasa* and the second with a holy woman, yet both are intermediate stages of liberation and symbolize Râma's spiritual growth. First, Râma comes across Kavandha, a *Râkshasa* without head and neck, but his breast has a huge mouth and one eye; once he is killed by Râma, the curse is broken and Kavandha regains his freedom and his initial status of handsome *Gandharva*.[2] Then, Râma reaches the hermitage of Savari who was working on her *tapas*; she said: "Just now, on your pleasing manifestation before me my ascesis is accomplished," and she throws herself into fire, being thus raised to heaven.[3]

Following Kavandha's advice,[4] Râma starts the next phase, which is the quest for Sugrîva, the king of *Vânaras*, and Hanumân, the counsellor of Sugrîva, will be Râma's vehicle in the Quest. Hanumân plays a special and complex role in this initiatory tale,[5] symbolizing Râma's "humanity" (characterized by *manas*, which is what gives the name *man* to a human being), but we have to see Hanumân not only as the "mental force" but also as the intellectual intuition, *Buddhi*, regarded from the human being's perspective, namely the Intellect projected as *manas* and *prâna*.[6] In fairy tales, the spiritual vehicle is often the

---

[1] *Râmâyana*, pp. 193, 197, 211. The golden deer represents the temptation inherent in any initiatory journey and here it made Râma lose his *palladium*; on the other hand, the golden deer and her sacrifice (Râma kills her) represent an initiatory trial found also in other tales (see, for example, *The Story of White Arab* in *Folk Tales from Roumania* or the Grail stories where the white hart plays a significant role).

[2] *Râmâyana*, pp. 223-225.

[3] *Râmâyana*, pp. 227-228. These two "liberations" are, in essence, Râma's transitional liberations.

[4] Like in fairy tales, each stage brings advice and direction for the hero.

[5] We mention that Sri Râmakrishna took Hanumân as model for his devotion and tried to behave as Hanumân.

[6] We could consider Râma ready for the *Greater Mysteries*, a stage Guénon explained as follows: "At a much higher degree are situated those who, having extended their conscience to the extreme limits of the integral individuality,

horse, which flies with the speed of the wind and of mental thought; in the *Râmâyana*, Hanumân is the same vehicle and he is described like thought: "Hanumân who could assume any desired form," and wind: "Hanumân, best among monkeys, the intellectual son of Vâyu." We notice as well that Râma's army is composed of monkeys (*Vânaras*) and bears (*Bhallûkas*), because they are the most similar in appearance to man, and the bear is the symbol of the *Kshatriya*.[1] The next stage of the Greater War is the "discrimination trial." The power of discrimination (symbolized by *Hamsa* in the Hindu tradition[2] and by the *Qur'an*[3] in Islam) guarantees the right choice between heavenly (supernal) and terrestrial (infernal) symbols, between the immortal and mortal twin, between the wheat and the darnel[4]; it means to achieve the spiritual power of discrimination (Sanskrit *viveka*) between the truth of Brahma and the illusion of the world, as Shankarâchârya explained in a whole book.[5] In the *Râmâyana*, the power of discrimination is applied with regard to Sugrîva and his identical brother Valî, who abducted Sugrîva's wife; slaying Valî, Râma destroys the illusion of duality and reveals

---

are capable of seeing directly the superior states of their being, without though effectively participating to them; we are here in the initiatory domain, but this initiation, real and effective with regard to the extension of the individuality in its extra-corporeal modalities, is nonetheless only theoretical and virtual with respect to the superior states, because it did not accomplish the actual possession of them" (*Aperçus sur l'initiation*, p. 171).

[1] *Râmâyana*, p. 282. See Guénon, *Symboles fondamentaux*, p. 180.

[2] *Hamsa*, the Hindu tradition says, is the symbol of *viveka*, because from a mixture of water and milk he is capable to drink only the milk, the spiritual white beverage (Ananda K. Coomaraswamy, *Pour comprendre l'art hindou*, Tradition Universelle, 1926, p. 104).

[3] The *Qur'an* is defined as *al-Furqân*, "the Instrument of Discrimination."

[4] *Matthew* 13:24-30.

[5] Shri Shankarâchârya, *Vivekachûdâmani*, Advaita Ashrama, Calcutta, 1974. In *The Story of White Arab*, the hero has to discern the Maiden from an illusory identical copy. See also Boron, *Merlin and the Grail*, pp. 16-17, where the Judas' kiss is explained as a way to differentiate Jesus from his cousin James the Lesser, who "looked very much like Jesus"; this is very interesting, since here the kiss has a metaphysical meaning, concerning the "discrimination" between immortal and mortal.

the real one.[1] With this, the intellectual intuition is activated, and the next step is Hanumân's quest for Râvana's center and for Sîtâ. We would have expected to see Râma embarked on this quest, but, like in fairy tales, since it is primarily an inner spiritual realization, a different integral being's component intervenes with each stage, the higher the stage, the higher the component. Hanumân, as fast as wind and thought,[2] represents, of course, not the complete and effective spiritual realization, but rather a theoretical, virtual and mental one, a preparation for real and everlasting realization[3]; however, Hanumân's voyage is not a simple one, and comprises higher and essential phases of Râma's Greater War.

There are a number of symbolic trials for Hanumân: "This glorious son of Vâyu, going by the name of Hanumân is flying over the ocean. You obtain a horrible mountain like demonic appearance and make a face with fearful tusks, red-brown eyes and as vast as the sky, and create an obstacle to him for an instant. We desire to find out if by his strength and also courage and intelligence he can win over you or obtain sorrow." Beside this, Hanumân is swallowed by Surasâ, the mother of the serpents (Nâgamâtr), and then by the Râkshasi Sinhikâ, both trials meaning a death and a rebirth. "Hanumân then saw the City of Lankâ having a resemblance of Amarâvati, the capital City of Indra, the heavenly city."

Reaching the center, Hanumân has to deploy again the power of discrimination, or rather to comprehend the mystery[4]

---

[1] *Râmâyana*, pp. 238-252. We see how this apes Sîtâ's abduction; it represents an intermediate initiatory level, reflecting the supreme one, when Râma kills Râvana like he kills Vali here.

[2] "I will go to the city of Lankâ, ruled by Râvana, just like an arrow released by Râma will go, with wind-like speed."

[3] As Guénon said, this stage is when the initiate realizes the light, not only through its reflections and shadows, but through its rays, yet still an effective realization has to come during which the neophyte will reach the source of light (*Aperçus sur l'initiation*, p. 171).

[4] We use the word "mystery" to stress that we have here something that is not unknowable but inexpressible (see Guénon, *Les états multiples de l'être*, Guy Trédaniel, Paris, 1984, p. 94).

of the "many into One," which could be symbolized by the well known geometrical image of the circle, where the indefinite number of points on the circumference traveling along the radii to the center will become One in the very center, but will still be potentially many. Hanumân will notice in the center Râvana's innumerable wives: "Women of royal sages, Brâhmanas and Daityas, and of Gandharvas, of Râkshasas – all those unmarried girls surrendered from lust to Râvana. All those women had been stolen by Râvana with a desire for war, some together with heat of youth obtained Râvana being desired by god of love. There, even one woman had not been obtained forcefully by the strong Râvana, except for that daughter of Janaka, Sîtâ."[1] To mark even stronger the reality of One and the illusion of many, the story tells us that Sîtâ was not with the many in the center, but alone in another center – the hidden and most "central" center (the Ashoka garden or forest): "The strong Hanumân observing girls from Dêvas, Gandharvas and girls from Nâgas did not see Jânakî. He then not seeing her there and seeing other best women then started to think deeply going far from there."[2] Hanumân reaches the Ashoka garden, finds Sîtâ, and, to stress the reality of One, destroys the garden, leaving untouched only the tree (the *Axis Mundi*) sheltering Sîtâ.[3]

---

[1] *Râmâyana*, p. 322. We notice that the only one abducted is Sîtâ. We could also say that the multiplicity loves Râvana, or that Râvana, at the end of the cycle, became overwhelmed by multiplicity (like Solomon, in a way).

[2] *Râmâyana*, p. 325.

[3] *Râmâyana*, pp. 362-363. The tree, which is the symbol for the *Axis Mundi*, but also indicates the center as temple, is often present in the Grail stories, usually in connection to a damsel who represents a *Dryad* or an equivalent "nymph of the tree" like the Hindu *Yaksha*. Ananda K. Coomaraswamy explained the symbolism: "*Yaksha* is the invisible spirit that indwells and manifests itself in the Tree of Life ... The identification of the Tree with Brahman ... takes us back to the question asked in *RV* X.31.7 and X.81.4, 'What was the Wood, and what the Tree, of which they fashioned Heaven and Earth' ... and the answer in *Taittirîya Brâhmana* II.8.9.6, 'The Wood was Brahman, Brahman the Tree, whereof they fashioned Heaven and Earth; it is my considered word, ye knowledgeable men, that there stands the Brahman, world-supporting.' Bearing in mind the dual nature of the Brahman, 'in a

Nevertheless, we should not forget that we have here a *Kshatriya* initiation and the spiritual realisation is a Greater War; therefore, Hanumân will carry out four battles, and at one moment he would be bound by Indrajît, Râvana's son: "Indrajît, who knows the true nature of divine weapons, bound that Hanumân, the son of wind-god ... Hanumân became motionless and fell down on the ground. Realizing that he had been bound by a weapon presided over by Brahmâ the Lord of creation that Hanumân, failing to keep his swiftness, considered it to be a favour of Brahmâ the creator done to him. Knowing it to be a weapon presided over by Brahmâ the creator and consecrated by spells sacred to Brahmâ, the creator, Hanumân then recollected a boon got by Lord Brahmâ, the grand father of the entire creation: 'I have no capacity to liberate from the bondage of the weapon due to the power of Brahmâ the father of the world. Thus knowing the bondage, through the weapon presided over by Brahmâ the self-born creator imposed by the enemy, it must be obeyed by me.' ... that Hanumân obeyed the command of Brahmâ the grand father of the entire creation. 'Since I am being protected by Brahmâ, Indra and the wind-god, I do not have fear, even though I am fastened by the weapon. Even if I were captured by the Râkshasas, a great advantage is foreseen. There will be a dialogue with Râvana. Therefore, let the enemies capture me.'"

There is no clearer example of how the Art of *Brahma* works. Like in the case of Troy, Râvana's center is only superficially a

---

likeness and not in any likeness,' the relation of the Brahman-Yaksha to the Brahma-tree can easily be understood; the Brahman-Yaksha is both the unseen source or root of the Tree, and the manifested growth of the Tree itself, in which the radical possibilities of manifestation are realised. And this is why the Tree is at the same time 'an everlasting support of the contemplation of Brahman' (*Maitri Up.* VII.11) and a Tree to be cut off at the root (*Bhagavad-Gîtâ* XV.3). It is from the former point of view that the *cult* of trees can best be understood. For just as the World-tree is the Brahman in a likeness, a theophany and an epiphany, so can any designated tree be regarded as the visible form of its indwelling *yaksha*, who may or may not upon occasion also assume another and human form within and beside the Tree itself' (*Yakshas, Essays in the Water Cosmology*, Indira Gandhi National Centre for the Arts, 1993, p. 11).

"demonic" center, since Indrajît uses divine weapons and everything is supervised by Brahmâ himself. Hanumân is tied with the "bonds of Brahmâ [Varuna]" and his release means an important step of Râma's spiritual realization: "A release from the bonds of Varuna, it is also a return to Varuna, to the Brahman."[1] In the end, Hanumân will set Lankâ on fire, an anticipation of the *Ragnarök*. As Guénon said, this phase is when the initiate realizes the light, not only through its reflections and shadows, but through its rays; yet still, an effective realization has to come during which the neophyte will reach the source of light, and this is the next phase when Râma, after listening to Hanumân's report, will march against Lankâ. Now the Greater War is in full development and, after crossing the ocean of ephemeral passions and worldly changes,[2] Râma and his army will start killing one after another of Râvana's heroes. In these battles, Râma and Lakshmana die and are resurrected a few times,[3] thus

---

[1] Coomaraswamy, *Trad. Art*, p. 447.

[2] The son of Vishwakarma, the Great Architect of the Universe, will build a bridge over the ocean. The symbolism of the bridge is famous, and the *pontifex maximus* title for the spiritual authority is based on this symbolism. Crossing the bridge means reaching the center. The symbolism of navigation has a similar meaning, and we mention here the Grail stories, where the Fisher King is presented in a boat, and, to reach the Grail Castle, the hero has to cross the water (see Robert de Boron, *Merlin and the Grail*, D. S. Brewer, 2007, p. 140, Chrétien de Troyes, *Perceval or The Story of the Grail*, The University of Georgia Press, 1983, pp. 82-83, 195-200, *The Quest of the Holy Grail*, Penguin Books, 1969, pp. 254, 256); see also *The Chemical Wedding of Christian Rosenkreutz*. See Guénon, *Autorité spirituelle*, pp. 106-108.

[3] *Râmâyana*, pp. 443, 447, 462, 491, 493. Similarly, Dante, in his initiatory voyage, died (fainted, fell asleep) each time he crossed to another level; see, for example, "E caddi come corpo morto cade" (*Inf.* V, 142). "Any change of state [level] has to be accomplished in the darkness." "Because similar considerations are applicable to any change of state, and because the following and successive degrees of the initiation correspond also to changes of the states, it is possible to say that ascending to each of them means death and birth, even though the 'cutting' is less evident and less fundamental than in the case of the primary initiation." "However, it is obvious that the changes suffered by the being during its development are indeed indefinite in number" (Guénon, *Aperçus sur l'initiation*, p. 179); therefore Râma's spiritual realization is illustrated by numerous trials.

passing from *degree* to *degree*, and eventually, when they fall dead
("E caddi come corpo morto cade") under Indrajît's arrows,
"lying inert as dead,"[1] Hanumân will bring them the redeeming
plants: "O valiant Hanumân! In the midst of these two peaks,
you will see a blazing and unequally brilliant herbal mountain,
containing all kinds of herbs. O foremost of monkeys! Sprouted
on the head of that mountain, are four blazing herbs. You can
see them, illuminating the ten quarters. ... You can see there,
Mrita Sanjîvanî (capable of restoring the dead to life),
Vishâlyakaranî (capable of extracting weapons and healing all
wounds inflicted by weapons), Suvarnakaranî (restoring the
body to its original complexion) and Sandhâni, the great herb
(capable of joining severed limbs or fractured bone). O
Hanumân! Bring all those herbs quickly. O son of wind-god!
Bring succour by injecting lives into them."[2]

There are three more fundamental phases in this Greater
War that deserve our attention: the first one is the battle against
Kumbhakarna; the second is the illusory Sîtâ; the third is
Râvana's death.

Kumbhakarna, Râvana's brother, is charged with a complex
symbolism, which is, in a way, connected to the previous
episode regarding the clashing mountains. From one point of
view, Kumbhakarna is the Universal Man or the Self, which
now, at the end of the initiatory journey, becomes from virtual
(asleep) real (awake); from another point of view, he is Kâla, the
Time that devours the universal manifestation[3] and then
devours itself,[4] his mouth (*mukha*) being the "Sun door" (*sûrya-*

---

[1] *Râmâyana*, p. 493.
[2] *Râmâyana*, p. 494. A similar initiatory phase occurs in various fairy tales, like
in *The Story of White Arab*, where the horse (Hanumân's equivalent) will bring
from the clashing mountains the water of life and the water of death, which
will resurrect the beheaded hero (*Folk Tales from Roumania*, p. 56); the two
mountains are the two peaks in the midst of which Hanumân finds the healing
plants. About the clashing mountains symbolizing the "Sun door" see
Coomaraswamy, *Traditional Art*, pp. 521 ff.
[3] See Guénon, *Symboles fondamentaux*, p. 359.
[4] See Guénon, *Le règne*, p. 217. Therefore, the end of the world is "the end of
time."

dwâra): "His mouth yawning horribly resembled hell and appeared like the sun rising under the high peak of Mêru Mountain [*Kâla-mukha*]. That figure of Kumbhakarna, rising up, stood out resembling Time at the dissolution of the world, prepared to devour all beings. His huge eyes, resembling flames of fire, with a glitter equal to that of lightning, appeared like great blazing planets." "Seeing the mighty Kumbhakarna with ghastly eyes and a spear in hand, the celestials were not able to kill him, having confused to think that he was Yama the god of Death."

Râvana wakes up Kumbhakarna, who was forced to sleep in order to keep the universal manifestation alive (otherwise he would devour it),[1] and the ogre enters the war; yet, battling

---

[1] Brahmâ spoke as follows: "He will indeed sleep for six months and wake-up for a day [the Day of Judgement]." The description we have about the ogre's awakening suggests the end of the world and the noise is the counterpart of the *Parashabda*: "They together tried to awaken Kumbhakarna who was sleeping nastily like a spread-out mountain in a great slumber. ...Then, those powerful Râkshasas, in order to satisfy him, placed a heap of venison as high as Mount Mêru, in front of Kumbhakarna. Those excellent demons piled up a great mass of wonderful food with the meat of deer, buffaloes and pigs. Then, the demons placed pots of blood and various kinds of meat in front of Kumbhakarna. They rubbed Kumbhakarna the scourge of his foes with the rarest sandalwood and refreshed him with celestial and fragrant garlands as well as sweet-smelling perfumes. They burnt incenses and hymned the praises of that warrior who proved fatal to his foes. They cried out noises which burst forth on every side like thunder. They blew couches which were as bright as the moon and with impatience, made with impatience, made sounds tumultuously all at once. Those Râkshasas made sounds by clapping their hands, in order to awaken Kumbhakarna and shook him too, creating a great clamour. The birds passing through the sky fell down soon on hearing the sounds of the couches, drums, gongs, clapping of hands and leonine roars. Then, the cruel Râkshasas struck that sleeping Kumbhakarna on his chest with mountain-tops, pestles, maces, hammers and their fists. Even with all their strength, the Râkshasas could not stand upright before the breathing winds of Kumbhakarna, the Râkshasa. Then, the terribly strong Râkshasas firmly seated themselves round him and began to beat drums, cymbals, kettle-drums and myriads of couches and trumpets. Even then, he did not wake. As they were unable to rouse him by these means, they resorted to more energetic and ruthless methods. They beat horses, camels, donkeys, and

Râma, Kumbhakarna, without discrimination, kills *Vânaras* and *Râkshasas*, announcing the total conflagration – the end of the cycle. Eventually, Râma destroys the "monster," cutting off first his arms and legs,[1] and then his head.[2] The end of time is also the end of "illusion" and, from a macrocosmic standpoint, this is the meaning of the illusory Sîtâ that was created and killed by Indrajît[3]; from a microcosmic perspective, the illusory Sîtâ is the last temptation before the conclusion of the spiritual voyage and we should mention that in *The Story of White Arab* the hero, at the end of his initiation, has to discern between the real Maiden and the illusory one. The illusory Sîtâ episode comes to an end with Lakshmana beheading Indrajît, a secondary sacrifice preceding the supreme one, which is, of course, the destruction of Râvana and the total dissolution of the cycle: "Râma, coming in the form of either Rudra the lord of destruction or Vishnu, the lord of preservation, or Indra the lord of celestials who performed one hundred ritual sacrifices, or otherwise Yama, the Lord of Death himself, is killing us … Râma is occupying us, as the Death occupies at the time of dissolution of the universe. We do not find any one now, who can give protection to us in this world."

Now, the Greater War is at its apex: "Râma and Râvana after some circuitous movements again faced each other and began to fight desperately … Râma grew exceedingly enraged and cut down Râvana's head by aiming a terrible shaft like a dreadful snake. The inhabitants of the Three Worlds saw that Râvana's

---

elephants with sticks whips and thongs, so that they trample upon him and blasted kettle-drums, couches and drums."

[1] This transforms him back into the primordial dragon, which means that the manifestation is retracted into non-manifestation.

[2] This head will become the sun of the new manifestation. It means also the "liberation" of the Self. Kumbhakarna is compared to Vritra, which underlines what we just said: "By killing Kumbhakarna, who tormented the army of celestials and who was not defeated at any time in great battles, Râma was rejoiced in the same way as Indra the lord of celestials was rejoiced in killing Vritra, the great Asura." Kumbhakarna should also be compared to Humbaba, the Sumerian monster from the *Epic of Gilgamesh*, and to Grendel from *Beowulf.*

[3] *Râmâyana*, pp. 505-506.

head was actually rolling on the ground, but immediately another head grew up in its place. Thus, though Râma cut down hundred heads of Râvana, still Râvana did not die!" In the case of the Trojan War, nine and a half years the Greeks could not conquer Troy, where 9 (nine) symbolizes the cycle and 1 (one) the center. "The circle, with its central point, symbol of the number ten, is at the same time the symbol of the cyclical perfection, a perfection that represents the integral realization of the possibilities involved in a state of existence (world)," Guénon tells us.[1] Râvana, it is said, had ten heads, and this cyclic beheading represents the indefinite manifestation, the indefinite helix of the cycles, and a metaphysical "jump" is needed to pass from multiplicity to One, into the Center, and therefore only when Râma pierced Râvana's heart [center], this one was deprived of his life.[2] Sîtâ is liberated, and together with Râma they return to Ayodhyâ,[3] where Râma is crowned king; the Greater War is over and the new cycle starts: "The earth her kindly fruits supplied,/ No harvest failed, no children died./ Unknown were want, disease, and crime:/ So calm, so happy was the time."

---

[1] *Le symbolisme de la croix*, p. 46.
[2] *Râmâyana*, pp. 537-538. Now the "reversal of the poles" occurs; now the Great Change takes place, which means "taking the limit," a limit that is beyond the indefinite series of states or cycles, a limit reached only by a jump, by breaking the continuity of the indefinite helix of the Universal Existence.
[3] As Guénon said, the "return" is usually just mentioned, without many details.

V

THE HOLY GRAIL

Râvana's beheading and his death bring out other facets of the symbolism of the center, considering the fact that both the head and the heart, together with the navel, are well known "central" marks, sometimes "threaded on a string," a string that is *sûtrâtma*, "the thread-self," or, in the Masonic tradition, "the chain of union," a string mapping the initiatory path from center to center. This is the meaning in fairy tales of the wrestle between the hero (*dêva*, angel) and the dragon (*asura*, titan), with its three degrees, the hero burying the titan in the earth, first to its waist, then to its breast, and lastly to its neck (and then the beheading occurs); this is also the hidden meaning of the *prânâyâma*; and it is the meaning of the Masonic penalties, where the initiatory journey from an Entered Apprentice to a Fellow Craft and finally to a Master Mason degree is equivalent to a quest for the center from head to heart and then to the navel.[1] We have already mentioned the symbolism of the center as heart and navel,[2] but, in addition, the head could be regarded as

---

[1] The penalty for the Entered Apprentice degree should be compared to Tristan's deed, when, in order to acquire Iseult, he kills the dragon and cuts its tongue out, while his substitute will behead it. Jean Dauphin, in *Rites maçonniques et processus spirituals*, tried, unconvincing, to explain the three Masonic penalty signs (Études Traditionnelles, 1960, no. 361, pp. 220-222). As Guénon said, the "signs" used in Masonry or other initiatory organizations are related to the "location" in the human being of the subtle "centers," and their "awakening" represents a way to acquire an effective initiatory knowledge (*Aperçus sur l'initiation*, p. 95).

[2] About the symbolism of the heart see our *The Everlasting Sacred Kernel*. With regard to the navel as center see what we already quoted from the *Midrash*

an emblem of the center, as it is in the Christian tradition, where the skull of Adam is placed at the foot of the Cross,[1] and where the "keystone" or "angle–stone" is the "head of the angle" (*caput anguli*).[2]

The head's symbolism is complex, as it should be, and follows all the rules governing the fundamental symbols of the traditional societies: it contains various meanings at various levels; it presents two apparent opposed main significances; and it has a triple purpose with regard to the triad Cosmos – Year – Man. These three purposes are: a cosmogonic one (the production of the World), a cyclic one (the rotation of the World) and an initiatory one (the Liberation), which allows us, from this perspective, to understand the act of beheading as a cosmogonic act, as a generator of the cycles, and as a synthesis of the initiatory realization.

Ananda K. Coomaraswamy has extensively studied the sacrificial act of beheading and it would be best for the reader, as in the case of René Guénon, to refer directly to his texts; however, it is beneficial for the present work to "capitalize" on Coomaraswamy's studies, highlighting some crucial elements.[3]

The dragon's beheading as a cosmogonic act represents the "cutting" or the "secession" of the Primordial Man, his head becoming Heaven and his feet Earth[4]; it is the Biblical *Fiat Lux*, when God divided the light from the darkness and the waters

---

Tanhuma: "As the navel is set in the center of the human body, so is the land of Israel the navel of the world."

[1] The word *Golgotha* was translated in Latin as *Calvary* and in Greek as *Kranion*, both meaning "skull" ("And they bring Him unto the place Golgotha, which is, being interpreted, The place of a skull," *Mark* 15:20) (see also Guénon, *Symboles fondamentaux*, p. 269). The skull is present in the Masonic initiation.

[2] See Guénon, *Symboles fondamentaux*, p. 278. The head of the pillar is a *chapiter* or a *capital*, from Latin *capitulum* (diminutive of *caput*, head). In the Hindu tradition, Agni is, at the same time, "head of heaven" and "navel of the earth," "Agni is head and height of heaven" (*Rig Véda* I.59.2, VIII.44.16).

[3] We have already discussed the various aspects of the act of beheading in our *The Everlasting Sacred Kernel*.

[4] See Ananda K. Coomaraswamy, *La doctrine du sacrifice*, Dervy, 1978, p. 106 and *Sir Gawain and the Green Knight: Indra and Namuci*, Speculum, Vol. 19, No. 1, Jan. 1944, p. 106.

from the waters; it is what Nicholas of Cusa calls "explication" and Coomaraswamy "extroversion" (*pravritti*), while the restoration of the head is the "complication" or the "introversion" (*nivritti*).[1] Coomaraswamy underlined that the dragon's head rolled (Sanskr. *vrit*) and became the Sun, which suggests a fourth meaning, the head symbolizing the Principle and the Center.[2] In addition, the rotation of the head is an illustration of the Year, and the beheading, one by one, of the dragon's multiple heads alludes to the doctrine of the cosmic cycles. From Man's point of view, the beheading is a sacrifice that produces Liberation (the liberation or the disenchantment of the Self), yet at the same time the head could represent the *ego* with its arrogance and ignorance.[3] As we mentioned in a previous chapter, the total spiritual realization implies, besides the ascendant journey, a descendant phase (Ibn 'Arabî's "return"), which is represented by the restoration of the head.[4]

---

[1] Coomaraswamy also uses the terms "procession" and "recession," which are equivalents for explication-complication. See *La doctrine du sacrifice*, p. 103 and *Sir Gawain*, p. 105.

[2] The dragon's head becomes the turning sun of the new Cosmos, with "one thousand" rays (Coom., *La doctrine du sacrifice*, pp. 26, 32 and *Angel and Titan: An Essay in Vedic Ontology*, Journal of the American Oriental Society, Vol. 55, No. 4, Dec. 1935, pp. 375, 378, "set Heaven's gem [the Sun] a-rolling"). The rest of the body remains "emptied of creatures" ("beardless") and without "powers."

[3] "Our head is our self, and to cut off one's head is self-abandonment, self-denial, self-naughting" (Coom., *La doctrine du sacrifice*, pp. 128-129, *Sir Gawain*, pp. 119-120). The decapitation and the skinning are interchangeable ways of releasing the enchanted being from the form in which he or she is concealed (Coom., *La doctrine du sacrifice*, pp. 110-111, *Sir Gawain*, pp. 108-109). As an initiatory realization, it represents a new birth, when the old skin is put off and the beautiful, shining new person is released; it is the passage from snake-like to solar-like. Cosmogonically, it represents the birth of Light from the dragon, of manifestation from non-manifestation, it is the liberation of the sun from the darkness, but it also describes the passage from One to multiplicity. From a Hindu point of view, Coomaraswamy stressed, all procession is from an ophidian to a footed form; it is an established pattern that "The Serpents abandoning their inveterated skins, move on, put off death, and become the Suns" (Coom., *Sir Gawain*, pp. 107-108).

[4] In the *Satapatha Brâhmana* (XIV, I), there is a tale about the sage (*rshi*) Dadhyac threatened by Indra with beheading if he unveils the secret initiatory

The head of *Yajna* (the Sacrifice), for example, after the sacred act of beheading, became the Sun; the rite *Pravargya* will operate the restoration. As in the case of the horse's head, so the sun at the beginning of the cycle and of the world leaves the World Tree (the beheading) and comes back at the end of times; René Guénon affirmed that, in different traditions, the sun represents the fruit of the World Tree, the tree being indeed the "sun's station,"[1] and the Chinese character signifying the sunset depicts the sun resting in the tree at the end of the day.[2]

The solar head[3] on top of the tree is equivalent to the pillar's chapiter and, as the tree's fruit, is comparable to the Golden Fleece or to the Golden Apples, symbolizing Tradition and divine Knowledge, which means, from this perspective, that being headless describes someone for whom the Tradition was lost, someone antitraditional, or even worse, someone belonging to the counter-initiatory forces.[4]

---

lore (*madhu-vidya*); hence, the Ashwins, twin brothers, having the Sun as father and the mare as mother, will replace *brâhmand*'s head with a horse's head, and this very horse's head will transmit the esoteric teaching. Indra will behead Dadhyac, and the horse riders Ashwins will bring back the initial head.

[1] This is the meaning of "solstice." In the Chinese tradition, the ideogram for a tree's fruit shows the sun as fruit (Léon Wieger, *Caractères chinois*, Kuangchi Cultural Group, 2004, p. 280):

[2] The ideogram for sunrise (Wieger 282) shows the sun in a tree (we should notice the tree's symbol, with three roots and three branches):

[3] In Masonry, the known figure of the Mason composed of his tools has the Sun as head (see the illustration in Patrick Geay, *Mystères et significations du Temple maçonnique*, Dervy, 2000, p. 79).

[4] On the contrary, the gods are only heads, as the Hermetic tradition declares: "as to the celestial gods, it is admitted by all men that they are manifestly generated from the purest part of matter, and that their astral forms are heads, as it were, and heads alone" (*Hermetica*, Shambhala, 1993, p. 339). Meister

We saw in the previous chapter that Râma's Quest starts
with the encounter with Kavandha, a *Râkshasa* without head
and neck, though his breast has a huge mouth and one eye, this
headlessness or *acrania* illustrating the "demonic" state.
Coomaraswamy explained that *Râkshasas* mean "guardians"[1] (of
soma) and they acquired "their pejorative sense of 'demon' only
from the fact that in their capacity as Soma-guardians the *raksha*
is inimical to the Sacrifice."[2] In the Hindu tradition, the seven
Soma-guardians are "a company of Gandharvas," described as
Âsîvishâh, venomous serpents or basilisks, which Ananda K.
Coomaraswamy compares to the ophidian three-headed Azhi
Dahâka,[3] helping us to see Sîtâ corresponding to the Holy Grail
or *soma*, guarded by the ten-headed Râvana and his *Râkshasas*.[4]
However, the state of headlessness also indicates a revolt
against the normal order, a separation from the center, a
transfer of power from the spiritual authority (*brâhmana*, Golden
Age = head, mouth) to the temporal one (*kshatriya* = breast,
arms)[5]; the headless dragon is the emptied and exhausted
"demon," which could find shelter in our viscera, and waits to
be reunited with its head,[6] while the headless magicians

Eckhart also said: "the little spark of the intellect is the head of the soul, called
the 'groom' of the soul."
[1] The root *raksh* means "to protect, to guard."
[2] Ananda K. Coomaraswamy, *Guardians of the Sun-Door*, Fons Vitae, 2004, p. 5,
and *Headless Magicians; And an Act of Truth*, Journal of the American Oriental
Society, Vol. 64, No. 4, Oct. - Dec. 1944, pp. 216-217 ("acquiring its evil
significance only because the hymns are naturally constituted from the point
of view of the mundane Gods and men whose well-being depends upon the
due performance of the rites for which the possession of Soma is
indispensable"; see *La doctrine du sacrifice*, pp. 172-173).
[3] *Guardians*, p. 9.
[4] When Kavandha was killed by Râma, the curse was broken and he regained
his freedom and his initial status of handsome *Gandharva*.
[5] The beheading also symbolizes the "schism of the Sacerdotium (*brahma*)
from the Regnum (*kshatra*)" (Coom., *Sir Gawain*, p. 107, *La doctrine du sacrifice*,
p. 108). A headless king (Coom., *Sir Gawain*, p. 114, *La doctrine du sacrifice*, p.
121) is, like the mutilated Fisher King, an expression of the end of the cycle.
[6] This reunification is the "sacred marriage" (*daivam mithunam*) (Coom., *Sir
Gawain*, p. 107, *La doctrine du sacrifice*, p. 109); see also our *About the Yi Jing*, p.
133, *The Everlasting Sacred Kernel*, p. 13.

mentioned by Coomaraswamy are projections of this dragon, manipulating the inferior powers and the erring forces by using their capacity to move their heads at will. As Ananda K. Coomaraswamy affirmed, "the Dêvas are often victorious over the Asuras precisely in that they adhere to *satyam* [the truth],[1] while the Asuras follow *anritam* [the disorder, the falsehood]"; the Act of Truth determines the god "to fell 'the crestless and headless,'" and what we have here is more than the beheading of the dragon, since it is already headless (which means it is truthless, and the headless magicians belong to this category).[2]

The Act of Truth is present in various sacred stories[3] and, in fact, each initiatory degree and each new station of the initiatory realization represent such an Act: in the *Odyssey*, the final station is described by the archery contest, the revealing of Ulysses, and the killing of the suitors[4]; in some fairy tales,[5] at the end (again the final station), the three brothers throw into the sky three swords or lances and the older brothers (who represent the dragon or the *ego*) are killed; in the tale of Tristan, the hero must prove that he is the one who has smitten the dragon.

In the *Ancient and Accepted Scottish Rite*, there are many similarities between its rites and the initiatory elements of fairy tales. We know the general mentality, which has little interest in the esoteric aspect of these tales, considering them either

---

[1] The "Golden Age" is the Age of Truth (*satya-yuga*).

[2] See Coom., *Headless*, pp. 215-216, *La doctrine du sacrifice*, pp. 170-171.

[3] "And the Gileadites took the passages of Jordan before the Ephraimites: and it was so, that when those Ephraimites which were escaped said, Let me go over; that the men of Gilead said unto him, Art thou an Ephraimite? If he said, Nay; Then said they unto him, Say now Shibboleth: and he said Sibboleth: for he could not frame to pronounce it right. Then they took him, and slew him at the passages of Jordan: and there fell at that time of the Ephraimites forty and two thousand" (*Judges* 12:5-6). This Act of Truth is part of the Masonic ritual (Macoy, *A Dictionary of Freemasonry*, p. 349).

[4] The suitors represent our lowest passions and appetites. They are also the residues of the dying cycle. Killing them, Ulysses purifies his own heart and also ends the old world. Then he abandons the "dark snake skin," the beggar clothing, and reveals himself as the spiritual Sun.

[5] This kind of tales is common in the Near West.

"children's literature" or, in the best case, vestiges of lost traditions, but the Holy Grail stories, the *Odyssey*, or even the *Râmâyana* in a way, are also such vestiges; however, they all have guarded a most valuable symbolism, which could help us understand the initiatory process and the sacred rites. In fairy tales,[1] the treacherous elderly brothers try to destroy (kill) the youngest one, but in the end the hero will be resurrected and the evil brothers will be punished (the Act of Truth),[2] such an initiatory scenario being more or less universal and found, as expected, in the Masonic rites, where we witness a similar plot: the older brothers are Hiram's three assassins,[3] and they will be beheaded.

In the Ninth Degree, the first murderer is found hiding in a cave (the center) and he is beheaded, but, of course, this act has little to do with a mundane "revenge," since it is about sacrificing the dragon, which usually dwells in a cave and is, for the candidate, the criminal *ego*. In the ritual presented by Blanchard,[4] it is said that King Solomon, who wanted the assassin caught alive, would condemn the punisher (the candidate) by decapitation, and even if in the end this one is

---

[1] The same scenario is valid for the maiden's initiation. See, for example, *The story of Cinderella*.

[2] See also *The Story of White Arab* where the hero is called *Harap Alb*, the "White Moor" or the "White Arab" (*Folk Tales from Roumania*, Routledge and Kegan Paul, 1952). Here, the elderly brothers are replaced with a bald and beardless character, who will behead the solar hero: it is a "ritual death" belonging to the initiatory process, followed by a resurrection, "the second birth." Indeed, the Virgin (the emperor's daughter) will restore *Harap Alb*'s head and the hero will be resurrected; at the same time, the hairless character is punished (killed).

[3] In fairy tales, there are two older brothers (corresponding to *Corpus* and *Anima*); in the *Scottish Rite*, though there are three killers, they will be separated into two groups: one assassin will be punished in the Ninth Degree and the other two in the Tenth Degree. However, in the Hindu tradition, we find four "masons": Twashtri and the three Ribhus, where Twashtri is the Great Architect (*sthapati*) and the Ribhus are the Fellowcrafts (the carpenter, *sûtragrâhi*; the mason, *vardhaki*; the joiner, *takshaka*); yet here also we find the oscillation between 3 and 4, since the three Ribhus crafted four cups from Twashtri's unique cup (*pâtra*). See Guénon, *Symboles fondamentaux*, pp. 263-264.

[4] John Blanchard, *Scotch Rite Masonry Illustrated*, Kessinger, I, p. 167.

forgiven, we have to assume that he was beheaded and resurrected, like *Harap Alb* or other fairy tale heroes.[1]

In the Tenth Degree, the two other assassins are beheaded, and all three heads are set up on posts, placed at the southern, eastern and western gates.[2] Coomaraswamy wrote: "But it is sometimes overlooked that the decapitation of an enemy or criminal is, strictly speaking, a sacrifice, and the setting up of the head on a spear or post at a city gate is not a further disgrace but an honour paid to the deceased who is 'despatched to the Gods' and 'deified' … The placing of a head or skull on a spear or post is, in fact, only another way of restoring the head to the body or trunk, and involves at the same time an assimilation to the Sun, regarded as a 'sky-supporting post,' as a pillar together with its capital supports a roof."[3]

In the present work, our interest in the head's symbolism is mainly with regard to its "central" significance and, without question, the head or skull placed on a spear or post suggests the center[4]; but, we should not forget that the center is also the

---

[1] The apron of the Ninth Degree bears a decapitated head; we mention the close relation between the signs of the Masonic apron and Heraldry.

[2] Blanchard, I, 205.

[3] *Sir Gawain*, p. 113, *La doctrine du sacrifice*, p. 119. In some fairy tales, this symbolism is explicitly described, the center being marked by 99 posts with 99 heads, while the 100th one is waiting for the hero's head; on Trajan's Column (metope XLII), two Dacian heads placed on spears could be seen. The apron of the Tenth Degree bears the three heads placed on posts (Blanchard, I, 189). We should add a text from *The History* of Herodotus: "[the Tauroi], whatsoever enemies they have conquered they treat in this fashion: each man cuts off a head and bears it away to his house; then he impales it on a long stake and sets it up above his house raised to a great height, generally above the chimney; and they say that these are suspended above as guards to preserve the whole house" (IV.103) (the chimney, as the stake, is a symbol of the *Axis Mundi*).

[4] This significance is made obvious in the mentioned fairy tale where there are 99 + 1 posts ("I say unto you, that likewise joy shall be in heaven over one sinner that repenteth, more than over ninety and nine just persons, which need no repentance," *Luke* 15:7). The post is the *Axis Mundi*. In Chrétien's *Erec et Enide*, the center is described as the middle of a garden, where "on sharpened stakes, there stood bright and shining helmets, and each one had beneath the rim a man's head. But at the end there stood a stake where as yet

contact point between Heaven and Earth,[1] the "furthest" or the "highest"; it is the station *terminus*, governed by the Roman god Terminus, who was represented as a stone pillar supporting his head. The Romans considered Terminus a "boundary stone," like a *landmark*, but, at the same time, they included the ancient Terminus stone in the Capitoline Temple, that is, in the center (there was a small hole in the ceiling directly above the Terminus stone, symbolizing *brahma-randhra*,[2] the "solar gate" and the "eye").[3] Coomaraswamy, who could not overlook the significance of Terminus, specified that *brahma-randhra* is precisely what is called the *foramen*, and Ovid used this word "to denote the hole intentionally left in the roof of the temple of Jupiter, immediately above 'old Terminus, the boundary stone,'" and Coomaraswamy clarified that, "whereas *termini*, as boundary posts in the plural, are placed at the edges of a delimited area, the *Terminus* of all things occupies a central position."[4] This center is, like *brahma-randhra*, a boundary between This World and The Other World, between beneath and beyond the Sun; in this center a jump takes place, a break, a trespassing from

---

there was nothing but a horn" (Chrétien de Troyes, *Arthurian Romances*, J. M. Dent & Sons Ltd., 1982, p. 75). In the Islamic tradition, there are 99 divine attributes and the 100th one is the "Name of the Essence," residing in Paradise (that is, in the Center) (Guénon, *Symboles fondamentaux*, p. 372).

[1] Guénon, *Écrits*, p. 112.

[2] During the Alchemical Wedding, Christian Rosenkreutz had his hair cut precisely at the top of his head.

[3] The Capitoline Hill (*Collis Capitolinus*) was the highest of Rome's seven hills; a "legend" explains the name *Capitolinus* as being a derivation from *caput* (head), since, when the first temple was built, in the year 509 BC, the head or skull of Tolius was discovered there. The temple (of Jupiter Optimus Maximus), the most important temple of ancient Rome, evidently indicated the center, but we see that the head or skull was also considered to be marking the same center. See also Coom., *Traditional Art and Symbolism*, pp. 441, 450 ff.

[4] Terminus was in the center of the central shrine of the temple. We should add that the god Terminus was the guardian of Peace and the witness of Justice (the main attributes of the Lord of the World) and he was also called Placidus, a name symbolizing the *principial* immutability.

"here" to "beyond," and a "(tress)passing to the limit."[1] On the other hand, the *termini* emphasize the "cutting" or the boundary of the sacred land, like the stones that became the limits of the *haram*, but they were primary "guardians of the holy land" in the way the Greek *hermae* or the Templars (and also the *gargouilles* of the cathedrals) were.

René Guénon explained how the Order of the Temple had precisely this function of guarding the holy land, where the "holy land" is, at the same time, the center (supreme or subordinate) and the tradition conserved or emanated from this center, where center and tradition are closely associated. This double sense, Guénon stressed, is to be found in the symbolism of the Holy Grail, which is both a cup (*grasale*) and a book (*gradale* or *graduale*), and, for this reason, referring to the "Knighthood of the Holy Grail" is the same thing as referring to the "guardians of the holy land."[2] Guénon's avowal is the most lucid and truthful definition possible for the Holy Grail and its symbolism: the Holy Grail symbolizes the Center and the Tradition, and all the other fantasies written in the last centuries about the Grail are pure nonsense.

The "guardians," Guénon added, are placed at the boundaries of the spiritual center (understood as holy land), that is, at the "cutting" that separates the center from the "outside" world. The Templars had this function, but, because they were both knights and monks, René Guénon considered them among the "guardians" not of a secondary center but of the Center of the World; and, when the Order was destroyed, the Occident lost the connection with the Center. The Templars as "guardians" had two other functions: first, they constituted the "outer cover" for the center; second, they supported various external relations and maintained the connection between the Primordial Tradition and the secondary traditions, which meant

---

[1] To trespass meant originally "to pass beyond or across." The Latin *terminus* comes from a root *tr* and is related to the Sanskrit *tarana*, "to trespass," and to *avatarana*.

[2] *Symboles fondamentaux*, p. 110.

that they were in contact with various similar organizations belonging to other traditional forms.[1]

As René Guénon mentioned many times, only in the Middle Ages could we witness a traditional civilisation in the Occident comparable to the Oriental civilisations, even though the metaphysical aspect was not developed at a similar level.[2] Therefore, in the Middle Ages we find the Templars and the Holy Grail stories and the sacred symbols similar to those of the Oriental traditions; and, also the Middle Ages was the period that accepted and understood the influence of the Orient, facilitated by the Arabs.[3] At the end of the Middle Ages though,[4] after the 13th Century, the "demonic" aspect of the head dominated,[5] when Islam retransmitted various symbolical images; but, also the Greek and Roman glyptic was a rich source,[6] and we witness a proliferation of the so-called *grylli*, represented as moving heads (heads with legs) or as multi-headed characters, or headless monsters with a face on their

---

[1] *Symboles fondamentaux*, pp. 111-113.

[2] See *Orient et Occident*, Guy Trédaniel, 1993, pp. 164, 191, *Introduction générale*, pp. 69, 116.

[3] Guénon, *Introduction générale*, p. 19. Earlier, the Alexandrine Age was a period when the Occident received the influence of the Orient directly. See also our *The Near West*, Sophia, Vol. 9, No. 1, 2003, where, besides the essential contribution of Islam to the Western Middle Ages, we showed the importance of the Byzantine Empire as a source for the Islamic civilization. It is interesting that Chrétien de Troyes considered Byzantium the origin of Chivalry, which then "passed to Rome, together with that highest learning which now has come to France," *Arthurian Romances*, p. 91. Chrétien started *Cligés* by mentioning the Emperor of Constantinople and his two sons, Alexander and Alis.

[4] The true Middle Ages, Guénon affirmed, lasted from the reign of Charlemagne to the beginning of the 14th Century (*La crise du monde moderne*, Gallimard, 1975, p. 29).

[5] This aspect perpetuated over the centuries, and any metaphysical meaning was forgotten. For example, the head with legs was used to represent the devil in the Last Judgment scene painted on the wall of the Probota Monastery (Moldavia, 1530). See also Hieronymus Bosch.

[6] However, we should keep in mind that ancient Greece got a lot of inspiration from Egypt, Phoenicia, Chaldea, Persia and India (Guénon, *Introduction générale*, p. 16).

breast.[1] However, the *grylli* as "guardians" and the gems as paradisiacal stones had an apotropaic function, similar to that of the Greek *hermae*. In traditional societies, the precious stones had a sacred function: they were considered of celestial origin or miraculously generated, being related to various constellations (as gold corresponds to the sun) and having thaumaturgic powers, which explains the role of the "talismans" in the Hermetic tradition; moreover, the Holy Grail was itself a precious stone.

We mentioned the *hermae* for two reasons: first, because a *herma* represented a head placed on a pillar; second, because Hermeticism constituted an essential part of Occidental Middle Ages esotericism. In ancient Greece, the *herma* was a quadrangular pillar with Hermes' head set on top and had a similar function as the god Terminus, the *hermae* being placed as guardians at crossings, country borders, land boundaries, and road margins. The Greek god Hermes has very rich symbolism, related to that of other traditions,[2] but Hermeticism is based on

---

[1] See for all this Jurgis Baltrušaitis, *Le Moyen Age fantastique*, Colin, 1955. The author presented how, mainly after the pillage of Constantinople in 1204 by the Crusaders, the interest in gems and glyptic increased and spread in Europe. Regarding the Islamic influence, Baltrušaitis highlighted its contribution to Romanesque and Gothic art and he listed the geometrical and heraldic themes, the "monsters," the Alexandrine lapidaries; Baltrušaitis said: "it is known how strongly the Islamic thinking acted upon the whole medieval thinking," and his book contains numerous examples to support this assertion.

[2] His birth in a cave, the stealing of Apollo's herd, his vegetal footwear, the invention of the lyre, his winged sandals and winged hat (*petasus*), the caduceus, his equivalence with Nabu, Budha, and Odin, the fact that he gave Ulysses *moly*, the miraculous white and black plant, and his function as gods' messenger, are some of Hermes' important symbolic elements, similar to those found in the Hindu tradition, and each one would necessitate lengthy comments. Regarding the Greeks' capacity to assimilate foreign influences, we should mention that probably Hermes was first a Thracian god: "Their [Thracians] kings, however, unlike the rest of the citizens, worship Mercury [Hermes] more than any other god, always swearing by his name, and declaring that they are themselves sprung from him" (Herodotus, *History*, 5.7). Also, we should compare Hermes' function to that of the *Shekinah* (the zodiacal house of the Virgin is the planet Mercury).

the identification of Hermes with the Egyptian Thoth and represents "a tradition of Egyptian origin, dressed in a Hellenic form, during the Alexandrine Age, and transmitted such as, in the Middle Ages, at the same time to the Islamic and the Christian world, and it must be added that to the second mainly through the intermediary of the first."[1] Hermeticism, as it was understood in the Alexandrine Age, was not the complete Egyptian tradition, but that part related to the intermediary world, corresponding to the cosmogonic knowledge and to the Royal Art, with Alchemy as its "technique."[2]

The Masonic symbolism was attached to Hermeticism,[3] and so was Heraldry,[4] the Holy Grail stories, Chivalry and the Rose-Cross. The Rose-Cross, René Guénon affirmed, were people who effectively accomplished the *Lesser Mysteries*, and the Rosicrucian initiation, inspired by them, was a particular form attached to Christian Hermeticism.[5]

---

[1] Guénon, *Formes traditionnelles*, p. 120. See also *Aperçus sur l'initiation*, chapter XLI.

[2] It would be interesting, Guénon added, to find out how this part of the Egyptian tradition could remain isolated and survive in an independent manner, and later be incorporated in the Islamic and Christian esotericism of the Middle Ages (*Formes traditionnelles*, pp. 121-123).

[3] Guénon, *Franc-Maçonnerie*, I, p. 17, II, p. 43, 74-75. For Guénon, the junction of Hermeticism with Masonry occurred long before 1646. Guénon also pointed out the resemblance between the name Hermes and Hiram (*Formes traditionnelles*, p. 129). See also Guénon, *L'ésotérisme de Dante*, pp. 18-21, where he presented the hermetic influence upon the High Degrees of the *Scottish Rite*, which originated in the close relation between the Hermeticism and the Orders of Chivalry, during the times of the Crusades; see also Geay, *Mystères et significations du Temple maçonnique*, pp. 20-21.

[4] Heraldry was part of the Royal Art (see for example Jean Vassel, *Le symbolisme des "couleurs" héraldiques*, Études Traditionnelles, 1950, p. 26 ; for Vassel, heraldry was a silent language of the initiates, the heraldic colours illustrating the initiatory process, pp. 28-9, 313, 368-369). See also Guénon, *Franc-Maçonnerie*, II, p. 147, where he underlines the contribution of the knights themselves to the esoteric composition of the coats of arms.

[5] Guénon asked the question: did the Orders of Chivalry receive the Hermeticism from the Orient, or from the beginning they had an esotericism and their own initiation allowed them to establish contact with the Oriental organizations? And Guénon admitted that he has no answer to this question (*L'ésotérisme de Dante*, p. 21). Later on, he said: "It is admitted that there were

The initiates of Christian esotericism, after the brutal disappearance of the Order of the Temple, seemed to have saved themselves and reorganized, in accordance with Islamic esotericism, but in a very secretive, invisible manner, having no visible institutions as support. The *Superiores Incogniti* who inspired this reorganization were, it seems, the Rose-Cross, the genuine Rose-Cross, so different from the later Rosicrucians, and the "legend" of Christian Rosenkreutz apparently illustrates this reorganization. The Rosicrucians, on the other hand, were selected individuals, operating within the framework of visible organizations, yet no one had acquired the spiritual degree of a Rose-Cross. It is said that, after the end of the "thirty years

Islamic influences at the origins of the Rosicrucianism... yet, the real origin of the Rosicrucianism are precisely the Orders of Chivalry" (*ibid.* p. 43). René Guénon wrote: "The history of this Hermetic tradition is intimately related to that of Chivalry; and, at the epoch we mentioned [at the beginning of the 14th Century], this tradition was preserved by initiatory organizations as *Fede Santa* and *Fedeli d'Amore* [to which Dante belonged], and also as *Massenie de Saint Graal*" (*L'ésotérisme de Dante*, p. 35). Guénon also considered that the transformed Templarism produced the Rosicrucianism, as Dante suggested: "Then, in form of a white rose, the host of the sacred soldiery [*milizia santa*] appeared to me, all those whom Christ in his own blood espoused" (*The Paradiso*, XXXI, 1-3) (*L'ésotérisme de Dante*, p. 26). There is a great difference between Rose-Cross and Rosicrucianism (Guénon, *Aperçus sur l'initiation.*, pp. 241 ff., 259). The true Rose-Cross never constituted a visible organization; all the groups that were born, starting with the 17th Century and which could be qualified as Rosicrucian, did not have among their members a Rose-Cross, since the Rose-Cross functioned invisibly, similar to the messengers of Agarttha. The name Rose-Cross designates an initiatory degree, a spiritual state, and was not an association, an organization, or an identifiable group. The symbol of Rose-Cross (the rose in the center of the cross) expresses the perfection of the human state, describing the reintegration of the being in the center of this state, and the full expansion of human possibilities starting from this center. The initiatory state of Rose-Cross refers to the Earthly Paradise and to the *Lesser Mysteries*, and only analogously we can transpose it to the *Greater Mysteries* and to Heavenly Paradise; as we said before, Hermeticism also is about cosmology and not metaphysics. The name "Rose-Cross" was used, we should take note, for some particular spatial and temporal conditions, that is, for Christian society starting with the 16th Century; in other circumstances there would have been a different name. Everything, Guénon stated, is indicated by the "legend" of Christian Rosenkreutz, who must not be considered a historical character, but rather a "collective entity."

war" and the Peace of Westphalia, in 1648, the last genuine Rose-Cross retired to the Orient, wherever this "Orient" might be.[1]

The legend[2] tells us how the young Christian Rosenkreutz, yearning to complete the holy pilgrimage to Jerusalem, heard about the sages of Damcar (located in *Arabia Felix*) and travelled there, where he became the disciple of some Arabic masters, similar to Gahmuret, who went to Baldac (Baghdad) to serve the powerful Baruc,[3] all these suggesting the Islamic influence in the esoteric field.[4] Back in Europe, Rosenkreutz established a "brotherhood" of four members, who built the "Temple of the Holy Spirit," an invisible temple, like Agarttha, symbolizing the Center. In the year 1459, when he was 81 years old, Christian Rosenkreutz was admitted to participate in the Alchemical Wedding, dressed in a white robe with a red cruciform ribbon (alluding to the Templars and the Grail Knights). He passed various gates, one guarded by two statues, one happy and one sad (*congratulator* and *condoleo*)[5]; entered a miraculous castle (the center); and witnessed, like in the Grail stories, a scene involving a unicorn and a lion near *fons vitae*, the lion breaking a sword,[6] after which a series of beheadings

---

[1] Sédir, *Histoire et Doctrines des Rose-Croix*, Bibliothèque des Amitiés Spirituelles, 1932, p. 40. Guénon confirmed Sédir's sayings.

[2] For this legend we use Jean-Valentin Andréae, *Les Noces Chymiques de Christian Rosencreutz*, Éd. Traditionnelles, 1994, and Frances Yates, *La lumière des Rose-Croix*, Retz, 1978.

[3] Wolfram von Eschenbach, *Parzival and Titurel*, Oxford Univ. Press, 2006, p. 8.

[4] The Rose-Cross, like the Templars, were a link between Orient and Occident, being in contact (a spiritual relation) mainly with the Muslim Sufis.

[5] In fact these are two pillars, like in the Masonic Lodge.

[6] This happens on the third day ("there came forward a beautiful snow white Unicorn, with a golden collar, engraved with certain letters, about his neck. He bound himself down upon his fore-feet, as if hereby he had shown honour to the Lyon, who stood so immovably upon the fountain that I took him to be stone, or brass, but who immediately took the naked sword which he bare in his paw, brake it into two in the middle"); on the fourth day, Rosenkreutz is purified with water from *fons vitae* belonging to *Hermes Princeps* and having the inscription *bibite Fratres, et vivite*. We mention the hermetic importance of the lion in the Grail stories. At one moment, Perceval reaches a center (the middle

occurred. This is not the place to insist on the Rosicrucian legends and symbolism, but we have to highlight the importance of the head's symbolism, as related to Hermeticism. On the fourth day of his initiation, Rosenkreutz participated in the following *mysteries*: in a rectangular hall he saw thrones, and "in each throne sate two persons; in the first sate a very ancient King with a grey beard, yet his consort was extraordinarily fair and young. In the third throne sat a black King of middle age, and by him a dainty old matron, not crowned, but covered with a veil. But in the middle sate two young persons, who though they had likewise wreaths of laurel upon their heads, yet over them hung a large and costly crown."[1] Similar to the Grail stories, a banquet took place: "All the Royal Persons, before meat, attired themselves in snow white glittering garments. Over the table hung the great golden crown, the precious stones whereof, without other light, would have sufficiently illuminated the hall. All the lights were kindled at the small taper upon the altar. The young King frequently sent meat to the white serpent, which caused me to muse." And "finally, there stepped in a coal-black, tall man, who bore in his

---

of an island) and sees a serpent carrying a lion cub and followed by a lion; he will help the lion to defeat the serpent. Later on, during his sleep, Perceval saw two ladies riding a lion and a serpent (*The Quest of the Holy Grail*, pp. 114-118). In Chrétien's *Yvain*, the hero witnesses, in a forest, the fight between a lion and a serpent, and helps the lion, killing the serpent (*Arthurian Romances*, pp. 223-4); the lion becomes Yvain's best friend, but, of course, this lion is his inner self. It is worth to mention that, as Guénon said, the lion and the serpent could signify, at the same time, and depending on the specific situation, Christ and Satan (*Symboles fondamentaux*, p. 44).

[1] Then follows a picture worthy of Dürer: "Before the Queen stood a small but inexpressibly curious altar, wherein lay a book, velvet black covered, only a little overlaid with gold. By this stood a taper in an ivory candlestick, which although very small, burnt continually, and stood in that manner, that had not Cupid, in sport, now and puffed upon it, we could not have conceived it to be fire. By this stood a sphere or celestial globe, which of itself turned about. Next this was a small striking watch, by that a little crystal pipe or siphon-fountain, out of which perpetually ran a clear blood-red liquid liquor, and last of all there was a skull or death's head, in which was a white serpent, of such length, that though she crept circle-wise about the rest of it, yet her tail still remained in one of the eye-holes until her head again entered at the other."

hand a sharp axe. Now after that the old King had been brought to the seat, his head was instantly whipt off and wrapped in a black cloth, the blood being received in a great golden goblet, and placed with him into the coffin that stood by, which, being covered, was set aside. Thus it went with the rest, so that I thought it would have come to me too, but as soon as the six Royal Persons were beheaded, the black man retired, another following that just before the door beheaded him also, and brought back his head, which, with the axe, was laid in the little chest. This indeed seemed to me a bloody Wedding."

Beyond the specific Alchemical meaning, there is in this text a universal symbolism, related to the doctrine of the sacrifice, so well explained by Coomaraswamy with regard to the Hindu tradition, the above quotation proving how the symbolism of the head continued its journey as a sacred heritage of the Middle Ages.[1] From this perspective of the head's symbolism, we should mention the well known Hermetic *Rebis*, composed of a body with two heads, one masculine (the sun) and one feminine (the moon),[2] the first half holding the compass and the second a square, which indicates the universality of the Masonic symbols.[3] Even though there are two heads (from the point of view of the universal manifestation), *Rebis* the Androgyne is a "unique thing" in its essence (where the wedding of the heavenly and terrestrial virtues takes place),

---

[1] In this Rosicrucian text, the Moor's head is used to produce the "lovely great snow white egg," that is, the "philosophical egg." A direct connection between the "Knighthood of the Holy Grail" and the Rose-Cross can be found. There is also a symbolic similitude between the Masonic *ashlar* and the Hermetic philosophical stone.

[2] *Tabula Smaragdina* said about *Rebis*: "the sun is its father and the moon its mother" (see Guénon, *La Grande Triade*, p. 131).

[3] In the Chinese tradition, this primordial Androgyne is represented by Fu Xi (who holds the square) and Niu Wa (who holds the compasses). See Guénon, *La Grande Triade*, p. 131 and Patrick Geay, *Mystères et significations du Temple maçonnique*, pp. 21-23.

which means that we have the possibility of accepting a unique head gathering the lights of the sun and the moon.[1] The Hermetic Androgyne corresponds to the "primordial state" (the center), with its realization symbolizing the restoration of this state, and is equivalent to the term "Rose-Cross."[2] It represents the accomplishment of the *Lesser Mysteries*, when the being, reaching the Earthly Paradise, is virtually "liberated," even though he must pass through the *Greater Mysteries* before it is effectively so[3]; therefore, *Rebis* of the *Rosarium Philosophorum* has under its feet the moon or the dragon, symbolizing the complete realization and domination of the individual state, and the readiness to climb the ladder of the superindividual states.[4] On the other hand, the lunar crescent is a symbolic equivalent for the cup,[5] which, in addition, signifies Christ's heart and the sun.[6] To this "unique thing" not only Hermeticism alluded but also *The Book of Revelation*: "A great and wondrous sign appeared in heaven: a woman clothed with the sun, with the moon under her feet and a crown of twelve stars on her head" (12:1-2), a quotation that could be illustrated by the lunar cup containing the solar (spiritual) nutriment.[7]

Coomaraswamy wrote: "It has been usual to identify the Grail vessel with the Moon (Soma); but actually the Moon is a food that the Sun receives and assimilates, and this food corresponds to what is put into Buddha's begging bowl which, like the Sun, is the Grail *qua* receptacle."[8]

---

[1] This "duality in one" is understandable since Hermeticism refers to the cosmogonic domain, beyond which we cannot consider the androgyne anymore, but the neutral Brahma (Guénon, *Le symbolisme de la croix*, pp. 146-147).

[2] René Guénon, *Aperçus sur l'ésotérisme chrétien*, Éd. Traditionnelles, 1983, p. 77.

[3] Guénon, *Aperçus sur l'initiation*, pp. 252-253.

[4] Guénon, *Aperçus sur l'ésotérisme chrétien*, p. 77.

[5] Guénon, *Symboles fondamentaux*, p. 45.

[6] Guénon, *Symboles fondamentaux*, pp. 39, 407.

[7] In the Islamic tradition, the cup is the *haram* and its circumference, and the nutriment is the cubic Kaaba in the center (Guénon, *Aperçus sur l'ésotérisme islamique*, p. 32).

[8] *Sir Gawain*, p. 118, *La doctrine du sacrifice*, p. 127.

As we already mentioned, Guénon gave us the most lucid and truthful definition possible for the Holy Grail and its symbolism: the Holy Grail symbolizes the Center and the Tradition, and therefore we should examine next the Quest for this Center. However, since we presented in this chapter the various elements related to the symbolism of the Holy Grail, we have to elucidate one more aspect, before to dedicate our attention to the Quest: we have in mind here the Holy Bottle of Rabelais and its significance.

VI

LA DIVE BOUTEILLE[1]

In the era when Gutenberg started his adventure as a typographer, there were active guilds in the city of Mainz, with the guild of the *Küfers* among them, a guild that had a compass and two mallets as coat of arms, while the guild of the masons had three mallets.[2] The German word *Küfer* is related to the French "coffre" and the English "coffer," but also to the English "cooper" ("a person who makes or repairs barrels"), and this last word clarifies the significance of the *Küfers'* guild, considering that "cooper" derives from "cup." At one point in the stories of the Grail, the Holy Grail is deposited, following Jesus' order, in a coffer, and we can easily see the equivalence between the cup and the coffer, especially given that the word "coffer" is related to "cup."

The *Küfers* were craftsmen (*artifices*) manufacturing all types of containers, videlicet various objects which could keep or hold "contents," such as boxes, vessels and barrels; in Gutenberg's, making barrels was the main activity of a *Küfer*. Interestingly enough, the barrel became part of Gutenberg's métier, as it started to be used for the transportation of the prints: before being bound, the printed books were shipped in barrels filled with unbound copies.[3]

---

[1] The Holy Bottle.
[2] City of Mainz, *Gutenberg, Man of the Millennium*, 2000, p. 39. We may note the closeness between the two guilds, with respect to their symbolism.
[3] *Gutenberg, Man of the Millennium*, p. 153.

As the word "grail" means both "cup" (*grasale*) and book (*gradale*),[1] the barrel filled with books is a striking illustration of this double meaning. Yet the barrel allows for an even deeper analogy with the Holy Grail: the Grail vessel is known to have been considered a sort of continuation of the Celtic cauldron,[2] which makes the barrel a credible symbol of the Holy Grail, since the barrel could easily replace the cauldron and it was often used to keep the wine.

Generally speaking, the Holy Grail chalice should contain Christ's blood; nonetheless, from an initiatory viewpoint, what the Grail contained was *soma*, "the beverage of immortality," the spiritual drink that gives the initiate the "sense of eternity."[3] At one moment in time, the wine substituted *soma*, and the equivalence between wine and blood is well known in the Christian tradition. Guénon explained that the wine symbolizes the true initiatory tradition, and that, in Hebrew, *iain* (wine) and *sod* (mystery) are words with the same numerical value; in Sufism, the wine symbolizes the esoteric knowledge, a doctrine reserved only for the elite.[4] This symbolic meaning of the wine, Guénon added, is to be found in the legend of Dionysus or Bacchus, who, according to some traditional data, apparently came from India.[5]

The Templars clearly understood the holiness of the wine, even though the expression "to drink like a Templar" became something vulgar over the years; Guénon wrote: "the proverbial expression 'to drink like a Templar,' taken by the profane people in the most vulgar and literal sense, had, without any doubt, the same meaning: the wine the Templars drank was

---

[1] René Guénon, *Le Roi du Monde*, Gallimard, 1981, p. 45.
[2] Rabelais was very fond of the Celtic tradition (M. Bahtin, *François Rabelais*, Editura Univers, rom. tr., 1974, p. 433).
[3] Guénon, *Le Roi*, p. 46.
[4] See also J.-H. Probst-Biraben, *Rabelais et les secrets du Pantagruel*, Editions des Cahiers Astrologiques, Nice, 1949, p. 64.
[5] Guénon, *Le Roi*, p. 47.

identical with the wine drank by the Jews of the Kabbalah and by the muslim Sufis."[1]

All these features form the foundation of a famous work: *Gargantua and Pantagruel*, where François Rabelais has eulogized the wine, not in a vulgar, but in an initiatory sense. As in the case of Boccaccio's Decameron, only deceptively Rabelais's œuvre is "shameless" and "spicy," in reality under the cloak of coarseness, a sacred initiatory kernel is hiding[2]; and that is why Rabelais at one point mentioned the expression "to drink like a Templar" (*Ie boy comme un templier*).[3]

From the beginning Rabelais, like Dante, warns the reader not to be fooled by appearances. He gives Socrates as example who, although ugly in appearance, with rude manners and coarse clothing, hid golden wisdom, like a coffer sheltering a treasure. Similarly, as Rabelais underlined, the book about Gargantua hides precious elements, in spite of its coarse coat;[4] it is like a bone sheltering the marrow, *la substantificque mouelle*, the sacred and initiatory kernel.[5]

---

[1] René Guénon, *Aperçus sur l'Ésotérisme chrétien*, Éditions Traditionnelles, 1954, p. 62.

[2] See Guénon, *Aperçus sur l'Ésotérisme chrétien*, p. 107, and *Études sur la Franc-Maçonnerie et le Compagnonnage*, I, p. 17.

[3] "-I drink no more than a sponge. -I drink like a Templar knight. -And I, *tanquam sponsus.*" (I.5).

[4] *C'est pourquoy fault ouvrir le livre: et soigneusement peser ce qui y est deduict. Lors congnoistrez que la drogue dedans contenue est bien d'aultre valeur, que ne promettoit la boitte.*

[5] "Therefore is it, that you must open the book, and seriously consider of the matter treated in it. Then shall you find that it containeth things of far higher value than the box did promise; that is to say, that the subject thereof is not so foolish as by the title at the first sight it would appear to be... Or, did you ever see a dog with a marrowbone in his mouth, - the beast of all other, says Plato, the most philosophical? If you have seen him, you might have remarked with what devotion and circumspectness he wards and watcheth it: with what care he keeps it: how fervently he holds it: how prudently he gobbets it: with what affection he breaks it: and with what diligence he sucks it. To what end all this? What moveth him to take all these pains? What are the hopes of his labour? What doth he expect to reap thereby? Nothing but a little marrow. True it is, that this little is more savoury and delicious than the great quantities of other sorts of meat, because the marrow (as Galen testifieth) is a

Eschenbach, in *Parzival*, described how Kyot found in
Toledo a "heathen writing," the Grail story, written by "a
heathen, Flegetanis," who "was of the stock of Salomon."
Somewhat similarly the book of Gargantua was found: in a
bronze coffin, on which was written *Hic bibitur* ("we drink
here"), nine bottles arranged in a cross shape were discovered,
and under the middle bottle was lying the book (*gros/ gras/
grand/ gris/ ioly/ petit/ moisy/ livret, plus mais non mieux sentent que
roses*); to be noted the equivalence bottle – book, like in the
Grail case.

Throughout his five books, Rabelais keeps reiterating the
importance of the bottle and of the wine. He passionately
eulogizes the wine, as shown in the Prologue to the third book,[1]
where it is not difficult to understand that he does not have in
mind the corporeal wine but the spiritual one. And he eulogizes
the bottomless barrel,[2] the inexhaustible barrel, source of

---

nourishment most perfectly elaboured by nature. In imitation of this dog, it
becomes you to be wise, to smell, feel and have in estimation these fair goodly
books, stuffed with high conceptions, which, though seemingly easy in the
pursuit, are in the cope and encounter somewhat difficult. And then, like him,
you must, by a sedulous lecture, and frequent meditation, break the bone, and
suck out the marrow,—that is, my allegorical sense, or the things I to myself
propose to be signified by these Pythagorical symbols, with assured hope, that
in so doing you will at last attain to be both well-advised and valiant by the
reading of them: for in the perusal of this treatise you shall find another kind
of taste, and a doctrine of a more profound and abstruse consideration, which
will disclose unto you the most glorious sacraments and dreadful mysteries, as
well in what concerneth your religion, as matters of the public state, and life
economical" (The author's Prologue to the First Book). Guénon, writing
about the inner and outer in the Islamic tradition, remarks that the outer,
shariyah, is the "body," while the inner, *haqîqah*, is the "marrow," (*el-mukh*),
similar to Rabelais' marrow, *la substantifique moelle* (*Aperçus sur l'Ésotérisme
islamique et le Taoïsme*, Gallimard, 1973, p. 30).

[1] *C'est belle chose veoir la clairté du (vin & escuz) Soleil* ("It is a gallant thing to see
the clearness of (wine, gold,) the sun").

[2] *De ce poinct expédié, à mon tonneau ie retourne. Sus à ce vin compaings. Enfans
beuvez à plein guodetz. Si bon ne vous semble, laissez le. Tout beuveur de bien, tout
Goutteux de bien, alterez, venens à ce mien tonneau, s'ilz ne voulent ne beuvent: s'ilz
voulent, & le vin plaist au guoust de la seigneurie de leurs seigneuries, beuvent franchement,
librement, hardiment, sans rien payer, & ne l'espargnent. Tel est mon decret. Et paour ne
ayez, que le vin faille, comme feist es nopces de Cana en Galilée. Autant que vous en tireray*

"living water," and compared with the horn of plenty, which is obviously an equivalent of the Grail chalice.[1] And to be sure that we understand what he is saying, Rabelais continues with the eulogy of the blood, which is made of bread and wine, the two initiatory and Eucharistic ingredients.[2]

---

par la dille, autant vous en entonneray par le bondon. Ainsi demeurera le tonneau inexpuisible. Il a fource vive, & vène perpetuelle. Tel estoit le brevaige contenu dedans la couppe de Tantalus representé par figures entre les saiges Brachmanes: telles estoit en Iberie la montaigne de sel tant celebrée par Caton: tel estoit le rameau d'or sacré à la deesse soubterraine, tant celebré par Virgile. C'est un vray Cornucopie de ioyeuseté & raillerie. Si quelque foys vous semble estre expuysé iusques à la lie, non pourtant sera il à sec. Bon espoir y gist au fond, comme en bouteille de Pandora: non desespoir, comme on buffart des Danaïdes. ("Having despatched this point, I return to my barrel. Up, my lads, to this wine, spare it not! Drink, boys, and trowl it off at full bowls! If you do not think it good, let it alone. I am not like those officious and importunate sots, who by force, outrage, and violence, constrain an easy good-natured fellow to whiffle, quaff, carouse, and what is worse. All honest tipplers, all honest gouty men, all such as are a-dry, coming to this little barrel of mine, need not drink thereof if it please them not; but if they have a mind to it, and that the wine prove agreeable to the tastes of their worshipful worships, let them drink, frankly, freely, and boldly, without paying anything, and welcome. This is my decree, my statute and ordinance. And let none fear there shall be any want of wine, as at the marriage of Cana in Galilee; for how much soever you shall draw forth at the faucet, so much shall I tun in at the bung. Thus shall the barrel remain inexhaustible; it hath a lively spring and perpetual current. Such was the beverage contained within the cup of Tantalus, which was figuratively represented amongst the Brachman sages. Such was in Iberia the mountain of salt so highly written of by Cato. Such was the branch of gold consecrated to the subterranean goddess, which Virgil treats of so sublimely. It is a true cornucopia of merriment and raillery. If at any time it seems to you to be emptied to the very lees, yet shall it not for all that be drawn wholly dry. Good hope remains there at the bottom, as in Pandora's bottle; and not despair, as in the puncheon of the Danaids").

[1] In conection to the barrel, at the end of the first chapter of the fifth book, Pantagruel regards the barrel as a primordial matrix: "If we must fast, said Pantagruel, I see no other remedy but to get rid of it as soon as we can, as we would out of a bad way. I'll in that space of time somewhat look over my papers, and examine whether the marine study be as good as ours at land. For Plato, to describe a silly, raw, ignorant fellow, compares him to those that are bred on shipboard, as we would do one bred up in a barrel, who never saw anything but through the bung-hole."

[2] In both cases, of wine and of bread, the multiplicity becomes One. *La vie consiste en sang. Sang est le siège de l'ame. Pourtant un seul labeur poine en ce monde, c'est*

Much has been written about Rabelais and his work; even in the 16th century, "keys" were published, trying to decipher the hidden meaning of the work, and, like Dante's *Divine Comedy*, the meanings contained in *Gargantua and Pantagruel* were countless.

Rabelais, growing up among Franciscans, a medical student (of the famous university of Montpellier), chaplain of a Masonic organization, great scholar, connoisseur of Platonism and of Pythagorean lore,[1] knowledgeable in alchemy and astrology, follower of Hermeticism in general, he demonstrated in his work a great spiritual ability to recover the initiatory elements of his predecessors, elements that were preserved (as is usually the case), especially by the common people (the people being an honest and faithful receptacle).[2]

---

forger sang continuellement. En ceste forge sont tous membres en office propre: & est leur hierarchie telle que sans cesse l'un de l'autre emprunte, l'un à l'autre preste, l'un à l'autre est debteur. La matière & metal convenable pour estre en sang transmué, est baillée par nature: Pain & Vin. En ces deux sont comprinses toutes espèces des alimens. ("The intention of the founder of this microcosm is, to have a soul therein to be entertained, which is lodged there, as a guest with its host, (that) it may live there for a while. Life consisteth in blood, blood is the seat of the soul; therefore the chiefest work of the microcosm is, to be making blood continually. At this forge are exercised all the members of the body; none is exempted from labour, each operates apart, and doth its proper office. And such is their heirarchy, that perpetually the one borrows from the other, the one lends the other, and the one is the other's debtor. The stuff and matter convenient, which nature giveth to be turned into blood, is bread and wine. All kind of nourishing victuals is understood to be comprehended in these two").

[1] Probst-Biraben (p. 173) assumed that Rabelais belonged to a neo-Pythagorean branch; or that he was even a Rosicrucian (p. 175).

[2] For Probst-Biraben (p. 176), Rabelais was a great initiate, hidden under a buffoon mask. In the third book of *Gargantua and Pantagruel*, Rabelais tells us that "the emperors and the fools are born under the same Zodiacal sign" and "As he who narrowly takes heed to what concerns the dexterous management of his private affairs, domestic businesses, and those adoes which are confined within the strait-laced compass of one family, who is attentive, vigilant, and active in the economic rule of his own house, whose frugal spirit never strays from home, who loseth no occasion whereby he may purchase to himself more riches, and build up new heaps of treasure on his former wealth, and who knows warily how to prevent the inconveniences of poverty, is called a worldly wise man, though perhaps in the second judgment of the intelligences

Yet for us, the interesting part is the esoteric meaning hiding in Rabelais' work, a meaning that Rabelais himself suggested, and we would like to quote Guénon's review (year 1950) of Probst-Biraben's book about Rabelais,[1] in which he gives us some insight into this esoteric meaning:

On a assez souvent parlé de l'ésotérisme de Rabelais, mais généralement d'une façon plutôt vague, et il faut bien reconnaître que le sujet est loin d'être facile ; on a bien, dans maints passages de ses oeuvres, l'impression de se trouver en présence d'un « langage secret », plus ou moins comparable à celui des Fedeli d'Amore, *quoique d'un autre genre ; mais il semble bien que, pour pouvoir le traduire, il faudrait une « clef » qui jusqu'ici n'a pas été retrouvée. Cette question est d'ailleurs étroitement liée à celle de l'initiation qu'aurait reçue Rabelais : qu'il se soit rattaché à l'hermétisme, cela ne paraît pas douteux,[2] car les connaissances ésotériques dont il fait preuve appartiennent manifestement à l'ordre « cosmologique » et ne semblent jamais le dépasser ; elles correspondent donc bien au* domaine *propre de*

---

which are above he be esteemed a fool,—so, on the contrary, is he most like, even in the thoughts of all celestial spirits, to be not only *sage*, but to *presage* [!] events to come by divine inspiration, who laying quite aside those cares which are conducible to his body or his fortunes, and, as it were, departing from himself, rids all his senses of terrene affections, and clears his fancies of those plodding studies which harbour in the minds of thriving men. All which neglects of sublunary things are vulgarily imputed folly."

[1] J.-H. Probst-Biraben, *Rabelais et les secrets du Pantagruel*, Editions des Cahiers Astrologiques, Nice, 1949. René Guénon has admited that Rabelais' work shields an esoteric kernel, "which could be interesting to be studied more closely" (*L'Ésotérisme de Dante*, Gallimard, 1981, p. 33). As a trivia, let us note that Eliphas Lévi believed that he was a reincarnation of Rabelais (René Guénon, *L'Erreur Spirite*, Éd. Traditionnelles, 1984, p. 66).

[2] Gargantua's emblem is the Androgynous (a sort of Rebis): *Pour son imaige avoit en une plataine d'or pesant soixante & huyt marcs, une figure d'esmail competent en laquelle estoit portraict un corps humain ayant deux testes, l'une tirée vers l'aultre, quatre bras, quatre piedz, & deux culz, tel que dict Platon in Symposio, avoir esté l'humaine nature à son commencement mystic & au tour estoit escript en letres Ioniques: ΑΓΑΠΗ ΟΥ ΖΗΤΕΙ ΤΑ ΕΑΥΤΗΣ* ["true love demands no reward"; obviously the "true love" is the Love of the Templars and of Dante] ("For the jewel or brooch which in his cap he carried, he had in a cake of gold, weighing three score and eight marks, a fair piece enamelled, wherein was portrayed a man's body with two heads, looking towards one another, four arms, four feet, two arses, such as Plato, in *Symposio*, says was the mystical beginning of man's nature).

l'hermétisme, mais encore serait-il bon de savoir plus exactement de quel courant hermétique il s'agit, et c'est là quelque chose de fort complexe, car, à cette époque, les hermétistes étaient divisés en des écoles diverses, dont certaines étaient déjà déviées dans un sens « naturaliste » ; sans vouloir entrer plus avant dans cette question, nous devons dire que précisément, sur l'orthodoxie initiatique de Rabelais, les avis sont assez partagés… il y a chez lui un grand nombre de symboles qui relèvent nettement de l'hermétisme, et l'énumération en est fort curieuse et pourrait donner lieu à bien des rapprochements ; il y a aussi des allusions éparses à l'astrologie, mais surtout, comme on devait s'y attendre, à l'alchimie, sans compter tout ce qui fait du Pantagruel *un véritable « répertoire de sciences conjecturales »… Une des choses les plus extraordinaires, mais aussi les plus ouvertement apparentes, ce sont les descriptions d'un caractère évidemment initiatique qui se rencontrent dans le Ve livre de* Pantagruel *; il est vrai que certains prétendent que ce livre n'est pas de lui, parce qu'il ne fut publié que dix ans après sa mort, mais le plus vraisemblable est seulement qu'il le laissa inachevé et que des disciples ou des amis le complétèrent d'après les indications qu'ils avaient reçues de lui, car il représente bien réellement le couronnement en quelque sorte normal de l'oeuvre tout entière.*[1] *Une autre question qui présente un intérêt tout particulier est celle des rapports qu'eut Rabelais avec les « gens de métier » et leurs organisations initiatique*[2] *; il y a chez lui bien des allusions plus ou moins déguisées, mais malgré tout assez claires encore pour qui connaît ces choses, à certains rites et à certains signes de reconnaissance qui ne peuvent guère avoir une autre provenance que celle-là, car ils ont un caractère « compagnonnique » très marqué, et, ajouterons-nous, ce peut fort bien être aussi de ce côté qu'il recueillit, sur la tradition pythagoricienne, les connaissances que paraît indiquer l'emploi qu'il fait très fréquemment des nombres symboliques ; qu'il ait été affilié à quelqu'une de ces organisations en qualité de chapelain,*[3] *c'est là une hypothèse très vraisemblable.*[4]

Already in the first book Rabelais, similar to Dante, fights the academic scholars and the wicked monks and priests, because these, with their ignorance, have killed esotericism and

---

[1] See also Probst-Biraben 65, and G. Mallary Masters, *Rabelaisian Dialectic and the Platonic-Hermetic Tradition*, State Univ. of New York Press, 1969, p. 101.

[2] See also Probst-Biraben 67, 145.

[3] See also Probst-Biraben 68, 110, 174.

[4] *Franc-Maçonnerie*, II, pp. 113-115, 158, 171. Guénon was very kind in his review, since Probst-Biraben was a collaborator to *Le Voile d'Isis*, but we must say that his work is a disappointment (he quotes Fulcanelli, assumes the existence of a "Mediterranean tradition," and insists on presenting Rabelais as a "humanist" concerned with the social order).

they continue to do so even today. Like in Dante's case, it is not a revolt against the legal order, against the spiritual authority and the temporal power, but an uprising against those who managed, manipulated by suspect forces or by simple stupidity, to bury the initiatory significance of the Grail stories, as well as everything related to initiation and esotericism.

A medieval tradition indicates that Merlin created Gargantua, which to some extent makes Rabelais the continuator of the Grail tales. Gargantua, like any *avatâra*, was born miraculously: through the ear and after 11 months; and immediately becomes addicted to drinking.[1]

The first book, which is the book of Gargantua, ends with the description of the famous Abbey of Thélème – an imitation of Paradise, because the real center is where the Holy Bottle is.[2] The monastery is built following the wish of Prester John, a companion of Gargantua and Pantagruel, and nicknamed *frère Iean des Entommeures*, namely Friar John the Ripper,[3] who is described akin to a Templar, that is he is both a monk and a warrior, while his name and function allude to Prester John of India (or Ethiopia) and his kingdom where the Holy Grail disappeared in the end.

The Abbey of Thélème has a hexagonal shape, with six towers, indicating the cardinal points (and thus being "oriented"), with interior spiral stairs, like the stairs of Salomon's temple, and in the middle there is a fountain with three white fairies, and everything obeys, like in the Grail stories, the women's wishes.

---

[1] To be born through the ear is nothing new; in the Hindu tradition, two titans ("demons") *râkshasa*, Madhu and Kaitabha were born from Vishnu's ear. We should mention that both Gargantua and Pantagruel are "giants," similar to *asuras* and the Greek giants, but here it is rather suggested that they belong to the subtle domain.

[2] We find the same scenario in *Râmâyana*.

[3] The translation of the word "entommeures" is not so simple, and therefore in English we also see "Friar John of the funnels and gobbets"; probably Rabelais used this word because it is related to "temple" and also because is similar to "entonner" (to drink greedily from a barrel").

A prophecy about the end of times, written on a bronze
tablet, was discovered at the foundation of the abbey,[1] a
prophecy[2] that was similar to the one recorded by the Hindu
tradition about the *Kali-yuga*; its finding in this center, an
imitation of the Paradise, unmistakably implies that, just like
what happens in *Râmâyana*, there is a need for an initiatory
journey to start a new cycle, a new "Golden Age," the center
Thélème sealing a world in agony The various traditional data
depict how the end of times will be accomplished by the
concerted deadly actions of the primordial elements, water
(flood), earth (quake), fire (volcanoes) and air (hurricanes), and
such a picture Rabelais presented in front of us, closely related
to what *Bhagavata Purana* presented, a dying world with people
displaying chaotic and aggressive behaviour, a battle with
friends against friends, relatives against relatives, son against
father, with vassals attacking the masters, with honor and
honesty, rank and order vanished, and then the flood, the
darkness (no sun), the fire and the quake will come.[3]

---

[1] The bronze tablet appears also in the Christian Rosenkreutz's story. The
prophecy could be compared to the prophecy stated by the Lord of the
World. Friar John affirmed that he has recognized "the style of the prophet
Merlin" (the very end of the first book).

[2] The author could have been Mellin de Saint Gelais.

[3] Here is the prophecy or the "enigma," as Rabelais calls it: "Poor mortals,
who wait for a happy day, Cheer up your hearts, and hear what I shall say: If it
be lawful firmly to believe That the celestial bodies can us give Wisdom to
judge of things that are not yet; Or if from heaven such wisdom we may get
As may with confidence make us discourse Of years to come, their destiny
and course; I to my hearers give to understand That this next winter, though it
be at hand, Yea and before, there shall appear a race Of men who, loth to sit
still in one place, Shall boldly go before all people's eyes, Suborning men of
divers qualities To draw them unto covenants and sides, In such a manner
that, whate'er betides, They'll move you, if you give them ear, no doubt, With
both your friends and kindred to fall out. *They'll make a vassal to gain-stand his
lord, And children their own parents; in a word, All reverence shall then be banished, No
true respect to other shall be had* [our *Italics*]. They'll say that every man should have
his turn, Both in his going forth and his return; And hereupon there shall arise
such woes, Such jarrings, and confused to's and fro's, That never were in
history such coils Set down as yet, such tumults and garboils. Then shall you
many gallant men see by Valour stirr'd up, and youthful fervency, Who,

The second book starts with Pantagruel's birth, Pantagruel being an *alter ego* of Gargantua, similar to Galahad, Lancelot's son, who was an *alter ego* of his father. Pantagruel has solar characteristics as well: he is the Widower's son, and grows, like the fairy tales heroes, with uncommon speed. His name means, Rabelais explained, "totally thirsty" because *panta* in Greek means "all" and *gruel* in Arabic means "thirsty." At his birth, he was hairy like a bear, and he torn a bear into pieces when he

---

trusting too much in their hopeful time, Live but a while, and perish in their prime. Neither shall any, who this course shall run, Leave off the race which he hath once begun, Till they the heavens with noise by their contention Have fill'd, and with their steps the earth's dimension. *Then those shall have no less authority, That have no faith, than those that will not lie; For all shall be governed by a rude, Base, ignorant, and foolish multitude; The veriest lout of all shall be their judge, O horrible and dangerous deluge!* Deluge I call it, and that for good reason, For this shall be omitted in no season; Nor shall the earth of this foul stir be free, Till suddenly you in great store shall see *The waters issue out*, with whose streams the Most moderate of all shall moistened be, And justly too; because they did not spare The flocks of beasts that innocentest are, But did their sinews and their bowels take Not to the gods a sacrifice to make, But usually to serve themselves for sport: And now consider, I do you exhort, In such commotions so continual, What rest can take the globe terrestrial? Most happy then are they, that can it hold, And use it carefully as precious gold, By keeping it in gaol, whence it shall have No help but him who being to it gave. And to increase his mournful accident, *The sun, before it set in th' occident, Shall cease to dart upon it any light, More than in an eclipse, or in the night,* - So that at once its favour shall be gone, And liberty with it be left alone. And yet, before it come to ruin thus, *Its quaking shall be as impetuous* As Aetna's was when Titan's sons lay under, And yield, when lost, a fearful sound like thunder. Inarime did not more quickly move, When Typheus did the vast huge hills remove, And for despite into the sea them threw. Thus shall it then be lost by ways not few, And changed suddenly, when those that have it To other men that after come shall leave it. Then shall it be high time to cease from this So long, so great, so tedious exercise; For the great waters told you now by me, Will make each think where his retreat shall be; And yet, before that they be clean disperst, You may behold in th' air, where nought was erst, *The burning heat of a great flame to rise,* Lick up the water, and the enterprise. It resteth after those things to declare, That those shall sit content who chosen are, With all good things, and with celestial man (ne,) And richly recompensed every man: The others at the last all stripp'd shall be, That after this great work all men may see, How each shall have his due. This is their lot; O he is worthy praise that shrinketh not!"

was still a boy in a cradle; we don't know what Rabelais was thinking, but the bear is a symbol of the warriors and of the royal caste, and the name Arthur means bear. Pantagruel is described as being wiser than Salomon, and he was the founder of the Stone used as a table, alluding clearly to the symbolism of the Round Table.[1]

Rabelais applied a method commonly used in the sacred writings, substituting the principal hero (Pantagruel) with Panurge, and we saw how, in *Râmâyana*, Hanumân was Râma's substitute. Panurge must be regarded as Pantagruel's expression and for this reason he is the one who competes with the wise man from England, a mute competition, using signs, an allusion maybe to the Masonic ritual.

In this second book, Rabelais once again referred to the end of times, because he also presented, like Dante, the Hell, described as an upside-down world[2] where the Knights of the Round Table are porters.[3] And Rabelais promised that, in the following books, we will find out about Panurge's wedding (in fact a preview to Pantagruel's sacred wedding), about Pantagruel finding the philosophical stone and who he married

---

[1] *Une grosse roche ayant environ de douze toyzes en quarre, & d'espesseur quatorze pans. Et la mist sur quatre pilliers au millieu d'ung champ bien à son ayse, affin que lesdictz escholliers quand ils ne sçauroient aultre chose faire passassent le temps à monter sur ladicte pierre, & là banquetter à force flacons, iambons, et pastez: et escrire leurs noms dessus avecques un cousteau: et de present l'appelle on la Pierre levée.*

[2] Even Gargantua's birth is "upside-down" since he goes up to the ear.

[3] And the same for the others: *Xerces crioit la moustarde. Romule estoit saunier. Numa, clouatier. Tarquin, tacquin. Piso, paisant. Sylla, riveran. Enéas, meusnier. ... Achilles, teigneux. Agamemnon, lichecasse. Ulysses, fauscheur. ... Lancelot du Lac estoit escorcheur de chevaulx mors. Tous les chevaliers de la Table Ronde estoient pauvres gaignedeniers, tirans la rame pour passer les rivières de Cocyte, Phlegeton, Styx, Acheron et Lethé, quand messieurs les diables se veulent esbattre sur l'eau, comme sont les bastelieres de Lyon et gondoliers de Venise. Mais, pour chascune passade, ilz n'en ont qu'une nazarde, et, sus le soir, quelque morceau de pain chaumeny. ... Le pape Jules, crieur de petits pastis ; mais il ne portoit plus sa grande et bougrisque barbe. Jean de Paris estoit gresseurde bottes. Artus de Bretaigne, degresseur de bonnetz. Perceforest porteur de coustrets. Boniface pape huitiesme estoit escumeur de marmites. Nicolas pape tiers estoit papetier. Le pape Alexandre estoit preneur de ratz. Le pape Sixte, gresseur de vérole* (the second book, ch. XXX).

the daughter of the mysterious Prester John, all these being important initiatory elements.

The third book treats almost in its entirety Panurge's wedding, yet underlines a characteristic specifically applied to the Holy Grail, namely the oracular power. A series of most varied oracles are asked about the future wedding, from the oracles of Horace and Vergil, to the book of dreams, from the fortune-teller of Panzust to Herr Trippa (who probably is Cornelius Agrippa); the advice of a mute, of Friar John,[1] of the fool Triboulet (who has a wooden sword) is heard. Finally, after this long preparation, the decision is to ask the oracle of the Holy Bottle, at which point the voyage to the Center and the quest of the Grail begin.

The initiatory voyage takes place at sea, the navigation being symbolic, like Ulysses' voyage, and the "heroes" travel form center to center, that is from island to island, each center being different and described in a style à la Rabelais, like the island where the "incest" is unreserved, since nobody knows who the mother, the father, the sister, etc., or the Tohu-Bohu island are. The final destination of the voyage is India, because that is where the temple of the Holy Bottle is located, which is remarkable since that is where the Holy Grail retreated in the end. The voyage is marked by the colours white and red, which are the hermetical colours, but also the colours of the Templars.

The initiatory voyage is strewn with many details, many with hidden significance, like the letter Y for example, or the fundamental cyclic number 108,[2] or the name Ruah given to an

---

[1] Friar John urges Panurge to speed the wedding because the end of times is coming and the Antichrist was already born.

[2] Rabelais introduces 9720, which is 108 x 90. Yet 108 is also the number of stairs descending to the temple of the Holy Bottle, with the half 54 based on the Pythagorean tetraktys: starting from 1, two branches open, one composed of 2, 4 (the square), 8 (the cube), the other one composed of 3, 9 (the square), 27 (the cube), the sum being precisely 54.

island, or the spiritual influence in the shape of a celestial book written by Cherubim, or the pope's portrait.[1]

Further, the fifth book describes the end of the initiatory voyage, marked by the county of the Quintessence, the Entelechy (the perfection), the golden-silver chess, the golden fleece of Jason and the skin of Apuleius's golden ass, the county of Lights where the travellers received a lantern to guide them to the Holy Bottle.[2]

In the end, the Temple of the Oracle of the Holy Bottle is introduced, a subterranean temple, resembling Agarttha, where the "heroes" descend, as Christian Rosenkreutz descended, and now we witness a cascade of very powerful symbols, all illustrating the Center. Here are gathered all the varieties of vine and wine and all kinds of bottles, barrels, bowls and pitchers; here, in the center, is gathered what was scattered, here the multitude of vessels is gathered in the unique vessel of the Grail. And we now discover the explanation of an esoteric meaning, which René Guénon also exposed later: to reach the center of the center, where the altar of the Holy Bottle is located, the neophytes must step on the vine leaves, showing that they are mastering and possessing the wine and not the wine is possessing them (the same as Jesus who, riding the donkey, showed how he masters the evil).

Furthermore, Rabelais explained the apocalyptical image of the Virgin standing on the lunar crescent as proof that the Virgin masters the world of forms, that is the sublunary world, in comparison with most women who are "lunatics" (having in their heads three quarters of the moon).

At the same time, Rabelais suggested an initiation related to the Mysteries of Dionysus or Bacchus, mentioning that Bacchus is painted on the temple's ceiling as conqueror of India;

---

[1] The icon represents an ideal pope, a hidden icon which, to be seen, 32 locks and 14 padlocks had to be opened; we should compare this to Heraclius' coffer.

[2] Gold, perfection, quintessence and light, are all elements of the Center.

however, he did not forget to remember Pythagoras' teaching (which Rabelais particularly cherishes).[1]

The temple's gates are sealed with a huge diamond, while the lintel reads *in vino veritas*; nonetheless, as Rabelais carefully suggested on various occasions, this adage is not a profane and vulgar one, but clearly indicates that the wine is the beverage of immortality, and therefore of the Truth (and this wine the Templars drank).

The temple itself has a floor that, like the Masonic temple,[2] is in the shape of mosaic, but here the mosaic is composed of all sorts of precious stones, alluding to the Heavenly Jerusalem. Although subterranean, the spiritual sun of midnight illuminates the temple: "an admirable lamp that dispensed so large a light over the entire temple that, though it lay underground, we could distinguish every object as clearly as above it at noonday" (ch. XLI); in the center of the temple there is the fountain of youth, as found in various other traditions:

While we were admiring this incomparable lamp and the stupendous structure of the temple, the venerable priestess Bacbuc and her attendants came to us with jolly smiling looks, and seeing us duly accoutred, without the least difficulty took us into the middle of the temple, where, just under the aforesaid lamp, was the fine fantastic fountain. She then ordered some cups, goblets, and talboys of gold, silver, and crystal to be brought, and kindly invited us to drink of the liquor that sprung there, which we readily did; for, to say the truth, this fantastic fountain was very inviting, and its materials and workmanship more precious, rare, and admirable than anything Plato ever dreamt of in limbo... On the top of the cupola, just over the

---

[1] "We went down one marble step under ground, where there was a resting, or, as our workmen call it, a landing-place; then, turning to the left, we went down two other steps, where there was another resting-place; after that we came to three other steps, turning about, and met a third; and the like at four steps which we met afterwards. There quoth Panurge, Is it here? How many steps have you told? asked our magnificent lantern. One, two, three, four, answered Pantagruel. How much is that? asked she. Ten, returned he. Multiply that, said she, according to the same Pythagorical tetrad" (the fifth book, ch. XXXVI).

[2] In the fifth book, Rabelais mentioned the password Shiboleth (ch. XIX).

centre of the fountain, were three noble long pearls, all of one size, pear fashion, perfectly imitating a tear, and so joined together as to represent a flower-de-luce or lily, each of the flowers seeming above a hand's breadth. A carbuncle jetted out of its calyx or cup as big as an ostrich's egg, cut seven square (that number so beloved of nature), and so prodigiously glorious that the sight of it had like to have made us blind, for the fiery sun or the pointed lightning are not more dazzling and unsufferably bright. (ch. XLII).

The lily and the carbuncle both symbolize the Holy Grail. Yet the center of the center is, of course, the Holy Bottle:

When she had thus accoutred my gentleman, she took him [Panurge] out of our company, and led him out of the temple, through a golden gate on the right, into a round chapel made of transparent speculary stones, by whose solid clearness the sun's light shined there through the precipice of the rock without any windows or other entrance, and so easily and fully dispersed itself through the greater temple that the light seemed rather to spring out of it than to flow into it. The workmanship was not less rare than that of the sacred temple at Ravenna, or that in the island of Chemnis in Egypt. Nor must I forget to tell you that the work of that round chapel was contrived with such a symmetry that its diameter was just the height of the vault. In the middle of it was an heptagonal fountain of fine alabaster most artfully wrought, full of water, which was so clear that it might have passed for element in its purity and singleness. The sacred Bottle was in it to the middle, clad in pure fine crystal of an oval shape, except its muzzle, which was somewhat wider than was consistent with that figure. (ch. XLIII)

The oracle of the Holy Bottle utters just one word: *trink*, which means "drink" in German and evidently refers to the act of "drinking" the absolute knowledge, of "drinking" the beverage of immortality. Like the Holy Grail, the Holy Bottle is not only a vessel, but also a book, because the translation of the word the oracle uttered was found in the Great Book, a silver book, which miraculously becomes a carafe full of wine. And again Rabelais eulogizes the "wine" that comes from the "divine," a wine that gives wisdom, science and truth.

Before leaving the Center, the priestesses of the Holy Bottle came with gifts for the "heroes," three leather bottles with enchanted water; yet, in some versions, the third bottle contains water "taken from the well of the Indian sages, which is called the Barrel of the Brahmans.[1] Even though this specification is probably a later addition, it deserves our consideration because it brings back the image of the barrel as Holy Grail, as Center, as Tradition. This Center is identical to the Principle.[2]

---

[1] Rabelais, *Gargantua & Pantagruel*, Penguin Books, 1969, p. 711.

[2] For Rabelais, God is also the intelectual infinite sphere, with the center everywhere and the circumference nowhere, as Hermes Trismegistos said (Rabelais underlined): *Ceste infinie & intellectuale sphaere, le centre de laquelle est en chascun lieu de l'univers, la circunference poinct (c'est Dieu scelon la doctrine de Hermes trismegistus) à laquelle rien ne advient, rien ne passe, rien ne dechet, tous temps sont praesens.* And the same definition was given in the last chapter of the fifth book: "and may that intellectual sphere whose centre is everywhere and circumference nowhere, whom we call GOD, keeps you in his almighty protection." Nicolaus Cusanus and then René Guénon were also very involved with this definition.

VII

THE HOLY GRAIL AS CENTER

There is no doubt that the Holy Bottle is an equivalent of the Holy Grail, but it is more accurate to say that it is an explication of the Grail, revealing one main aspect, namely the Grail as the cup containing the beverage of immortality.

From this angle, the Holy Grail is a symbolic equivalent to the sacred and sacrificial head, with all the significances presented in chapter V, as Coomaraswamy pointed out more than one time.[1] The "full vessel" (*pûrna pâtra*, *kalasha*) of the Hindu tradition, identified with the Head,[2] is to be regarded as the Grail vessel, and that is why "an almsbowl is so often called a 'skull-cup' (*kapâla*), and why in fact the almsbowl may be actually made from a skull"; and, "of such relics, as is well known, the head or skull is the most important, and this has been so from the Stone Age to those of 'poor Yorik.'"[3]

---

[1] See, for example, *Sir Gawain*, pp. 115-118, *La doctrine du sacrifice*, pp. 122-127.

[2] "When Prajâpati is beheaded, 'he survives this woe,' and because of that the Soma vessel (*drona-kalasha*) is called the 'surviving vessel,' for 'it is Prajâpati's head that was struck off,' and Prajâpati, the Sacrifice, is King Soma, who 'was Vritra'" (Coom., *Sir Gawain*, pp. 110-111, *La doctrine du sacrifice*, pp. 114-115).

[3] Coom., *Sir Gawain*, p. 113. The sacred relics of the Magi are three skulls; also, the main relic at Saint-Maximin-la-Sainte-Baume is Mary Magdalene's skull. However, the heart also is the cup: "this Soma I am bearing in my heart" (*Rig-Vêda*, X.32.9). Herodotus said in his *History*: "The skulls of their enemies, not indeed of all, but of those whom they most detest, they treat as follows. Having sawn off the portion below the eyebrows, and cleaned out the inside, they [the Scythians] cover the outside with leather. When a man is poor, this is all that he does; but if he is rich, he also lines the inside with gold: in either case the skull is used as a drinking-cup" (IV.65).

Coomaraswamy, after stressing that "Makha's head becomes the Sun" and "Vishnu's head becomes 'yonder Sun,'"[1] explained: "In SB. IV. 4. 3. 4 we find 'Now Vritra was Soma. When the Angels smote him, his head whirled up (*udvavarta*) and became the *drona-kalasha*,' i.e. the soma-vessel, cf. PB. VI. 5. 7. 'the vessel of the Angels.' That the head becomes a vessel explains the designation of certain vessels as *kapâla*, 'skull-cup.' 'Vessel of the Angels' would appear to be the Sun, rather than the Moon, which would be the vessel of the Asuras."[2]

The Holy Grail as Head corresponds, as Coomaraswamy noted, to the Sun, but also to the Moon,[3] and, evidently, to Soma, but, essentially, it is a "unique thing," and sometimes the moon is the cup containing the solar *soma*, and sometimes the sun is the cup containing the lunar *soma*.[4]

"The dragon's head detached from his body, and mounted on a pillar, would be, of course, the Sun; and one cannot but think of the Indian Pravargya ritual, with its repeated 'For Makha's head art thou,'[5] with reference to the heated bowl that is the 'head of the sacrifice,'[6] and equated with the Sun."[7] In addition, Soma was considered to be the Sun and the *soma* juice was conceived as a liquid fire ("fire-water"),[8] even though the

---

[1] *Angel and Titan*, pp. 377-378, *La doctrine du sacrifice*, pp. 28-29.

[2] *Angel and Titan*, p. 382, *La doctrine du sacrifice*, p. 33.

[3] "Vritra survives as the Sun or Moon" and "Soma was Vritra" (Coom., *Sir Gawain*, p. 111, *La doctrine du sacrifice*, p. 115). In the Judaic tradition, Mount Horeb and Mount Sinai were, it seems, the solar and lunar aspects of the same mountain.

[4] Râma, the heir of the solar dynasty, is called Chandra; the solar Krishna has a lunar father. Charbonneau-Lassay mentioned *l'Estoile Internelle*, which is, like the emerald stone of the Grail and the "keystone," a stone with facets, and is placed in a cup (Guénon, *Symboles fondamentaux*, pp. 286-287).

[5] About this see in detail *Sir Gawain*, p. 116, *La doctrine du sacrifice*, p. 124.

[6] But the sacrifice is also the navel as center: "this sacrifice of ours is the navel of the earth" (*Rig-Vêda*, I.164.35).

[7] Ananda K. Coomaraswamy, *Guardians of the Sun-Door*, Fons Vitae, 2004, p. 60. "Head of the earth is Agni in the night-time; then, as the Sun, at morning springs up and rises" (*Rig Vêda* X.8.6).

[8] Coom., *Sir Gawain*, pp. 105-6, *La doctrine du sacrifice*, p. 105. In the Hermetic tradition, it is also mentioned the "fire-water" or the "liquid fire."

god Soma is a lunar deity.[1] There is, as we see, a continuous *hierogamos* between the sun and the moon[2] and we shouldn't be surprised that the Virgin, symbolizing the supreme *Sophia*, often appears as a lunar Maiden.[3] Coomaraswamy also wrote: "King Soma is the victim: Agni the eater, Soma the food here below, the Sun the eater, the Moon his food and oblation above[4]; when when eater and food (*adya, purodâsha*, sacrificial cake) unite, it is called the eater, not the food. ... It is the marriage effected on the night before the new moon's rising... There are inseparable connections between initiation, marriage, and death, and alimentary assimilation."[5]

The symbolism of *soma* helps us understand that of the Holy Grail. Both are, above all, the "beverage of immortality," and we saw how skilful Rabelais expressed this meaning; both are, as the Rosicrucian tradition would say, *veram medicinam*: "I took some Soma when the Sun rose up. That is the sick man's medicine"[6]; like the blood of the Grail, *soma* is an igneous liquid[7]; and both descended from heaven.[8] Soma,

---

[1] Soma is identical to the god Chandra. The full moon is the time to collect and press *soma*; the moon is also the cup from which the gods drink *soma*. Soma has the Nakshatras as wives; the Vedic astronomy (*jyotishavedanga*) describes the 27 *nakshatras* as lunar houses (if we multiply 27 by 16, the parts of the moon, the cyclic number 432 results).

[2] "The terrestrial marriage is in the hymn X, 85 [*Rig Vêda*], especially in the verses 36 and 38, assimilated to the celestial marriage between Sûryâ and Soma" (Abel Bergaigne, *La Religion Védique d'après les Hymnes du Rig-Véda*, Vieweg, 1878, I, p. 123). About Soma as Sun and Moon see Bergaigne 155-161.

[3] In the Hindu tradition, Damayanti, miraculously born, with the help of a *brâhmana*, represents the divine Maiden. She is described as a luminous being, a pearl, a lightning, and especially as the moon; she is compared to the full moon that drives away the darkness, to the lunar crescent, to the moon among the clouds, to the chaste Rohinî, the lunar god's favourite wife.

[4] See *The Śatapatha Brâhmana*, Motilal Banarsidass Publishers, Delhi, 1995, part IV, p. 398 and part V, p. 16 (X, 6, 2, 1-3, XI, 1, 6, 19).

[5] *Metaphysics*, p. 110, *La doctrine*, pp. 195-196.

[6] *Rig Vêda*, VIII.61.17.

[7] Bergaigne 165, 168 ("*soma* is fire in a liquid state"). "Soma is the life-blood of of a Dragon-tree" (Coom., *Guardians*, p. 5).

[8] Bergaigne 170-171.

Coomaraswamy specified, "is at once a 'person' and the tree, plant, food or Water of Life of the gods," and it is comparable to the Golden Fleece, Golden Apples and the Grail, the Vessel of Plenty.[1]

There is a Grail story, *Peredur Son of Efrawg*,[2] where it is explicitly affirmed that the Holy Grail is a head. The story tells how Peredur (Perceval) reaches the Center, which is the castle of the Grail, and enters a hall and "there was a great iron column in the hall floor." The column is a symbol of the *Axis Mundi*, and, similar to fairy tales, the hero smote the column three times with the sword, "so that it was in two pieces, and the sword in two pieces. ... Peredur placed the pieces together and they were joined as before. ... Peredur placed them together the third time, but neither the column nor the sword would be joined."[3] This triple trial alludes to the beheading of the dragons' three heads and to the cosmogonic *Fiat Lux*, but here the primary significance is an initiatory one, the first two trials regarding the renovation of *Corpus* and *Anima*, and the third one aiming at *Spiritus*, for which Peredur is not yet prepared: "two thirds of thy strength hast thou come by, and the third is still to come."[4] And then, Peredur witnesses the Grail procession: "he could see two youths coming into the hall, and from the hall proceeding to a chamber, and with them a spear of exceeding great size, and three streams of blood along it. ... The man did not tell Peredur what that was, nor did he ask it of him. After silence for a short while, thereupon, lo, two maidens coming in, and a great salver between them, and a man's head on the salver, and blood in profusion around the head."

---

[1] *Guardians*, p. 2.

[2] *The Mabinogion*, Everyman, 1993, pp. 152 ff.

[3] We observe that column and sword have the same axial meaning. Guénon said: "it is important to note that most of the symbolic weapons, and especially the sword and the lance, are often symbols of the 'World Axis'" (*Symboles fondamentaux*, p. 200).

[4] *The Mabinogion*, p. 159.

Evidently, the head is the Holy Grail,[1] but we should remark that in this case the lance reveals its universal symbolism as *Axis Mundi*,[2] and we could say that the lance is the body from which the head was separated, the Grail and the lance representing together the head on a pillar or spear,[3] and they mark the Center.[4]

The Masonic Catechism registered in the Dumfries Manuscript gives the following dialog: "Q: Where lyes ye key of your lodge? A: In a bone box covered with a rough mapp. Q: Give ye distinction of your box. A: My head is ye box, my teeth are the bones, my hair is the mapp, my tongue is ye key." Here also the head, considered a (treasure) box, is comparable to the Holy Grail; but we see that the key is the tongue, and since Peredur failed to use his tongue and ask the proper question, he could not "open" the box, that is, he could not reach *Spiritus*.

---

[1] Grison also observed that the Grail was replaced by a head (Jean-Louis Grison, *Notes sur les œuvres de Chrétien de Troyes*, Études Traditionnelles, no. 442, 1974, p. 71).

[2] "The lance appears in the Grail legend a complementary symbol [of the cup] and is one of the many figures of the 'World Axis.' The complementarism of the lance and the cup is strictly comparable to that of the mountain and the cave" (Guénon, *Symboles fondamentaux*, p. 192).

[3] The blood connected to the head and the lance stresses this meaning.

[4] In *Sir Gawain and the Green Knight* (Penguin Books, 1968), the Quest for the Holy Grail is, in fact, the Quest for the Green Knight's head. After Gawain beheaded the Knight, the head tells Gawain to come at the Green Chapel (p. 40), which is the Center, at New Year (which is the center of the time). In *The Story of White Arab*, one of the hero's initiatory trials is to cut and bring the head of a miraculous stag; "the stag's head shone so brightly that they all thought White Arab was carrying the sun" (*Folk Tales*, p. 28); no doubt, the stag's head is an equivalent of the Holy Grail. Similarly, a damsel asks Perceval to bring her the head of the white hart in exchange for her love (Robert de Boron, *Merlin and the Grail*, D. S. Brewer, 2007, p. 126). The quest for the white hart is an ancient initiatory theme, used in the Grail stories. In *Erec et Enide* (Chrétien, *Arthurian Romances*), the story starts with King Arthur hunting, on Easter Day, the White Stag (and "whoever can kill the White Stag must forsooth kiss the fairest maiden") (p. 1). A white hart came at the wedding of King Arthur to Guinevere (Sir Thomas Malory, *Le Morte D'Arthur*, Penguin, 1981, I, p. 98). In *The Quest of the Holy Grail* (p. 243) and Malory (II, pp. 345-346), the White Stag is Christ. In Tristan's tale, the hart is the Universal Man (the hierarchy of the hart's parts is presented) (Strassburg 78-88, Bédier 7-8).

The head as Holy Grail marks the Center. Yet, again, a symbolic hierarchy of the spiritual Pole's successive approximations is revealed: the Grail castle is the center, and the table is the center of the center, and the Grail is the center of the center of the center.[1] Peredur was able to reach the two "exterior" centers, the castle and the table, but not the most inner center.[2]

---

[1] In Chrétien's *Cligés* it is said: "He through whose efforts the town [center] shall be taken is to have the cup" (*Arthurian Romances*, p. 111); we see the equivalence. The cup is made of gold and precious stones. Regarding the symbolic hierarchy of the spiritual Pole's successive approximations, we repeat Vulliaud's sayings: "the Tabernacle of the Holiness of Jehovah, the residence of Shekinah, is the Saint of Saints, which is the heart of the Temple, which is itself the center of Sion (Jerusalem), as the Holy Sion is the center of the Land of Israel, and as the Land of Israel is the center of the world." Guénon gave another example, from the Far-Eastern tradition: as the central province (called the "Median Realm" and where the Emperor resided) was in the center of the Empire, so the Empire was in the center of the world; and in the center of the "Median Realm" was situated the *Ming-Tang*. These approximations are based on the fact that everything is comprised in the Center (in the state of "complication") and, through successive explications, "images" of the center will develop as concentric circles. These two examples, regarding the Judaic and Far-Eastern traditions, also illustrate how any particular tradition considered its center as the only center (Guénon, *La Grande Triade*, pp. 137-138).

[2] With respect to the table as center, Herodotus said: "After this Cambyses planned three several expeditions, one against the Carthaginians, another against the Ammonians, and a third against the 'Long-lived' Ethiopians, who dwell in that part of Libya which is by the Southern Sea; ... and to the Ethiopians to send spies first, both to see whether the table of the Sun existed really ... Now the table of the Sun is said to be as follows: there is a meadow in the suburb of their city full of flesh-meat boiled of all four-footed creatures; and in this, it is said, those of the citizens who are in authority at the time place the flesh by night, managing the matter carefully, and by day any man who wishes comes there and feasts himself; and the natives (it is reported) say that the earth of herself produces these things continually" (III.17-18). With respect to the Ethiopians, it is well known that in the Middle Ages one of the locations for Prester John's Realm was considered to be Ethiopia (see Guénon, *Le Roi*, p. 15, Robert Silverberg, *The Realm of Prester John*, Doubleday & Co., 1972).

The table as center is not a Christian but a universal symbol[1] and could be found in various traditions, including the traditional ballads or the fairy tales.[2] René Guénon considered it a very ancient symbol, one of those that were associated with the idea of spiritual centers,[3] and the Grail stories diligently exposed the table as center, even though they used mostly Christian garments.[4] Of course, the Round Table is famous, but besides it, there are many other allusions to this symbolism of the table, and we notice a ritual in the stories, which, repeated over and over again, refers to washing the hands before sitting at the table, a gesture that is not about profane hygiene but about purification. "The King and his company came into hall. Called on with cries from clergy and laity, Noël was newly announced, named time and again.[5] ... All this merriment they made until meal time. Then in progress to their places they passed after washing, in authorized order, the high-ranking first."[6] "The knights washed and sat down to eat."[7] "They

---

[1] The cup also is a universal symbol, which belongs to the Primordial Tradition (Guénon, *Symboles fondamentaux*, p. 52).

[2] See, for example, *The Story of White Arab*, where the initiatory quest for the Maiden (the Red Emperor's daughter) is the result of the challenge made by a miraculous bird at the table of the Green Emperor and his knights. A similar episode is found in *The Quest of the Holy Grail* (Penguin Books, 1969, pp. 36-7), where Arthur and his knights are seating at the Round Table and an old man robed in white with a knight in red armour came in; the knight is Galahad, "the Desired Knight, from the noble house of King David," who is recognized as the Knight of the Holy Grail. Soon after, a maiden came and announced the appearance of the Holy Grail at the Table (p. 42); and when this occurred, "they began to look at one another, uncertain and perplexed. But not one of those present could utter a word, for all had been struck dumb" (p. 43) (see the *timor panicus* related to the Lord of the World, Guénon, *Le Roi*, p. 9).

[3] *Symboles fondamentaux*, p. 41, *Écrits*, p. 6.

[4] As Guénon said, the Round Table and its Chivalry illustrate the founding of an authentic spiritual center (*Franc-Maçonnerie*, II, p. 35).

[5] The center is also a "temporal" one, and Christmas is indeed "central."

[6] *Sir Gawain*, pp. 25-26. We note the importance of hierarchy and order.

[7] Chrétien de Troyes, *Perceval or The Story of the Grail*, The University of Georgia Press, 1983, p. 46. Even from the profane viewpoint, we see that the general opinion regarding the "dark ages" and the lack of "civilisation" and "hygiene" are inventions of the modern minds.

washed their hands in water, warmed, and then two squires, so
I'm informed, brought in the ivory tabletop, made of one
piece.[1] ... The trestles had two very special, rare properties,
which they contained since they were built, and which remained
in them forever: they were wrought of ebony, a wood that's
thought to have two virtues: it will not ignite and burn and will
not rot.[2] They laid the tabletop across the trestles ... No legate,
cardinal, or pope has eaten from a whiter[3] tabletop."[4] "The
young man [Perceval] ... found the great hall, level with the
ground. The king [Arthur] and knights were at the table."[5]

There are three important tables, Merlin said, in accord with
the Christian Trinity, but we can easily detect a deeper meaning.
The first is the table of the Last Supper; the second was
established in memory of the first one, with the help of Christ,
by the soldier "who took Jesus from the cross" and who
happened to be, afterwards, in a "desolate land," where a "great
famine" beset him and his people, "and on this table the knight
placed a vessel which he covered with white cloths so that he
alone could see it. This vessel separated the good people from
the bad. Anyone who was able to sit at this table found the
fulfilment of his heart's desires"; the third is the Round Table
established by Arthur's father, Uther Pendragon, to whom
Merlin said: "at the second table they called the vessel which
bestowed this grace the Grail. If you'll trust my advice, you'll
establish a third table in the name of the Trinity, which these
three tables will signify."[6] The symbolism of the center and the
connection between the table and the Holy Grail are obvious,
but there is more to learn: Merlin's sayings suggest how a center
is established, how the transmission is kept alive and unbroken,[7]

---

[1] "Made of one piece" has a symbolic meaning, referring to the "multiplicity in
One."
[2] It alludes to the immutability and eternity of the center.
[3] Here white = pure is an attribute of the center.
[4] Chrétien, *Perceval*, p. 90.
[5] Chrétien, *Perceval*, p. 29. Here the table is a center reached by Perceval at the
beginning of his spiritual journey.
[6] Boron, *Merlin*, pp. 34-36, 92.

unbroken,[1] and how the elected knights "once they've sat at the table they'll have no desire to return to their homes," becoming the "Grail's guardians."[2]

Perceval's aunt, an anchoress and former Queen of the Waste Land,[3] also tells the story of the three tables, and the Christian influence that adorns the story, which is normal[4] and should not deflect us from perceiving the universal esoteric kernel. The first was the table of Jesus Christ; the second was the table of the Holy Grail, "in memory and likeness of the first" and "in the days of Joseph of Arimathea"; the third was "the Round Table, devised by Merlin, to embody a very subtle meaning."[5] Despite the Christian envelope, we promptly perceive here the uninterrupted chain of spiritual transmission and the journey from one center to another,[6] this time not a spatial but a temporal journey. Furthermore, the unique and special seat is again brought to our attention. In the case of the second table, "the seat itself had been fashioned after the one in which Our Lord had sat at the Last Supper" and it was prepared for Josephus, the son of Joseph of Arimathea.[7] It is interesting that, like in fairy tales and the Masonic ritual, the "two brothers

---

[1] In the case of the second table, there is an explicit description of the end of a cycle and the birth of a new one. Joseph of Arimathea made the second table, and Bron, Joseph's brother-in-law, brought fish to the table; a seat was left empty, and the same empty seat is found in the case of the third table, a seat prepared for Perceval, Bron's grandson and Alain li Gros' son (Boron, *Merlin*, pp. 34-36); this is the Seat of Danger, reserved, in other stories, for Galahad (*The Quest of the Holy Grail*, Penguin Books, 1969, p. 37).

[2] Boron, *Merlin*, pp. 93-4.

[3] The "waste land" usually represents a "holy land" that became wasted when the spiritual influences left it.

[4] The Grail stories were part of the Christian esotericism and then, with the destruction of the traditional civilization of the Middle Ages, they became, more and more, "historical" and exoteric, trying to save what could be saved and to keep the traditional Chivalry going.

[5] *The Quest of the Holy Grail*, pp. 97-99.

[6] Each table (and the related cup) represents a center and a secondary cycle. "Jesus said: 'As I said at the table, several tables will be established in my service'" (Boron, *Merlin*, p. 22).

[7] Similar to the table (but not ide ntical), the seat, chair or throne is a symbol of the center.

of Josephus' lineage were eaten up with envy" and disputed Josephus' right to that special seat and "one of them sat there himself ... at once, by a miracle [the Act of Truth], the earth swallowed up the usurper," and the seat became the "Seat of Dread," which in the case of the Round Table was called the "Seat of Danger."[1]

In comparison to the seat, the Table and the Grail both have two emblematic attributes of the center that the seat does not: their fullness and an endless capacity to nourish,[2] where nourishment must be primarily understood as spiritual food,[3] just as the Round Table and the Holy Grail must be recognized as spiritual archetypes, of which any table and cup are mere projections and symbols. Therefore, only modern mentality, and especially the most deranged part of it, could promote a material cup as the Holy Grail, when, in fact, the Grail stories insisted on presenting an elusive Grail, in accord with the Primordial Tradition and its teachings.[4]

The Grail procession is nothing else but the "vision" of the center, represented by its essential elements: the head or the heart and the axis. The Holy Grail manifests its presence by nourishing[5] and healing people, without a material intervention,

---

[1] The "danger" evidently refers to the Act of Truth. We should also note how the name of the Round Table was explained: "For in its name it mirrors the roundness of the earth, the concentric spheres of the planets. ... The Round Table is a true epitome of the universe"; as we already said, the roundness of the earth was well known during the "dark ages," and the modern mentality maliciously invented the idea that the "flat earth" concept characterized medieval thinking.

[2] See A. J. Wensinck, *The Navel of the Earth*, Johannes Müller, Amsterdam, 1916, pp. 30, 34.

[3] Bede said: "Our creator has prepared us a table of knowledge to strengthen us in the true faith" (pp. 109-110).

[4] "Then Jesus spoke other words to Joseph which I dare not tell you – not could I, even if I wanted to, if I did not have the high book in which they are written: and that is the creed of the great mystery of the Grail" (Boron, *Merlin*, p. 22). The "high book" is, of course, the Tradition and not a material book.

[5] We usually did not refer to the works about Solomon's Temple or the Holy Grail that have nothing to do with the traditional perspective; but we would like to mention an "anti-guénonist" author, Bonnal, who wrote a terrible book about the Grail, in which he ludicrously said that the Grail is an eternal food

intervention, and this story about the Grail is more invisible than visible, like a perfume's fragrance.[1]

Nonetheless, the Holy Grail, which heals in miraculous ways,[2] could not heal the Fisher King, because this one

---

supplier because in those times there was a significant lack of food and poverty (Isabelle & Nicolas Bonnal, *Lancelot & La Reine*, Claire Vigne, 1996, pp. 210, 221); he reduced the Grail story to a "human" level, charged with sentimentalism, naturalism, and emotions, where Lancelot is "psychically instable," Guinevere "is a too human objective of his quest," Galehot is emotional, the Arthurian cycle was interested first in the European politics and then in initiation, the beheading is a barbarian custom, the Fisher King's infirmity makes him a chthonic symbol, the adultery is disastrous, *The Quest of the Holy Grail* is the most sacerdotal story of the cycle, the Grail is the famous treasure of the Templars, but first it is nourishment, and the list of errors could continue. At one moment, the author asked if "Tradition and the ultimate secrets of the world are not destined to be out of reach for us?" We can assure the author that, for him, they are out of reach.

[1] See, for example, how the Grail healed Lancelot, who was wounded by a boar (Malory, *Le Morte D'Arthur*, pp. 218-221). In *Perlesvaus*, a head heals King Arthur (*La légende arthurienne*, pp. 135-137). We should mention that in *Perlesvaus* the decapitated head plays a major role. First, at the feast of Saint John (we know the importance of Saint John for Masonry), when Arthur gathers back the dispersed Knights of the Round Table, a procession with three maidens arrives: the first girl, who is bald, carries a knight's head (this maiden is also the Grail bearer, and again the Grail is equivalent to the head); the second girl carries a queen's head, crowned with copper (we see the hermetic influence); and there is a cart, drew by three white harts, with heads of 150 kings (Roger Sherman Loomis, *The Grail*, Princeton Univ. Press, 1991, pp. 103, 106; Loomis also comments on this "strange narrative," but his profane viewpoint is of no help). Later on, Gawain, during his quest, met a damsel with a knight's head tied to her saddle (the head protects the girl when crossing the forest). From a Christian perspective, the archetypal beheading is obviously that of Saint John the Baptist, and therefore Gawain must start the quest for the sword that did this decapitation, and he acquires the sword in exchange of beheading a giant (pp. 142-143, 145, 152, 171-172, 180-182).

[2] A sick knight "dragged himself by the strength of his arms to the stone where the table stood that supported the Holy Vessel. He pulled himself up with his two hands until he could kiss the silver table and press his eyes to it. And immediately he knew relief from his suffering, and he groaned aloud and said: 'Ah! God, I am healed!'" (*The Quest of the Holy Grail*, p. 83); even in the Vulgate Cycle, the Grail heals by its presence and not by direct touch, since the knight kisses the table; the table with the vessel is, here again, a symbol of the center. "These four men and these ladies laid hand on Sir Launcelot, and

represents the king of the old cycle, namely, the dragon (without hands and feet) that guards *soma*, and his healing is a consequence of the Knight's spiritual realization, when a new cycle will start with a new king, and when the dragon will leave its old skin (the healing) and will shine, becoming one with the Knight. But the spiritual realization is not about exoteric salvation; it is a very complicated initiatory path, which the common knight, as much as he would follow the chivalric rules and the religious rites, cannot fulfill, and even though the Grail stories, with the passing of time, increasingly emphasized the religious characteristics, they could not smother the esoteric kernel, nor could they make disappear the initiatory symbolism intended not to any knight but to the chosen ones. Therefore, the Knight's failure to recognize the Holy Grail has to be understood as part of the initiatory process, which essentially differs from the exoteric knighthood education.

"The Fisher King had the Grail in his keeping. And I tell you, the Fisher King was so old and frail and beset that he could not move his hands or feet. ... And they had the tables set at once and the lord and Perceval sat down to dine. And as they were sitting there ... they saw a damsel, most richly dressed, come out of a chamber: she had a cloth about her neck, and in her hands she carried two small silver platters. After her came a boy carrying a lance, which shed from the head three drops of blood. They passed before Perceval and into another chamber. After this came a boy bearing the vessel

---

so they bare him into a tower, and so into a chamber where was the holy vessel of the Sangrail... and so by miracle and by virtue of that holy vessel Sir Launcelot was healed and recovered" (Malory, II, p. 221); the story tells how Launcelot fought against a boar and was hurt (for the symbolism of this fight, representing the revolt of the *Kshatriyas* against *Brâhmanas*, see Guénon, *Symboles fondamentaux*, p. 181). And later on, Launcelot witnesses how a knight kissed the holy vessel and was healed, but the episode was presented as a "vision," since Launcelot was asleep (p. 269; see also *The Quest of the Holy Grail*, pp. 81-83). If in *Perlesvaus*, Arthur is healed not by the Grail but by a severed head, in Eschenbach's *Parzival*, Gawan is healed by a salve from Munsalvaesche (which is the Grail center) (pp. 240-244) (similarly, Râma was healed by plants from the "herbal mountain").

that Our Lord had given Joseph in prison. ... Then the boy returned carrying the Grail, and passed back into the chamber from which he had first come; and the boy bearing the lance did likewise; and the damsel followed after – but still Perceval asked nothing. When Bron the Fisher King realised no question was going to come he was most distressed. He had had the Grail presented to all the knights who had lodged there, because Our Lord Jesus Christ had told him he would never be healed until a knight asked what it was for, and that knight had to be the finest in the world."[1]

Robert de Boron transmitted in writing a version of this decisive moment, when the Knight has the "vision" of the Holy Grail procession. We find in the quoted text all the symbolic ingredients with respect to the Cosmos, Year and Man: the cycle is dying, the world is close to its end and the dragon is waiting to be reunited with its head, just as the Grail needs to settle on top of the lance. Yet the efforts of the future new king are too feeble, and definitely not sufficient in this epoch of the *Kali-yuga*, to allow him to become the "citizen" of this center (table) of the integral human state, regarded with the total extension of its possibilities, and so, the Grail procession, which, in fact, is a complete "session" with two phases, procession and recession (the returning to the initial chamber), remains a "vision" of a metaphysical reality still to be reached. This "vision" teaches the neophyte how the Supreme Center sends its messengers – the spiritual influences who institute a new center, and how, if there is no response, it retracts them back in the darkness of the middle chamber.

Although in Boron's story the carrier of the Holy Grail is a boy,[2] usually the bearer is a maiden, like in Chrétien's *Perceval*: "Out of a room a squire came, clasping a lance of purest white; ... all saw him bear, with measured tread, the pure white lance.

---

[1] Boron, *Merlin*, p. 141. Asking the question is an essential element of the Grail initiatory path and should be compared to the knight's kiss needed to wake up the sleeping beauty; it refers to the one's intimate effort and profound desire to follow the spiritual realization.

[2] He is a boy and not a man.

From its white tip a drop of crimson blood would drip and run along the white shaft and drip down upon the squire's hand, and then another drop would flow.[1] ... Two more squires entered, and each squire held candelabra, wrought of fine pure gold with niello work design. ... The squires were followed by a maiden who bore a grail, with both hands laden ... and when she entered with the grail, the candles suddenly grew pale, the grail cast such a brilliant light as stars grow dimmer in the night when sun or moonrise makes them fade.[2] ... The grail, which had been borne ahead, was made of purest, finest gold and set with gems; a manifold display of jewels of every kind ... The jewels in the grail surpassed all other gems in radiance."[3]

Dante, a direct successor of the Templars and of the Grail stories,[4] presented a similar procession when he reached the Earthly Paradise,[5] with Ezekiel's four beasts and the Griffon (Christ), described thus: "its bird-like [eagle] parts were gold [the solar, *principial* nature]; and white the rest [the lion] with blood-red markings."[6] The "heavenly pageant" stops in front of

---

[1] The symbolism of white and red is well known in Hermeticism, and generally in Christian esotericism; we also find these colours at the Knights Templar and on the banner of St. James of Compostela. In Ovid's story about Pyramus and Thisbe (retold later by Shakespeare), there is a mulberry tree near a cold spring (the *Axis Mundi* and *fons vitae*), where Pyramus, "drawing his sword, plunged it into his chest. The blood spurted from the wound, and tinged the white mulberries of the tree all red"; the change of color from white to dark red suggests an Alchemical process, white and red being not only connected to the theological virtues, described by Dante, but they are also Hermetic colors symbolizing the *Lesser* and *Greater Mysteries* of Alchemy, *the white stage of the Work* and *the red stage of the Work*. The drops of blood falling from the Grail lance symbolize the spiritual influences, similar to the drops of luminous dew falling from the Tree (as in the Jewish Kabbalah) (Guénon, *Le Roi*, p. 41); there is equivalence between the tree and the lance (Ovid described how Romulus' lance changed into a tree, see *Metamorphoses*, book XV).

[2] We see here the Grail compared to the sun or moon.

[3] Chrétien, *Perceval*, pp. 87-89. We see the Grail described similarly to Heavenly Jerusalem.

[4] *The Divine Comedy* was written in the year 1300, soon after the Grail stories changed from oral to a written form.

[5] *The Purgatorio*, XXIX.

[6] *The Purgatorio*, XXIX, 112-114; "E bianche altre, di vermiglio miste."

Dante and, for his surprise, Beatrice is making her appearance: "within a cloud of flowers that rose like fountains from the angels' hands, and fell about the chariot in showers, a lady came in view: an olive crown wreathed her immaculate veil [white, faith], her cloak was green [hope], the colours of live flame played on her gown [red, divine love]."[1]

In the Christian Middle Ages, the Virgin was a symbol for esoteric spirituality; she was *Madonna Intelligenza*. In the Hindu tradition, in the Judaic Kabbalah, in Greek mythology and in fairy tales, the initiatory stories presented a supreme endeavour, the finding of the divine Maiden, who is the Virgin (even if, historically, she doesn't appear as such) and has various names: Helen of Troy, Beatrice, *Pistis Sophia, Madonna Intelligenza*, Sîtâ, Ariadne, etc., symbolizing absolute Knowledge, divine Light and heavenly Love.[2]

The medieval initiatory organization *Fedeli d'Amore*, to which Dante belonged,[3] venerated *Madonna Intelligenza*, who, for Dante, was Beatrice and, ultimately, the Virgin Mary. To permit the human mind to grasp somehow what is impossible to understand in a rational, discursive way, the Principle (even if unchangeable and immutable, without duality and immovable) is considered to act through his "energy" (*shakti*), which is feminine compared to him. *Shakti* is the divine Maiden, the lunar Virgin, *Sophia*, Helen of Troy, *Madonna Intelligenza*, and Dante's Beatrice, as the target of the spiritual realization.[4] In

---

[1] *The Purgatorio*, XXX, 28-33.

[2] See, among others, Grison, *Notes*, ET, no. 437-438, p. 161, where the author underlines that the Lady is "the figure of the tradition, of spiritual authority, of Wisdom and, at a higher lever, of the divine Will."

[3] It seems that Dante also was a leader of another initiatory organization, of Templar origin, *Fede Santa* (Dante was Kadosch); see Guénon, *Aperçus sur l'ésotérisme chrétien*, p. 67, *L'ésotérisme de Dante*, p. 14. Guénon discussed in details about *Fedeli d'Amore* and *Madonna Intelligenza* in his *Aperçus sur l'ésotérisme chrétien*, pp. 55-80. See also Luigi Valli, *Il linguaggio segreto di Dante e dei 'Fedeli d'Amore,"* Roma, "Optima," 1928. With regard to *Fede Santa*, Faith should be understood as Truth, since the Act of Truth is an Act of Faith (Coom., *Headless*, p. 215).

[4] *Shakti* is the "dark cloud" of the Judaic tradition, the Black Virgin as celestial celestial Queen who, due to the Principle's "non-active activity" (*wei wu-wei* of the Far-Eastern tradition), generates the spiritual influences; these influences

this case, the "divine center" is identical to *Amor* (Love), which is conquered in an *active* manner, and the *Kshatriyas* were well prepared to assimilate this symbolism.[1]

Consequently, we must admit equivalence between the Maiden and the Grail, already suggested by the fact that the Grail's bearer is a maiden and by the apocalyptic vision of the Virgin as "a woman clothed with the sun, with the moon under her feet and a crown of twelve stars on her head." Moreover, since Lancelot is as important as Perceval, who had the "vision" of the Holy Grail,[2] Lancelot's Quest of the Maiden (the Queen Guinevere), and never of the Grail, makes it equal to the Quest of the Grail.[3] Only later, when the exoteric issue regarding the

---

descend upon *Prakriti*, representing the divine Activity of *Purusha*, and consequently, *Prakriti* emerges from her indifference and produces the universal manifestation. *Prakriti* is *Shakti*'s projection and the Black Virgin is, at the same time, *Shakti* and *Prakriti*. "Shakti is the maternal 'power,' 'the divine Activity.' Therefore, she is inherent to Brahma or to the supreme Principle; she is incomparably higher than Prakriti; Prakriti is, in fact, only a reflection of Shakti in the 'cosmologic' order. We remark the inverted analogy: the supreme Activity is reflected in the pure passivity and the 'almightiness' of the Principle is reflected in the potentiality of *materia prima*. Shakti, as the abode of divine 'art' in the Principle, is identical to the 'Wisdom,' Sophia, and, in this case, she is the mother of *Avatâra*. Using the Western terminology, Shakti is *Natura naturans*, and Prakriti – *Natura naturata*, even though both are named *Natura*" (Guénon, *Hind.*, p. 102).

[1] Guénon, *L'ésotérisme de Dante*, p. 47. Guénon insisted on the word *active*, since usually the religious path is *passive*; this means that in the initiatory process there is not only communication with the super-individual states (as it happens in the religious domain), but also an *active* conquest and assimilation of these states, when the human being actually becomes the integral being (and does not remain an individual, even though opened to the divine revelation).

[2] Lancelot's initial name is Galahad (*Lancelot of the Lake*, Oxford University Press, 1989, p. 3), and so is called the son of Joseph of Arimathea (p. 57). Lancelot's son is also Galahad, and he is the future king of the Grail; it is safe to assume that, as often happens in fairy tales, the two are in fact one and the same.

[3] Similarly, Râma's Quest for Sîtâ is a "quest for the Grail," that is, a quest for the Center.

adultery overcame the esoteric meaning,[1] is Lancelot described as failing to reach the Grail.[2]

In Eschenbach's story, the queen Repanse de Schoye is the Grail's bearer: "Four ladies carried huge candles. The other four, without reluctance, carried a precious stone, through which by day the sun shone brightly. Its name was renowned: it was a garnet hyacinth, both long and broad. ... After them came the queen. Her countenance gave off such sheen that they all thought day wished to break. This maiden, they saw, wore phellel-silk of Araby. Upon a green achmardi she carried the perfection of Paradise, both root and branch. This was a thing that was called the Grail, earth's perfection's transcendence. Repanse de Schoye was her name, she by whom the Grail permitted itself to be carried.[3] The Grail was of such a nature that her chastity had to be well guarded, she who ought by rights to tend it."[4]

Eschenbach has introduced another important symbol of the center – the stone. Not only that a stone, a garnet hyachinth, participates in the pageant, but the Holy Grail itself is a stone. "It is well known to me that many a valorous hand resides by the Grail at Munsalvaesche. ... I will tell you of their food [!]: they live by a stone whose nature is most pure. If you know nothing of it, it shall be named to you here: it is called *lapsit exillis*.[5] ... Never was a man in such pain but from that day he beholds the stone, he cannot die in the week that follows immediately after. Nor will his complexion ever decline. ... If that person saw the stone for two hundred years, his hair would never turn grey. Such power does the stone bestow upon man

---

[1] This meaning was preserved by initiatory organizations as *Fedeli d'Amore*.

[2] Lancelot "never stirred at the coming of the Grail, and gave no sign that he marked it"; and later, in front of the door leading to the Holy Grail, he is rejected and only furtively could he see the Grail (*The Quest of the Holy Grail*, pp. 83, 262).

[3] Similarly, the Grail can be reached only by the one who is chosen by the Grail (Eschenbach, *Parzival*, p. 197).

[4] Eschenbach, *Parzival*, pp. 99-100.

[5] This stone is the center as temple. See Guénon, *Symboles fondamentaux*, p. 286.

that his flash and bone immediately acquire youth. That stone is also called the Grail."[1]

This stone, which gives the sense of eternity and is called Grail, appears equal to Paradise. We already discussed the "central" symbolism of the stone; therefore, it is enough to say here that we could expect to see the Holy Grail also represented by a stone, since the Grail is the Center. René Guénon took notice of the identity between the "keystone" or "angle-stone" (the "head of the angle," *caput anguli*) and the Grail stone (Eschenbach's *lapsit exillis* that could be interpreted as *lapis ex coelis*, the "stone descended from heaven"),[2] and even wrote an article called *"Lapsit exillis"*[3] in which he accentuated two more things: first, the Grail is at the same time a stone and a cup, since the Grail cup was made of the emerald stone that fell from Lucifer's forehead; second, the stone was an "oracular" stone, and so was the Grail cup (it had an inscription: "for the inscription on the Grail had named him [Parzival] as their lord"[4]).[5] We should add that like the Holy Grail, there were "oracular" heads, "speaking" heads, or "heads of wisdom," as, for example, the head of Mimir, of Orpheus, and of the Green Knight.

René Guénon also pointed out the correspondence between the Holy Grail and the "Holy Heart of Christ." Charbonneau-Lassay observed that the legend of the Holy Grail was a "prehistory of the Eucharistic Heart of Jesus,"[6] and Guénon developed this idea, showing how the Grail is similar to the Heart, symbolizing the Center.[7]

---

[1] Eschenbach, *Parzival*, p. 198.
[2] This stone is similar to the "philosophical stone" of Hermeticism (Guénon, *Symboles fondamentaux*, p. 290).
[3] *Études Traditionnelles*, 1946, published also in *Symboles fondamentaux*, pp. 292 ff.
[4] Eschenbach, *Parzival*, p. 333.
[5] Guénon, *Symboles fondamentaux*, pp. 292-293.
[6] Guénon, *Symboles fondamentaux*, p. 39.
[7] Guénon, *Symboles fondamentaux*, pp. 21, 40-41, 47, 85, 110.

There is no doubt that the Holy Grail can be identified to the Heart of Christ, symbolizing the Center of the World.[1] At the same time, the Grail is equal to the Maiden, to the Head, to the Stone, and even to the Bottle, and we can assume that Lucifer when, during his fall, lost the emerald stone of the Grail, he also "lost his head,"[2] since he drank the wine from the Holy Bottle without realising that this wine was not the "beverage of immortality" but just profane alcohol.[3]

---

[1] However, we should not forget that we have here an application of a universal symbolism and, therefore, when Guénon compared the Holy Grail to the "Heart of Christ" his point of view was that of the Primordial Tradition. "It does not matter if Chrétien de Troyes and Robert de Boron did not see, in the ancient legend they adapted to their epoch, all the significance it contained" (Guénon, *Symboles fondamentaux*, p. 47); the fact of the matter is, Guénon went on, that all the traditions considered the sacrificial cup to represent the Center or the Heart of the World. "We finish with a last remark regarding the importance of the Heart as a universal symbol and the particular form it took in the Christian tradition, that of the Sacred Heart. If the symbolism is, in its essence, in strict conformity to the 'divine plan,' and if the Sacred Heart is the center of the being, both actually and symbolic, this symbol of the Heart, as such or through its equivalents, must have a central place in all the doctrines derived more or less directly from the primordial tradition" (Guénon, *Symboles fondamentaux*, pp. 37-38).

[2] The real achievement is to recover this "lost head"; the word "to achieve" initially signified "to reach the chief," that is, the head (Guénon, *Symboles fondamentaux*, p. 284). In Masonry, this achievement is the keystone; in Alchemy, the philosophical stone (Guénon, *Symboles fondamentaux*, p. 290). In a Mathematical language, it means the passage to the limit (René Guénon, *Les Principes du Calcul infinitésimal*, Gallimard, 1977, p. 128).

[3] The same as the Grail chooses the one allowed to reach the Holy Vessel, so the wine becomes the "beverage of immortality" only for the "chosen" one, only for the truly initiate, remaining a common drink for the profane people.

VIII

LANCELOT

"And he said unto him, Son, thou art ever with me, and all that I have is thine. It was meet that we should make merry, and be glad: for this thy brother was dead, and is alive again; and was lost, and is found."[1] Along with the various meanings, this parable has a profound initiatory essence, related to the significance of the two Adams. Christ explained: "I say unto you, that likewise joy shall be in heaven over one sinner that repenteth, more than over ninety and nine just persons, who need no repentance." The 99 just persons are similar to the 99 pillars with heads, to Adam before the fall, and to Râma when he first married Sîtâ; the 100th person is equivalent to Râma after he found the lost Sîtâ, to St. Paul's second Adam, and, of course, to the Knight who found the lost Grail.

Christ's parable also teaches us why the initiatory process is necessary: when the "sense of eternity" was lost, the only way to change death to life was to find what was lost, which meant precisely a spiritual realization that contained death and rebirth and a quest for the lost center. The Holy Grail stories, given the unfortunate period of the cycle to which they belonged, presented over and over again the quest for something that was lost, either the maiden, or a knight,[2] or the Grail, and such a quest the crusaders crowned with the conquest of Jerusalem,

---

[1] *Luke* 15:31-32. And before this: "Rejoice with me; for I have found my sheep which was lost" (15:6).

[2] For example, Gawain's quest is the quest for Lancelot, which is considered "the most noble quest there has ever been, after that of the Grail" (*Lancelot of the Lake*, p. 256).

understood as a recovery of the center. Yet the center was lost again, mainly because of the increasing decadence in the Occident and the rising of the antitraditional mentality, which culminated with the destruction of the Order of the Temple and the loss of the Holy Grail forever.[1]

Indeed, we could say that the Grail stories describe, first and foremost, the terrible end of a traditional society and the loss of its center. The Grail itself is from the beginning related to the idea of something that was lost.[2] As Guénon retold the story,[3] when Lucifer fell from heaven, an emerald fell from his forehead, and here we have the first "loss," since Lucifer lost his status and the "sense of eternity."[4] The angels carved the Grail from this precious stone and the cup was entrusted to Adam inside the Earthly Paradise, revealing the center again; yet, when Adam fell, he, in his turn, lost the Grail and, of course, the center. The first quest for the lost center was Seth's, and he succeeded in reaching the Earthly Paradise and recovering the Grail; after that, Seth and his heirs established spiritual centers on earth, as images of the Center of the World (the Earthly Paradise), even though, as Guénon specified, the legend does not say where and by whom the Grail was guarded till the time of Christ. It is very probable that the druids were at one time guardians of the Grail (but not the only ones), which means that they were among the regular keepers of the

---

[1] Guénon noticed that the Round Table was prepared to receive the Holy Grail, but this event never occurred (*Franc-Maçonnerie*, II, p. 35).

[2] Masonry has the same idea expressed as the Lost Word at its core. The quest of the Holy Grail in Chivalry is equivalent to the quest of the Lost Word in Masonry (Guénon, *Franc-Maçonnerie*, II, p. 34).

[3] *Symboles fondamentaux*, pp. 40-43, *Le Roi*, pp. 41-46.

[4] Guénon compared the stone with *urnâ*, symbolizing the "third eye" of Shiva; this, Guénon stressed, perfectly clarifies the symbolism of the Grail, and also emphasizes the connection with the heart, since the heart is the center of the integral being, which means that the "sense of eternity" has to be connected to the center (*Symboles fondamentaux*, p. 40, *Le Roi*, p. 41). We observe how important the Grail symbolism is for René Guénon, given that in his very dense work *Le Roi du Monde* he dedicated a whole chapter to it, called *Le symbolisme du Graal*.

Primordial Tradition.[1] It is also very probable that the Grail was lost and recovered successively during this period of time. As Guénon explained, the loss of the Holy Grail meant the loss of the tradition with everything this implied, even though, in fact, this tradition became concealed rather than lost, or the tradition could have been lost only for some secondary centers, when these had ceased to be connected to the supreme center. With respect to this, the supreme center will always preserve intact and guard the repository of tradition,[2] which opens the possibility of recovering the Grail through initiation and spiritual realization.[3]

The legend of the Grail follows mainly the chain of transmission from Christ to King Arthur.[4] Even if "historically"

---

[1] It is generally admitted that the Grail stories have inherited essential elements from the Celtic tradition (see also Guénon, *La crise*, p. 45 and *Franc-Maçonnerie*, II, p. 54, *Symboles fondamentaux*, pp. 40, 51, 52, 56, about Christianity assimilating the Celtic elements).

[2] Guénon, *Le Roi*, p. 43.

[3] See Guénon, *Le Roi*, p. 69. Guénon resumed by affirming: "What we just said here allows us to interpret in a very specific way the words of the Gospel: 'And I say unto you, Ask, and it shall be given you; seek, and ye shall find; knock, and it shall be opened unto you' (*Luke* 11:9)." These words, of course, could apply to the Quest of the Grail.

[4] In Boron's story, *Joseph of Arimathea*, Joseph was Pilate's soldier. A Jew took the vessel of the Last Supper and gave it to Pilate, who gave it to Joseph, and Joseph collected Christ's blood in it. The Jews captured Joseph and put him in jail and Christ comes and makes him the vessel's keeper. After many years of prison, the emperor Vespasian found Joseph and liberated him: "he took a rope and clambered down. When he reached the bottom he looked all around, and in one corner of the dungeon he saw a brilliant light" (this scenario is common for fairy tales and Masonry). Joseph's brother-in-law, Bron, had 12 children (a symbolic number, see Guénon, *Le Roi*, p. 38), and one of them, Alain li Gros, received the prophecy of the oracular vessel kept by Joseph, a prophecy that named Bron as Fisher King and keeper of the Grail (*Merlin*, pp. 16-43, pp. 112-113). We find a similar story in the Vulgate Cycle (*The Lancelot-Grail Reader*, Garland Publishing, 2000, Ed. Norris J. Lacy, pp. 12-47), with some more details. For example, Christ instructed Joseph to make an "ark for My bowl" and to open this ark when he and his son Josephus wanted to speak to Jesus (and only they could see the bowl!). Joseph took the ark to Sarras (a name of the Center), between Babylon and Salamander, where Jesus

it would be more natural to consider the influence of Celtic esoteric heritage upon Christian society than the other way around, we must not forget that the legend is a "legend" only because it is a sacred story, a "mythical" story, where mythical refers to what Clement of Alexandria wrote about this: "And the disciples of Aristotle say that some of their treatises are esoteric, and others common and exoteric. Further, those who instituted the mysteries, being philosophers, buried their doctrines in myths, so as not to be obvious to all."[1]

Therefore, the transmission of the Grail from Christ to Arthur has to be understood primarily on a *principial* level, as a symbolic explanation of how the Tradition and the spiritual influences perpetuated from center to center and from cycle to cycle, where this explanation, as recorded in writing by Chrétien de Troyes, Robert de Boron, or Wolfram von Eschenbach,[2] is a

---

consecrated and anointed Josephus as bishop. See also *Perlesvaus* (*La légende arthurienne*, pp. 123-124).

[1] *The Writings of Clement of Alexandria*, T. and T. Clark, Edinburgh, 1869, vol. II, pp. 255-256, *Stromata* V, 9. The myth is a special type of symbol and represents symbolical tales, these myths being integrated in rites, as in the case of Free-Masonry. The myth, like the fairy tale, is far from being a product of individual fantasy; it has a non-human origin, and only cyclic decadence has caused its real significance and its function to be forgotten. In the Western Middle Ages, various symbolic tales accompanied the pilgrims, helping them on their spiritual voyage; fairy tales are vestiges of such initiatory symbols. The Greek word *mythos* derives from the radical *mu*, which indicates silence (Latin *mutus*); indeed, the myth, similar to other symbols, is an initiatory teaching instrument, teaching that operates first of all through silence; the myth transmits the incommunicable essence, translating the silence into human language as an allegory (Guénon, *Aperç. sur l'init.*, pp. 122 ff.). Our constant reference to the spirituality of fairy tales is a consequence of what we just said, and it is easy to observe that the Grail stories are similar to the tales and can be better understood through them (in fact, they could hardly be understood otherwise).

[2] As in the case of the Operative Masons, we know almost nothing about these authors (see Guénon, *Le règne*, chapter *Le double sens de l'anonymat* about the "super-human" sense of the anonymity, and *Initiation et réalisation spirituelle*, p. 226). Chrétien de Troyes could be a symbolic name related to Christianity (similar to Christian Rosenkreutz's name) and Troy (the center) (see Jean-Louis Grison, *Notes sur les œuvres de Chrétien de Troyes*, Études Traditionnelles, 1973, no. 437-438, about the importance of Troyes, where St. Bernard, in

rather tardy and weakened exposure of the oral lore concerning the Grail.[1] To the Christian and Celtic currents we should add the Oriental influence,[2] and, if we refer to the *Râmâyana* that we discussed in detail in the previous chapters, it is easy to observe the similitude regarding the Quest, the adventures in the forest, and the lost center.[3]

1128, got approval for his Rule of the Templar Order); in *Erec et Enide*, he presented himself as *Crestïens de Troies*, but we know nothing about his life (see Chrétien, *Arthurian Romances, Introduction*, p. VII, and *Notes*, p. 361, Martin Aurell, *La légende du Roi Arthur*, Perrin, 2007, p. 253). We should add, with reference to Troyes, that Marie de Troyes, the daughter of King Louis VII and of Queen Eleanor of Aquitaine, asked Andreas Capellanus to write *The Art of Courtly Love* (where the center is the "palace of Love" situated in the middle of the Universe). With regard to Robert de Boron, there are only guesses about him and his work; see Aurell, pp. 399-402. As in Boron's case, the only thing known about Wolfram von Eschenbach is circumstantial and from his own work. We add what is said about the author of the *The Quest of the Holy Grail*: "the identity of the author remains, and doubtless will remain, unknown" (p. 25).

[1] Guénon considered that, in comparison to Dante, the authors of the written Grail stories were much less conscious of the esoteric meaning of their works; and it is possible that behind them there was an initiatory organization that could have guided them, either directly (using some of its members) or by using suggestions or influences of a subtle order (which, even though less "tangible," were very real and efficient) (*Symboles fondamentaux*, p. 56). Such subtle influences could have participated at the foundation of the *Ordre du Temple rénové* (René Guénon was its commander), but we will never know what really happened.

[2] Geay considered the existence of an "Indo-European" source for the Grail stories, but his arguments are not the best (Patrick Geay, *Hiram et le Graal, René Guénon L'éveilleur 1886-1951*, Dervy, 2002, pp. 151-152); what should be stressed is that the Grail stories shelter a universal symbolism.

[3] Evola noticed that the Grail novels have few themes and a lot of repetitions (J. Evola, *Le Mystère du Graal*, Éd. Traditionnelles, 1984, p. 160); in fact, these repetitions are essential for the initiatory process, since they represent the numerous degrees the neophyte has to pass, and they are not identical but analogous. As Guénon said, the immediate realization belongs to the *Brâhmanas*, while the *Kshatriyas* follow the "Liberation by degrees" (*krama-mukti*) (Guénon, *L'homme et son devenir*, pp. 150, 175), and these degrees could be numerous (even innumerable), since the path of the *Lesser Mysteries* is very long (Guénon, *Initiation et réalisation spirituelle*, pp. 194-195). In his *Aperçus sur l'initiation* (pp. 179, 279), Guénon insisted that the changes suffered by the being during the initiatory process are in an indefinite multitude (as the

However, if we want to understand Masonry and the Orders of Chivalry, as they functioned in the medieval Christian society, where they developed and prospered, we have to regard the Grail stories from the Christian perspective, and use them to penetrate the traditional medieval mentality.[1] We have to keep in mind that any genuine traditional form must consolidate its particular characteristics, which makes the Christian appearance of the Grail stories a necessity and not a flaw; what became a flaw was the gradual forgetting of the esoteric kernel. There are opinions that consider Robert de Boron the one who made "the Grail clearly, unambiguously Christian"[2]; in fact, the symbolism of the Grail is universal, and Boron was only an exponent of the mentality of his time. Chrétien de Troyes, Robert de Boron, Wolfram von Eschenbach and others stressed the Christian aspect since the stories were meant to be catalysers for Christian knighthood,[3] but they also wanted either to cover the esoteric meaning, or, because this meaning became less comprehensible, they just recorded the exoteric significance.

We have to keep in mind that the Grail stories existed and were transmitted in oral form during the consolidation of the traditional Christian society,[4] and they emerged in writing when

---

modalities of the integral individuality are), and the initiatory degrees of the rituals belonging to various traditional organizations correspond to a sort of classification indicating only the main steps.

[1] It does not mean, of course, that Waite was right to consider the Grail legend of purely Christian origin (Arthur Edward Waite, *The Holy Grail*, University Books, 1961).

[2] Boron, *Merlin, Introduction*, pp. 4-7. Moreover, certain commentators, completely ignorant, considered the Grail "Chrétien's greatest invention" (Eschenbach, *Parzival, Introduction*, p. X).

[3] There is testimony that, by 1180, the Grail legend "had spread to the Crusader states of Antioch and Palestine" (Loomis, *The Grail*, p. 8. Loomis has a completely profane mind and understands nothing about initiation, tradition and symbolism; see, for example, pp. 95-97, which makes his work almost useless).

[4] In Boron's trilogy, there are clear indications about "hearing" the story (*Merlin, Introduction*, p. 10).

this society started to have problems,[1] in an effort to maintain it for as long as possible.[2] Unfortunately, the increasing preponderance of the exoteric aspect was not able to stop the decadence, and maybe we could say that, in fact, this religious prevalence, together with the conversion from oral to written form, was a consequence and not a conscious technique to fight it. The most striking example is, of course, the condemnation of Guinevere's adultery, which started to be regarded from the external moral point of view, the esoteric meaning being completely forgotten, and Lancelot became, as a result, an emblem of the sinner.[3] In *Cligés*, Chrétien tried to elude the

---

[1] The Christian traditional civilization culminated with the foundation of the Order of the Temple, which subsisted for less than two centuries, illustrating how rapidly this civilization crumbled (in comparison to other traditional civilizations). The written Grail stories emerged, probably, within a period of about fifty years (see Loomis 4).

[2] It seems that Chrétien wrote his work around the year 1180, and Eschenbach composed his around 1210. We note that the Order of the Temple was founded in 1119, that Jerusalem was lost to Saladin in 1187 and recovered for a short period of time, with the Templars' help, in 1229. Evola's opinion (also mentioned by Guénon in a review, see *Articles et comptes rendus*, p. 140), about an underground current that emerged at one moment (and became abruptly popular) and then suddenly retired, needs amendments, since we have to consider an uninterrupted oral tradition first (Evola 79), while the written texts announced the troubled final decades of the traditional Christian society. Charbonneau-Lassay (quoted by Guénon in a review, see *Articles et comptes rendus*, p. 234) suggested that the Grail legend was a sort of prophecy, related to a body of oral teachings, very traditional, guarded by a providential elite, and today concealed, which appeared intermittently to those on the outside, in the religious domain (these oral teachings were present at the beginning of Christianity, then appeared again during the reign of Charlemagne, and again emerged with a lot of force during the 11th and 12th Centuries).

[3] Lancelot is twice described as "harder than stone, more bitter than wood, more barren and bare than the fig tree," a formula defining the sinner and the unbeliever (see, for example, *Matthew* 21:19-21, "Jesus answered and said unto them, Verily I say unto you, If ye have faith, and doubt not, ye shall not only do this which is done to the fig tree..."). Lancelot will confess his sin to a hermit (who was "clad in the armour of Holy Church"): "I have sinned unto death with my lady, she whom I have loved all my life, Queen Guinevere, the wife of King Arthur. ... For her love alone I accomplished the exploits. ... I will nevermore sin with her" (*The Quest*, pp. 85, 89-94); Lancelot's repentance

moral issue raised by the adulterous love between Cligés and his
uncle's wife, Fenice, specifying that Fenice, even though Alis'
wife, remained a virgin[1]; Fenice said to Cligés: "If I love you,
and you love me, you shall never be called Tristan, not I Iseut;
for then our love would not be honourable ["honourable" from
an exoteric viewpoint, of course]."[2]

Evidently, Christian exotericism is part of Tradition, yet
considering the times (the end of the *Kali-yuga*), we witness an
apparent paradoxical situation: the increase of religiosity by
itself, without help from the esoteric kernel, instead of bringing
a restoration, led to the rejection of the initiatory organizations,
which were actually the inner strength of this very religion. This
could mean that the written Grail stories in the end did not
consolidate the traditional mentality, but rather dismantled it,
being only echoes of the Royal Art.[3] In all this, the case of
Wolfram von Eschenbach is somehow special, since he openly

---

is in fact the funeral of Christian esotericism. Obviously, the queen is the
Virgin, absolute Knowledge. The so-called "adultery" has to be associated
with the abduction of the queen, another initiatory theme, when Guinevere is
rescued either by King Arthur himself or another knight, who takes Arthur's
place (when this one, together with the cycle, changes in a dragon) (see, with
regard to the abduction theme, Chrétien, *Arthurian Romances*, *Introduction*, p.
XIII, *Notes*, p. 373, Aurell 49-50, 75). The moral issue (regarding the so-called
"adultery" or the "incest") never applies to sacred stories where the "one
thousand feet" are just masks of the "one foot." "The spouse of the Emperor
is not the spouse only, but sister and daughter best beloved!" Dante explains
(*The Banquet*, Anma Libri, 1989, III.12.14). In the Hindu tradition, Aditi is
Daksha's daughter, and Daksha is Aditi's son; Sûrya, the sun, is both Aditi's
husband and son. Boron said: "Our Lord was gentle and kind indeed, that to
redeem His sinners from Hell He made His daughter His mother" (*Merlin*, p.
15). Therefore, the "adultery" in Chrétien's *Cligés* and *Lancelot* has nothing to
do with the religious morality, and the profane commentators will never
answer the question of how he could write such a thing (see, for example,
Chrétien, *Arthurian Romances*, *Introduction*, p. XIV, Aurell 282-283, 331).
[1] Alis, the brother of Alexander, the Emperor of Constantinople, is an
usurper, who took Cligés' place, which helps to validate Cligés relation with
Fenice.
[2] Chrétien, *Arthurian Romances*, p. 159. Regarding the comparison to Tristan
and Iseult's love, we stress that Tristan's story is typically initiatory.
[3] This means that, if we carefully take away the exoteric cover, the initiatory
significance of the Grail could still be found.

discussed the Grail as a stone, the Islamic influence, the mountain as center, and the Templars as guardians of this center, but it seems that Germany was in charge of "unveiling," before everything was lost, some of the esoteric aspects, as the legend of Christian Rosenkreutz shows.[1]

Jesus Christ represented, for the Grail stories, the archetypal Hero of the spiritual realization[2]; in time, this viewpoint proved

---

[1] It was also said that the Teutonic Order was used as a vehicle for the Templar heritage, between the 14th and 18th centuries, when some of the Knights Templar found refuge in Germany (Jean Tourniac, *De la Chevalerie au secret du Temple*, Éd. du Prisme, 1975, p. 147).

[2] We should not forget that most probably Christianity was, originally, an initiatory doctrine, restricted to elite. Due to the agony of the Roman world, regeneration and the replacement of the old cycle with a new one were necessary; all these would require a sacred, divine kernel, and thus, "Christianity" accepted the task of sacrificing and unveiling itself to the crowd, passing from esotericism to exotericism. This "sacrifice," illustrated by Christ himself, has produced a strange thing though: the new tradition, perfectly orthodox and valid, remained without an esoteric side, even if a hidden and initiatory kernel continued to exist more or less dormant. Therefore, Hermeticism, Masonry, and Chivalry, rebuilding an initiatory marrow, grafted onto the Christian tree; but, maybe because of this "grafting" the marrow dried out after the 14th Century, and in our days it is almost dead (see Guénon, *Aperçus sur l'ésotérisme chrétien*, p. 27 and our *The Wrath of Gods*, pp. 10, 20). However, there are allusions in the Gospels to the original Christian initiatory rites, like the one related to Judas' role. In the initiatory ritual, an essential task is to realize the difference between the immortal Self (*Âtmâ*) and the perishable *ego* (*jîvâtmâ*), which in Masonry is the difference between Hiram and his murderers, and in fairy tales the distinction between the hero and the elder brothers. In *The Story of White Arab*, a bald and beardless man is the dragon dwelling within us, the *ego*, who will behead the hero (*Harap Alb*). Beheading the hero means, as we know by now, a spiritual sacrifice, the supreme step of the initiation, a "ritual death" followed by a resurrection, "the second birth," and, indeed, the Virgin (the emperor's daughter) will place back the head of *Harap Alb*; at the same time, with the hero's revival, the hairless character is punished (killed) (see our *The Everlasting Sacred Kernel*, p. 28). This initiatory ritual also existed, we can assume, in a Christian form, where Jesus is the hero and Judas the *ego*. The distinction between the two (who looked alike externally) is realized by a "kiss"; this esoteric gesture was guarded over the centuries and surfaced in Boron, *Merlin and the Grail*, pp. 16-17, where Judas' kiss is explained as a way to differentiate Jesus from his cousin James the Lesser, who "looked very much like Jesus" (in fact, the twin is Judas himself, who will die, while Jesus is resurrected). Moreover, we should point out the

to be one of the reasons why the initiatory significance became easily confused with an exclusively religious significance, even though, as it happens in the tales of Lancelot, there are clear suggestions about the coexistence of the two facets, esoteric and exoteric. Lancelot's mother, Helen, similar to Virgin Mary and Joseph, "was from the noble line of King David,"[1] while

---

important discrepancy, regarding the Eucharist, between the *Gospel* of St. John (13:21-27) and those of St. Luke (22:17-22) and St. Mark (14:22-25): in the former, the Eucharist is not present (like in the others); it only describes the exposure of Judas, with whom Jesus shares the food: "Jesus answered, He it is, to whom I shall give a sop, when I have dipped it. And when he had dipped the sop, he gave it to Judas Iscariot, the son of Simon. And after the sop Satan entered into him." Regarding the "kiss," *The Gospel of Philip* says: "And the companion of the [Saviour] is Mary Magdalene. Jesus loved her more than [all] the disciples [and used to] kiss her often on her [mouth]." There is a serious error to believe that this kiss alludes to something other than spiritual or initiatory. In the Hindu tradition, the Great Hero, drinks *soma* directly from Apâlâ's mouth, imitating a kiss; this kind of kiss symbolizes in fact the assimilation of the immortal beverage, *soma* (Coom., *La doctrine*, pp. 142, 144, 154-155). In fairy tales, the hero has to kiss the maiden to start the new cycle of manifestation. The kiss transmitted by Jesus to Mary is "spiritualization." *The Song of Songs* begins with, "Let him kiss me with the kisses of his mouth"; Saint Gregory of Nyssa, commenting on this line, said: "The spring is the Groom's mouth, from where emerge the eternal life's words, which fill the mouth that drinks them, similar to the Psalmist who drank the Spirit." Eventually, we should add St. Bernard's words: "I hold for certain that to so great and holy an *arcanum* of divine love not even the angelic creation is admitted. ... See the new Spouse receiving the new kiss, not, however, from the *mouth* but from the Kiss of *His mouth*. He breathed on them, it is said. There can be no doubt that Jesus breathed upon the Apostles, that is, upon the primitive Church, and said: *Receive ye the Holy Ghost*. That was, assuredly, a kiss. What? – the physical breath? No, but the invisible Spirit. ... And so it is enough for the bride if she is kissed with the *kiss* of the Bridegroom, even if she is not kissed with His *mouth*. Nor does she think it is a slight thing or a thing to be despised that she is kissed with a *kiss*, which is nothing else than to be filled with the Holy Ghost" (*Love of God*, p. 69). This is the "kiss" between Lancelot and Guinevere that inspired Dante (*Inferno*, V) and makes him *caddi come corpo morto cade*. See our *The Wrath of Gods*, p. 308.

[1] *Lancelot of the Lake*, pp. 18-19. This story was written in French by an unknown author (*Introduction*, p. VII). Virgin Mary was from the line of David through Nathan, where Joseph was the son-in-law of Heli (*Luke* 3:23-31); for Joseph, see *Matthew* 1:7-15.

Lancelot's adoptive mother, Niniane ("The Lady of the Lake"),[1] was a fairy, "a woman with a knowledge of magic," "who learned her magic from the prophet Merlin."[2] This fairy alone knew Lancelot's name,[3] while the others called him the "Handsome Foundling," "King's Son," and "Rich Orphan."[4]

The Grail stories present a very rich symbolism of the center, since the initiatory rites and the spiritual quest are indissolubly related to the center and could not exist without it. In the tale of Lancelot, the first center is Trebe, the only castle left to king Ban of Benwick, Lancelot's father,[5] and is, in fact, a

---

[1] In Malory's story, the Lady of the Lake asks for a knight's head, and this one will behead her (Sir Thomas Malory, *Le Morte D'Arthur*, Penguin, 1981, I, p. 64); we see again the role of the head.

[2] Even though Merlin is considered "the offspring of a woman and a devil," he is called a prophet. Here "devil" alludes to *asura* and the past traditions. In Boron's *Merlin* (pp. 45-60), Merlin is the child of a virgin (*déva*) and of a "devil" (*asura*, but also a *yaksha* or a *gandharva*); God granted him the knowledge of things to come (*déva*, *yang*), and the "devil" (Hequibedes, the demon of the air, a *djinn*) gave him "the power and intelligence to know everything that has been said and done." Too often it is forgotten that Merlin is not the "devil's son" but the Son of Heaven and Earth, since God gave him *Spiritus* and the devil *Corpus* (p. 55); and Merlin affirmed: "from the moment it pleased Our Lord to grant me His knowledge, I was lost to the devil" (p. 61).

[3] We don't have to stress the initiatory importance of the name, which also plays the role of the Lost Word. The whole story of Lancelot is about finding the name.

[4] Foundling, meaning orphan, and Handsome are typical names for fairy tales, and the status of orphan (*Lancelot of the Lake*, pp. 19, 21, "who is orphaned so young," "he has today become an orphan"), which is that of Melchizedek, is used to indicate an *avatarana*. "King's Son" suggests Christ. For other parallels, see Chrétien, *Arthurian Romances*, where Lancelot is a "saviour" (pp. 298-300, 374), while in *Cligés*, Fenice suffers death and then is resurrected (pp. 167-169, 368) (Cligés also is an "orphan," Chrétien, *Arthurian Romances*, p. 125). *Perlesvaus* is considered a "radical Christianized version" of a Celtic legend (*La légende arthurienne*, Introduction, p. 120).

[5] We need more than one volume to thoroughly comment on the symbolism of the Grail stories, and it is not our purpose to do so; our work is dedicated to the paramount importance of the center. However, we have to note, even transiently, the mythical and hermetical essence of Lancelot's tale. For example, there are two brothers, Ban and Bors, married to two sisters; king Ban was old, his wife young. Trebe is a unique castle, and could be compared

lost center, since the king has to leave furtively the castle,[1] together with his wife and the new born Lancelot (baptized Galahad), and we could draw a parallel with Aeneas' departure from Troy, and with Hagar's expulsion into the wilderness. The next center is a mountain, with a large lake at its foot; the king will climb to the top, where he dies watching his former center burning,[2] and his wife will remain with Lancelot in the valley.[3] Lancelot himself is a "central" character, since he combines the colours (multiplicity) into one,[4] and is made a knight "on the day of the feast of St. John," namely on the day of the winter solstice.[5] A quest connected to Lancelot is the quest for his

---

to Thebes and Troy. In the center of the castle is the palace (*Lancelot of the Lake*, pp. 3, 5, 11).

[1] The castle was burned by the enemy (which represents here the counter-initiatory forces).

[2] The center will be marked by the Royal Minster, a church built (by Masons) at the top of the mountain, where the king's body is taken (*Lancelot of the Lake*, pp. 22-24); no doubt, the Royal Minster alludes to the double power, spiritual and temporal, of the center (similar to the double power of the Knights Templar and of Prester John).

[3] There is another element, which deserves our full attention. The queen heard the squire's very loud cry, when he found the dead king, and "she gathered up her skirts, and rand up the hill"; then, she heard the baby crying, and "she leapt up like a madwoman, and ran towards where she left her son" (*Lancelot of the Lake*, pp. 18-21); this running, like the crying (the sound), is obviously part of a sacred ritual, and should be compared to *sa'y*, the septuplet running of Hagar. In fairy tales or in Dante's initiatory journey, there is no place for being slow; in fairy tales, running has a very precise symbolism, which we cannot develop here.

[4] "His face glowed with a natural ruddiness, in such just proportion that evidently God had put the white and the brown and the red there" (in the center, the complementary elements unite). Similar to fairy tales (where we have the Red, Green, or White Emperor), the Grail stories use wisely the symbolism of colours; Lancelot, for example, appears as the White Knight, Perceval as the Red Knight, and Cligés fights gradually in four armours: black, green, red and white (hermetic colours, even though the religious viewpoint made the change between red and white), etc. (*Lancelot of the Lake*, pp. 28-29, 59, 63, Chrétien, *Arthurian Romances*, pp. 151-156).

[5] *Lancelot of the Lake*, pp. 58-59. The importance of St. John for Masonry is well known (see Guénon, *Symboles fondamentaux*, p. 253); the same initiatory importance can be found in Chivalry. As to Lancelot, we notice that Queen Guinevere, not Arthur, is the one who gave him the sword he should belt on

name, which even Lancelot apparently does not know and
remains silent about it.[1]

A major initiatory step for Lancelot, in quest for the Lost
Word (his name), is the enchanted castle, called the Dolorous
Guard, representing evidently the center of this level, which can
be reached by climbing three degrees,[2] culminating with the
finding of the Name.[3] Yet, the inner center is, as astonishing as
it may seem, "a very strange cemetery,"[4] described as a fortress:
"it was enclosed on all sides by closely crenellated walls, and on
many of the battlements there were knights' heads in their
helms"[5]; and the center ("in the middle of the cemetery") of the
inner center is "a great slab of metal, wonderfully worked with

---

as a knight (*Lancelot of the Lake*, pp. 74, 92), which illustrates the feminine
aspect of the Royal Art. Also, it is worth mentioning that Lancelot wants to be
made a knight with his own clothes and arms; *Harap Alb* (the White Arab)
uses his father's clothes and arms and not new ones (*ibid.* 65-66).

[1] *Lancelot of the Lake*, pp. 71, 100. Knowing the name means reaching the
center. Here, Lancelot's silence is beneficent, since he is at the beginning of
the spiritual realization, the apprenticeship requiring this silence. For this
reason, Perceval could not ask the question.

[2] The three degrees are symbolized by three white shields with respectively
one, two and three red diagonal bands (white and red!), allowing Lancelot to
"rise to greater heights" (*ibid.* 110-111). At one moment, Lancelot will have a
red shield with a diagonal white band (p. 159), and later on, a white shield with
a black band (p. 194).

[3] The Lady of the Lake, who is Lancelot's spiritual master (we notice the
feminine aspect, typical for Chivalry) says (through her representative, a veiled
damsel): "you will learn your name and the name of your father" (*ibid.* 110);
for this to happen, Lancelot has to conquer the center and behead the ten-
headed dragon (similar to the ten-faced Râvana), represented by ten knights
who had to be all killed, otherwise others would take their place (like the
heads that will grow replacing the lost ones) (*ibid.* 112).

[4] The cemetery as center is also present in Chrétien's *The Knight of the Cart*
(Chrétien, *Arthurian Romances*, pp. 294-295). See Wensinck, *The Navel of the
Earth*, pp. 58-59, where the tomb is an equivalent of the navel. The so called
"Lodi Gardens," in New Delhi, shelter the tombs of members of Sayyid and
Lodi dynasties, tombs that have a square base, a spherical dome and an
octagonal shape between these two, each tomb therefore representing the
center (and the Three Worlds).

[5] We notice the heads.

gold and precious stones and enamel,"[1] which has, like the
Grail, oracular powers, and, as the "central" center, is the
keeper of the Name.[2] Of course, this cemetery has nothing to
do with modern mentality's aberrations about ghosts; it was
chosen as a symbol of the center to imply the importance of the
"initiatory death," and, indeed, the cemetery is true (from an
initiatory point of view) and false (from a profane or mundane
viewpoint), since the tombs, including Lancelot's, do not
contain dead knights.[3]

This center is comparable to the Earthly Paradise and we
could say that Lancelot, by finding the Name, has accomplished
his spiritual realization. The sacred significance of the place is
also emphasized by "gathering what was scattered": King
Arthur, Queen Guinevere, and the Knights of the Round Table,
come to the cemetery and castle, attracted by Lancelot's
assumed death.[4] Nonetheless, the *modus operandi* of a sacred
story, and the fairy tales are vivid examples of this, is special,
because, first of all, such a story narrates the unutterable, and
then, translates ineffable and simultaneous events in a series of
episodes occurring in time. For instance, reaching the center
means at the same time finding the Lost Word, gathering what
was scattered, and Liberation. Usually, the sacred stories use
repetition and multiple projections of the one hero to symbolize
what is inexpressible, and we see in Lancelot's tale exactly such
procedure, since the Dolorous Guard is doubled by the
Dolorous Prison,[5] where Gawain and other nine knights

---

[1] It alludes to Heavenly Jerusalem and to the Holy Grail.
[2] There was written on it that "the slab will never be raised by the hand or
efforts of any man, except the man who will capture this dolorous castle
[namely Lancelot, who will be able to raise the slab and read the inscription],
and the name of that man is written underneath here" (*Lancelot of the Lake*, p.
119). We should compare this description to the Masonic ritual.
[3] *Lancelot of the Lake*, p. 181. Gahmuret's tomb also illustrates the center of the
center: it was located in Baldac and "gold was lavished upon it, great wealth
applied in the form of precious stones ... The stone above his grave is a
precious ruby" (Eschenbach 46).
[4] *Lancelot of the Lake*, pp. 122-129.
[5] It is an emblematic description of a center, since the Dolorous Prison is a
castle on a high rock, on an island. Later on, Lancelot lives in a tower

become prisoners,[1] and Lancelot will liberate them. This liberation is in concert with the efforts of King Arthur and Queen Guinevere to enter the Dolorous Guard, a typically initiatory episode, composed of three degrees, each one marked by one of the three shields (in hierarchical order) and by an absent-minded Lancelot.[2]

As expected, the real "prisoner" is Queen Guinevere herself: she is the highest prize, namely the Grail.[3] This "captivity" of *Madonna Intelligenza*, of *Sophia*, is already suggested when Gawain, released by Lancelot, arrives at the castle (the Dolorous Guard) and the damsel representing the Lady of the Lake tells him she is held in captivity and "can only be freed by the knight that the king allowed to go," that is, Lancelot.[4] We witness two

---

(Galehot's fortress), in the middle of a dense forest, on the Lost Island (*ibid.* p. 359).

[1] We notice the number 10. For all this, see *Lancelot of the Lake*, pp. 122-191.

[2] These events have to be regarded both as simultaneous and in sequence. The episode of the Dolorous Prison harmonizes with the strange episode about the difficulties encountered by King Arthur and Queen Guinevere to enter the Dolorous Guard; yet, at the same time, the Queen is the real "prisoner" of the castle, who must be liberated at the end of the Quest. Regarding Lancelot's oblivion or trance, this element is often found in the Grail stories; in this particular case, it marks the passing from one degree to another and, since Lancelot forgets about the corporeal queen while profoundly thinking of her, alludes to the esoteric meaning of the queen as *Madonna Intelligenza* (*Lancelot of the Lake*, pp. 136, 147).

[3] "King Arthur let the knight [Lancelot] who had conquered the castle go [the story still does not tell the name of Lancelot, which is not known to the others]; and my lady [Queen Guinevere] had been brought to this encounter, and she lodged yesterday evening in the castle. Now they have made her a prisoner and they say that for all King Arthur's might, she will never get out until she makes the knight come back, just as the king let him go" (*Lancelot of the Lake*, p. 189).

[4] *Lancelot of the Lake*, p. 153. This topic is also to be found in Chrétien's *Lancelot* (or *The Knight of the Cart*), a story that starts with the challenge addressed to Arthur's knights that, if one of them is able to accompany and protect the Queen in the forest, all the prisoners will be released. Later, the Queen herself becomes prisoner of Meleagant, in Bademagu's kingdom (Chrétien de Troyes, *Arthurian Romances*, J. M. Dent & Sons Ltd., 1982, pp. 271, 299, 300). Lancelot releasing the prisoners is described like a Saviour (Lancelot is "he who is to deliver us all").

opposite movements: the scattering, the centrifugal movement, produced by King Arthur, who permitted Lancelot to leave the center,[1] and the gathering, the centripetal movement, produced by Queen Guinevere, who brings the hero back in the center, where Lancelot is the ultimate prisoner and his Self must be liberated.[2] The final "liberation" takes place in the center of the

---

[1] Even though King Arthur was in many stories the hero embarked on an initiatory path, here he plays the role of the "old king," of the "unworthy husband." The theme of a "family triangle" is typically initiatory. In the tradition of the ancient Greeks, for example, Hercules, one of the greatest initiatory heroes, has as parents a triad composed by Zeus and Alcmene, plus the "inferior husband," Amphitryon; the "triangle" is obvious since Zeus took Amphitryon's appearance. The superior and the inferior "husbands" appear as twins: the immortal-mortal pair or as father-son (*asura-dêva*). Another famous example is the pair Ulysses – Penelope. Penelope is not only the patron of spiritual realization, but she is also the cosmological activity of God. It is said that Penelope was weaving a shroud for Laertes (*Odyssey* II, 95). Each night she was undoing the work she did during the day. Weaving the web symbolizes the production of the World, the *Fiat Lux*, while dissolving the web during the night means the absorption of the Cosmos back into the Principle. Penelope is the divine Maiden and the suitors represent our lowest passions and appetites, the "inferior husband."

[2] Lancelot asked: "is my lady the queen free yet?" and the reply was: "yes, and you are here instead of her, and the enchantments of this place must be ended by you" (*Lancelot of the Lake*, p. 191). Of course, "liberating" or "saving" the Queen is the same thing as the initiate becoming himself "free." In Chrétien's *The Knight of the Cart*, at the end, Lancelot becomes the prisoner of the dragon Meleagant, who ordered his Masons to build a tower where Lancelot would be kept captive; the tower represents the *Axis Mundi* (*Arthurian Romances*, p. 347). There is another story related to the Masonic Art: the usurper Vortigern, afraid for his life, ordered the Masons to build the biggest and strongest tower (where he could have protection), but the tower kept collapsing, and the seven sages told the king that an orphan child had to be sacrificed. In fact, Merlin explained at the end, there were two dragons, a white and a red one, fighting under the tower (Boron, *Merlin*, pp. 65-75). In Chrétien's *Cligés*, John, an artisan, built a marvellous tower (Cligés said that John was his "serf," but we should understand that he was rather his "vassal"; however, we see the close relationship between Chivalry and Masonry) (*Arthurian Romances*, pp. 161, 163-164) (Geay is right in suggesting a similitude between Hiram's legend and the Grail data; see Geay, *Hiram et le Graal*, p. 151). The well known symbolism of the tower is related to the foundation of a kingdom; therefore, India's first Muslim ruler Qutb-ud-din Aibak ordered in 1193 (in a time when the Grail

center.[1] Lancelot is escorted to the cemetery, enters a chapel (the ultimate center, the center as temple), and descends into an underground vault,[2] where the "key of the enchantments" (representing the Lost Word) was kept. Lancelot passes through the Sun-Door, between the guardians (the clashing rocks) represented by "two knights cast in copper" armed with very heavy swords.[3] The description about Lancelot reaching the center goes on with more fundamental symbols. He has to defeat a knight "whose head was as black as ink, and blue flame leapt from his mouth, and his eyes glowed like two burning coals," and who was guarding a black and terrible well, holding

---

stories were written) that the tallest and most powerful tower, Qutab Minar, be built in New Delhi.

[1] What could confuse the reader is the "interminable repetition" (as Evola wrongly called it); in fact, there is no repetition but analogy of the various initiatory degrees, and therefore Lancelot is made prisoner more than once and must realize liberation more than once. In Chrétien's *The Knight of the Cart*, for example, Lancelot's initiation starts with him described as a "convict" and then, after he crosses "the stony passage," Lancelot is made prisoner "in a fortress which stood upon a fortified hill" (another center), from where he escapes with the help of a miraculous ring and performing this ritual: "holding the ring before his eyes, he gazed at it, and said: 'Lady, lady, so help me God, now I have great need of your succour!' This lady, a fairy, gave him the ring and cared for him in his infancy" (*Arthurian Romances*, pp. 299-300). The implications of this ritual are rather obvious from an initiatory viewpoint, but we would like to note that in a fairy tale the hero is presented as triple and each of the three characters had a third of the invocatory formula that would bring the fairy's help; the three parts are: "fairyma," "rycomeagain," and "iminpain," which uttered in sequence gives: "Fairy, Mary, come again, I'm in pain" (we may note that in Masonry the Word was composed of three syllables and each of the three Masters, i.e. Solomon, Hiram of Tyre, and Hiram-Abif, had to pronounce a syllable; see Guénon, *Franc-Maçonnerie*, II, pp. 45-6). Later on, Lancelot is taken prisoner again (by Bademagu's people, p. 322), and again (this time by Meleagant's seneschal, p. 338) and finally is imprisoned in the tower (p. 347).

[2] This symbolism, found also in Masonry, was mentioned earlier in this work. See also our *René Guénon et le Centre du Monde*, pp. 134-135, where we quote Guénon's sayings about the Masonic *Royal Arch* and the finding of the Lost Word in the ninth underground vault.

[3] Lancelot is wounded, but passes, and "never looked back" (an essential rule of the initiatory process).

in his hand an axe.[1] Eventually, Lancelot meets a "copper damsel,"[2] takes from her the keys of the enchantments, and goes to a "copper pillar, which was in the middle of the chamber," symbolizing the *Axis Mundi*.[3] The pillar had an inscription about the keys, and we find here a familiar pattern, regarding the oracular cup and the pillar's function as a keeper of the sacred knowledge.[4] Here Lancelot vanquishes the devils, realizing the final "liberation" and the castle becomes the Joyous Guard.[5]

At the same time, the story must somehow introduce the spiritual love between Lancelot and Guinevere as the apex of the initiation, and therefore Lancelot is again presented as a prisoner, this time in the power of the Lady of Malohaut, who offers him three degrees of ransoms: the most "inner" one, to reveal his name [the Lost Word]; the second one, to reveal whom he loves [Guinevere's name]; the "exterior" one, to tell if

---

[1] The black head is also part of the Rosicrucian legend. The well alludes to Hell, since in the center the initiate can go either way, up or down.

[2] The "copper damsel" represents Venus, since Venus' island was Cyprus, a name meaning "copper" (Guénon, *Aperçus sur l'ésotérisme chrétien*, p. 68). There is an interesting similitude between Lancelot's descent and Christian Rosenkreutz descent, on the Fifth Day of the *Wedding*. "Now after this door was opened, the page led me by the hand through a very dark passage, till we came again to a very little door… But the main and most glorious thing that I saw here was a sepulchre (which stood in the middle [the center!]) so rich that I wondered that it was not better guarded. This sepulchre was triangular, and had in the middle of it a vessel of polished copper; the rest was of pure gold and precious stones. I asked my page what this might signify. 'Here,' he said, 'lies buried Lady Venus, that beauty which has undone many a great man, both in fortune, honour, blessing and prosperity.' After which he showed me a copper door on the pavement. 'Here,' he said, 'if you please, we may go further down.' So I went down the steps, where it was exceedingly dark. Then I saw a rich bed ready made, hung about with curious curtains, one of which he drew aside, where I saw the Lady Venus stark naked."

[3] This pillar reminds us of the pillar of Vishnu, which can be seen near Qutab Minar, in New Delhi. The pillar is made of wrought iron and is immune to corrosion.

[4] See Enoch's pillars: "they made two pillars; the one of brick, the other of stone: they inscribed their discoveries on them both" (Josephus, *Antiquities of the Jews*, Book I, chapter II).

[5] *Lancelot of the Lake*, pp. 192-194.

he will do again extraordinary deeds of arms [the "lesser war"].[1]
Using the "external" ransom, Lancelot, as the Black Knight,
fights in battle and consequently meets the Queen[2] and unveils
his love and his name, as a result of a long series of questions
and answers (representing a ritual similar to the Masonic one).[3]
    The initiatory love between Queen Guinevere and Lancelot
is stressed by the curious episode regarding the shield split in
two, which the Queen has received from the Lady of the Lake;
when the Union of the two lovers will be completed then the
shield "will join together."[4]

---

[1] *Lancelot of the Lake*, p. 263.

[2] We mention again what an important role is played by contemplation, which
overcomes war and action, as Lancelot forgets about the battle while
profoundly contemplating in his mind (or heart) the Queen (*Lancelot of the
Lake*, pp. 271-273, 298). In Chrétien's *The Knight of the Cart*, the Quest for the
Queen is an intense contemplation. "King Arthur's thoughts were so
profound, he did not utter any sound"; "So Perceval fell in reflection till he
forgot himself outright. The red contrasted with the white complexion of his
lady-love in the same way the three drops of red blood contrasted with the
snow. The combination pleased him so… He thought about the drops and
passed the morning at it, till, at last, the squires came out of the tent. They saw
him musing, all intent, and they believed that he was sleeping" (Chrétien,
Perceval, pp. 29, 115-116) (the hermetic meaning of red and white, colours that
were adopted by the Templars, made Perceval meditate a long time; how
many are able today to meditate at least five minutes upon a colour?). The
story tells that Perceval continued to reflect even though he was interrupted a
few times, which suggests a combination of contemplation and action (he
fought and defeated Sagremore and Kay), with the action seconding the
contemplation (*ibid.* pp. 116-117). Tristan also, "leant upon his bow, and all
through the night considered his sorrow" (Bédier 78).

[3] *Lancelot of the Lake*, pp. 313-318. We insist in presenting all these elements
because they are closely related to the Chivalric and Masonic initiations, and
unveil a mentality (to which fairy tales belong), a way of thinking, and a special
logic, which are all lost for the modern world. Guénon specified the
importance of the "question" in Masonry and its equivalence with the Lost
Word (*Franc-Maçonnerie*, II, p. 37).

[4] *Lancelot of the Lake*, pp. 341-342. The same meaning is found in *Erec et Enide*,
where Erec, after liberating Enide, leaves with her riding on the same horse
(Chrétien, *Arthurian Romances*, p 64), and also in *The Quest of the Holy Grail*,
where Galahad, arriving at the Castle of Corbenic (an aspect of the Grail
center), "took the two parts of the sword and joined the severed edges, and at

A curious booklet related to the Judaic Kabbalah and contemporaneous with the written Grail stories could help us understand this love and union.[1] Man was created androgynous, male and female, Gikatila said, and at the same time with the male soul was created his partner, the female soul. Similar to the perfect union of the two sephiroth *Yesod* (male) and *Malkhut* (female), the man should realize the union with his partner, who is a woman with the soul that is the female half of the initial androgynous form; therefore, a quest is necessary to accomplish this union. In Plato's *Symposium*, Aristophanes described this androgynous form and said that "each of us when separated, having one side only, like a flat fish, is but the indenture of a man, and he is always looking for his other half"[2]; but Socrates (in fact, Diotima) rejected this definition of love, since real love is the love for the absolute Beauty (which is identical to the Principle).[3] Therefore, even if Gikatila's interpretation could be applied to the love between Lancelot and Guinevere, as we will show below, we must not forget that this explanation is only a secondary aspect and the main significance is the union between "the man with his passive intellect and the active Intelligence,

---

once the sections knit so perfectly..." (Perceval could not unite them) (pp. 274-275).

[1] The booklet was written by R. Joseph ben Abraham Gikatila and starts with these words: "Bathsheba was destined to be with David, from the six days of Genesis" (R. Joseph Gikatila, *Le secret du marriage de David et Bethsabée*, Éd. de l'Éclat, 1994, p. 10).

[2] It seems that the exterior teachings of the H. B. of L. contained a similar theory about the two halves trying to get together (see Joscelyin Godwin, Christian Chanel, John P. Deveney, *The Hermetic Brotherhood of Luxor*, Samuel Weiser, 1995, p. 51).

[3] "He who from these ascending under the influence of true love, begins to perceive that beauty, is not far from the end. And the true order of going, or being led by another, to the things of love, is to begin from the beauties of earth and mount upwards for the sake of that other beauty, using these as steps only, and from one going on to two, and from two to all fair forms, and from fair forms to fair practices, and from fair practices to fair notions, until from fair notions he arrives at the notion of absolute beauty, and at last knows what the essence of beauty is."

represented by the woman,"[1] since the woman symbolizes *Madonna Intelligenza, Sophia*, and absolute Beauty.[2]

Râma and Sîtâ were the two halves of the androgynous form, and when Sîtâ was abducted this form was split in two, like the shield sent to Queen Guinevere; Râma had to complete the quest for Sîtâ, in order to realize the re-union. For the same reason, from a traditional viewpoint (and illustrated in various sacred stories), the king and queen are twins, brother and sister.[3] Bathsheba's soul was the twin of David's soul, but sometimes, by mistake, a maiden marries the wrong man, and that is what happened in Bathsheba's case, which justified David's behaviour and his ardour to unite with Bathsheba.[4]

---

[1] Guénon, *Aperçus sur l'ésotérisme chrétien*, p. 76.

[2] See Guénon, *Aperçus sur l'ésotérisme chrétien*, pp. 63-64, about *Madonna* as "active Intellect" (the "solar Ray"; in the Hindu tradition, *Buddhi*), representing the link between God and man. As Guénon said, the Wisdom and Intelligence are not identical (see the difference between the *Hokmah* and *Binah*, of the Judaic Kabbalah), but *Madonna*, under one of her aspects, is also identical to the Wisdom. The previous quotation regarding the union between the passive male and the active female referred originally to the *Rebis* of the *Fedeli d'Amore* (and of Francesco da Barberino in particular), a *Rebis* represented as androgynous, but with the female situated at the right side (stressing the "activity"), and the male at the left side (illustrating the "passivity"), which reversal, Guénon said, also occurs in the Hindu tantrism, where *Shakti* is the active principle (*ibid.* p. 76); therefore, accepting Gikatila's interpretation about the androyginous form composed of pairs like Lancelot and Guinevere or David and Bathsheba, we should keep in mind the *Fedeli d'Amore*'s symbolism, where the feminine part of the *Rebis* is the active Intelligence (that is, *Madonna Intelligenza*). The Hermetic Androgyne corresponds to the "primordial state" (the center), with its realization symbolizing the restoration of this state, and is equivalent to the term "Rose-Cross" (*ibid.* p. 77).

[3] Gikatila said that this is "a great secret" (pp. 50-51); the twin symbolism is a universal theme.

[4] Gikatila 59, 60-61, 64-65. For Gikatila, the separation of the twin souls (and of the sephiroth *Yesod* and *Malkhut*) is a consequence of the primordial sin, and this sin was inherited by David, who lost Bathsheba as bride of the first wedding. Similarly, even though the story tells that Râma married Sîtâ, Râma's first wedding is soon broken and a quest is needed to accomplish the second wedding, when the union is actually realized. In Chrétien's *Cligés*, the theme of the twin souls is clearly suggested: "our hearts are here with us now, for my heart is altogether in your hands," Cligés said to Fenice, his uncle's wife; and Fenice specified in her reply: "In error I am called a wife" (Chrétien, *Arthurian*

Correspondingly, Lancelot's love for Queen Guinevere is justified by the fact that their souls were twins and destined to each other; and, in the same way, Uther Pendragon's love for Igerne, the duke of Tintagel's wife, represents the quest for the twin female soul.[1]

We may notice that Lancelot takes the King's place and his arms,[2] Arthur representing in this initiatory scenario either the dragon or the "unworthy husband" (the human aspect); however, Lancelot's formidable war leading to the conquest of the Rock,[3] and the liberation of Arthur, finalized with Guinevere's kiss in front of the King, and her statement that she belongs to Lancelot,[4] shows a descending spiritual realization, a "return" when everything is reintegrated in universal harmony and order.[5]

In Chrétien's *The Knight of the Cart*, Lancelot's Quest for the Queen and his Love for her are present from the beginning as the essence of the initiatory path. Guinevere is prisoner, and

---

Romances, p. 159). See also the union of Tristan and Iseult; Iseult said to Tristan: "fold your arms round me close and strain me so that our hearts may break and our souls go free at last" (Bédier 141).

[1] Boron, *Merlin*, pp. 94-103. Merlin with his powers made Uther Pendragon look like the duke of Tintagel and so the union with Igerne was realized and Arthur conceived (Uther is the divine husband, the duke the human or the "unworthy" one). In the Greek mythology, Zeus takes Amphitryon's place (and appearance) in Alcmene's bed; their son is Heracles.

[2] *Lancelot of the Lake*, p. 396.

[3] The Rock is a fortress; it has a significant name.

[4] This statement is the consequence of a most important initiatory trial, which we call the "twins trial." There are two identical Guineveres (twins) and Lancelot is the only one capable of finding out which is the real one (*Lancelot of the Lake*, pp. 415-417). See what we said about "Judas' kiss" (the Queen's kiss, p. 409, has a similar meaning; it is how Lancelot is "identified" as the "chosen one") Also, in *The Story of White Arab*, the hero's highest trial is to decide between two identical maidens which is the Emperor's daughter.

[5] At one moment Lancelot is considered "the crowned king of the entire world" (*Lancelot of the Lake*, p. 399). The real hierarchy regarding the Self and the ego is shown when Lancelot liberates Arthur and the latter "fell at Lancelot's feet and said: 'Sir, I put myself in your power, myself and my honour and my land, for you have given me back the one and the other'" (p. 406).

Lancelot starts his spiritual realization with an initiatory death, described as supreme humiliation, when he accepts to "get up into the cart," for the sake of the Queen.[1] Furthermore, the Quest is twofold: an outer journey (marked by battles and jousting) and an inner process (illustrated by a continuous contemplation),[2] since the Queen is a prisoner in Bademagu's kingdom, which is a spiritual center and a "holy land," not to be found in the corporeal world.[3] In the end, as expected, the

---

[1] "Whoever was convicted of any crime was placed upon a cart and dragged through all the streets, and he lost henceforth all his legal rights" (Chrétien, *Arthurian Romances*, p. 274). We have something similar in the Masonic initiation of an Entered Apprentice, with the same meaning: the profane world or the ego must die (at one moment, Lancelot tried to kill himself for the Queen, using a noose, p. 324). The owner of the cart is a dwarf, who promises to lead Lancelot to the Queen; the dwarf is a token of the subtle forces, indicating that it is about the initiatory process aiming at the supreme goal, the Queen. Also, we could compare Lancelot's humiliation (he is mocked by the people of a town, and is side wounded by a lance pp. 275-277) with the passion of the Christ, regarded not from a religious but initiatory viewpoint. In Lancelot's case the center is marked not by the cross but a bed; later, the story tells about another bed as center (p. 285) (Ulysses' bed is an excellent example of a center, *Odyssey* XXIII.190-200). For Grison, the cart is a vehicle of the soul's journey (*Notes*, ET, no. 440, p. 272), but we should keep in mind that the cart, in its highest significance, is the symbol of the universal manifestation as order, and all the other "instruments" used to apply justice (the wheel, the sword, the cross, the gallows with the noose, etc.) have similar meanings; the convict must be justly punished and his death, from a traditional point of view, is a restoration of order (and a reintegration of the convict in this order) and even a spiritual liberation (like in the case of the good thief from the Christian tradition). For the wheel, see as a famous example the "spiked wheel" of St. Catherine of Alexandria (whose center is Mount Sinai). Regarding the symbolism of the cart as universal manifestation see Guénon, *La Grande Triade*, pp. 192, 202, *Symboles fondamentaux*, pp. 266-267; as the "vehicle" of the being viewed in its state of manifestation see Guénon, *Études sur l'hindouisme*, p. 11.

[2] "His thoughts are such that he [Lancelot] totally forgets himself, and he knows not whether he is alive or dead, forgetting even his own name. Only one creature he has in mind, and for her his thought is so occupied that he neither sees nor hears aught else"; "he likes to think, but dislikes to talk" (Chrétien, *Arthurian Romances*, pp. 279, 287).

[3] To reach this center, a "water-bridge" or a "sword-bridge" must be crossed. For the symbolism, see Guénon, *Symboles fondamentaux*, p. 344.

Queen is liberated, their love prevails and Lancelot beheads
Meleagant, the dragon.[1] However, there is no explicit mention
of the Grail and we could consider Lancelot as the main
illustration of this specific initiatory path (followed a few years
later by Dante), where the target is *Madonna Intelligenza*. In the
Vulgate Cycle though, the old Lancelot is forgotten, likewise his
goal, and a new Lancelot, considered his son,[2] will be the hero
of the Quest of the Grail.

---

[1] Chrétien, *Arthurian Romances*, pp. 355-359.
[2] This son, Galahad (Lancelot's real name was also Galahad), looked identical
to his father ("Bors thought he had never seen anyone so like in looks to
Lancelot," *The Quest*, p. 33).

IX

THE GRAIL TALES

Galahad, the new Lancelot ("from the noble house of King David"), combines two key aspects: first, he is more religious than initiatory[1]; second, he is the king who participates in the withdrawal of the center from the West and its transformation into a permanent Lost Center. The first aspect allowed the Holy Grail to become the spiritual goal, while Queen Guinevere was, together with the old Lancelot, deprived of her profound symbolism[2] and condemned for adultery.

There is an episode where the predominance of the exoteric point of view is well illustrated, and the center is the Church, even though built by Solomon. The center is described as a miraculous ship,[3] reached by three knights of the Holy Grail:

---

[1] The hermetic symbols are now purely religious; the lion becomes Christ and the serpent carries the Synagogue (*The Quest*, pp. 121-122). However, the initiatory path is still there, but now it is openly unveiled: "For this is no search for earthly things but a seeking out of the mysteries and hidden sweets of Our Lord, and the divine secrets which the most high Master will disclose to that blessed knight whom He has chosen for His servant from among the ranks of chivalry; he to whom He will show the marvels of the Holy Grail, and reveal that which the heart of man could not conceive nor tongue relate" (*ibid.* p. 47). In fact, in this story exotericism prevails: everything is explained, unveiled, and Lancelot promptly tells his name (*ibid.* p. 136); it looks like an endeavour to "purify" the Chivalry of the 13th Century, and Lancelot is chosen as the exemplary sinner (*ibid.* pp. 137-159); the esoteric meaning of the chivalric war is forgotten (or not understood anymore), as well as the initiatory sense of the adventures, and only the exoteric teachings are considered spiritual.

[2] Grison rightly compared Guinevere to Wisdom (*Notes*, ET, no. 440, p. 270).

[3] It is well known that the Church is symbolized as a vessel.

Galahad, Bors and Perceval.[1] The Grail story insists on explaining how the Tradition was transmitted uninterrupted, from Adam and Eve to Solomon and then Christ,[2] and later to the Grail Knights; also, it is stressed that, even though Eve (and, generally, the woman) was the instrument of the "fall," the woman is also the means to redemption.[3] The story tells how Eve brought on earth a twig from the Tree of Life and thrust it into the ground, which suggests that, even though she was responsible for the "fall," she is the one who sows the seed of redemption. On the other hand, what we have here is the establishment of an earthly center and the implantation of the Tradition into the world, which transforms the "fall" into an *avatarana*.[4] The new tree grown from Eve's twig could not be destroyed by Noah's flood, which means that it is situated at the top of the Mount of Purgatory, and symbolizes the Center of the World; and so it was found by King Solomon.[5] Solomon

---

[1] *The Quest*, p. 214. For Loomis, this is a "most bizarre" episode (*The Grail*, p. 185).

[2] For Dante, Wisdom is related to the triad Christ, Adam, and Solomon.

[3] In Masonry, even though there are in the lodge only men, the woman is raised to the *principial* level, as Widow; and it is connected to the symbolism of *Madonna Intelligenza*. Francesco da Barberino, who belonged to the *Fedeli d'Amore*, mentioned a mysterious widow, symbolizing *Sapienza*, the Wisdom (see Luigi Valli, *Il linguaggio segreto di Dante e dei "Fedeli d'Amore"*, Optima, 1928, p. 242). Guénon, referring to Barberino's widow, added that the same symbolic widow was important for Giocchino di Fiore and Boccaccio (*L'ésotérisme chrétien*, p. 75).

[4] Eve's twig should be compared to the acacia twig planted on Hiram Abif's grave. The new tree was white, then, with the birth of Abel, became green, and then, with the sacrifice of Abel, became red. We observe the hermetic colours and Abel's sacrifice could be compared to Hiram's.

[5] Of course, the mention of King Solomon is not arbitrary. He is fully connected to *Sophia*, Chivalry, Masonry, the symbolism of the Temple, and now to the Grail. In *Sir Gawain and the Green Knight*, Gawain receives a shield, "with the Pentangle in pure gold depicted thereon," and the following explanation: "And I intend to tell you, though I tarry therefore, why the Pentangle is proper to this prince of knights. It is a symbol which Solomon conceived once to betoken true faith, which it is entitled to, for it is a figure which has five points, and each line overlaps and is locked with another; and it is endless everywhere, and the English call it, as I have heard, the Endless Knot" (p. 49).

will establish a new center, building a Ship (an equivalent of the Temple), predicting Christ's crucifixion, and also a bed supported by three beams (white, green and red) from the Tree of Life.[1]

The center Eve established with the twig brought from Paradise and, later, Solomon's ship, are both in fact "substitute" centers, and the idea of the "lost center" is present, even though not openly uttered. In *Sir Gawain and the Green Knight*, this idea is substantiated in relation to the doctrine of the cosmic cycles, where each cycle "fell" because of a woman: "For here on earth was Adam taken in by one, And Solomon by many such, and Samson likewise; Delilah dealt him his doom[2]; and David, later still, Was blinded by Bathsheba, and badly suffered for it."[3] We have here four cycles ruled by "these four [who] were the finest whom Fortune favoured of all under the Kingdom of Heaven who ever loved well"; King David, presented as the last ruler, is the spiritual father of the Grail Knights, who, even though the way to redemption was showed by another woman,[4] will lose the center again and again.

---

[1] We know the central meaning of the bed. Gahmuret's bed also marked the center (Eschenbach 16). In addition, the bed symbolizes the whole Universe, since the bed, like the cart (Guénon, *La Grande Triade*, p. 192), has a canopy (as in the case of the sacred bed found on the Miraculous Ship, *The Quest of the Holy Grail*, p. 213).

[2] About the symbolism of Samson and Delilah see our *The Everlasting Sacred Kernel*, p. 20.

[3] *Sir Gawain*, p. 120. We may add Noah to this list. In the *Qur'an* (66:10), Noah's wife is an example of an unbeliever (her name was Wâila, which should be compared to Wâhela, Lot's wife, who was in confederacy with the men of Sodom). The Gnostics developed the theme of Noah's wife; she appears under the name of Norea, the daughter of Adam and Eve. Norea set fire to the Ark, because God (Ialdabaoth for the Sethians, an inferior and arrogant God) did not want to let her survive the flood and because Noah's God is considered the evil God. In other Gnostic texts, this God, who sent the flood, is opposed by *Sophia*, the Wisdom that saved Noah in the Ark.

[4] The Virgin Hodegetria. We should also consider the role of Solomon's wife in building the Wondrous Ship (even if she was called an "evil wife," she was the "architect" of the ship) (Malory, *Le Morte D'Arthur*, II, pp. 338-340). In Eschenbach, exotericism corresponds to women and esotericism to men: "God sends the men out secretly; maidens are presented openly. ... Thus

The biggest "loser" is, of course, Perceval, who loses the Grail because he did not ask the question.[1] We could wonder why Lancelot is not enough for the Quest, and why there are others, like Gawain,[2] Yvain, Erec, Perceval, Bors and Galahad, who follow the same Quest. The fact of the matter is that, even though the principles of initiation are immutable, there are various modalities used to accomplish the goal, and there cannot be two identical initiations for two different individuals.[3] The Grail stories with many heroes and many adventures illustrate this basic initiatory concept and also another one, which refers to the multiple degrees that compose the path between the second and the third birth, each degree corresponding to a different modality of the being. Each hero follows a similar, but not identical path, consisting of many adventures, which could seem alike, but actually each adventure has its precise purpose in realizing the goal.

As we said, the Grail Knights are King David's "successors"; if Lancelot's mother "was from the noble line of King David," in Perceval's case, his initiatory beginning reproduces David's story. The reason why David and not Solomon is the "spiritual *pater*" goes beyond the fact that Jesus was from the "house of

---

maidens are given away openly from the Grail, the men secretly" (p. 208) ("The Grail is select in its choosing," p. 207). Similar to the finest four, Lancelot is considered doomed by his love for Queen Guinevere; even Perceval has problems because of his mother. However, in this particular Grail story, *Sir Gawain and the Green Knight*, Gawain during his Quest is tempted three times by the Knight's wife and he prevails over the temptations, which allows him to reach the center.

[1] At one moment, when Perceval is engaged in the quest of the white hart, he beheads it, but loses the head (Boron, *Merlin*, pp. 127-128).

[2] Without going into detail, we mention that Gawain's quest is related to the letter G. In one of his quests, Gawain (his horse is called Gringalet) is related to Guinganbresil, Greoreas, Garis and Guiromelant; also, his brothers are Agravain, Gaheris, and Gareth. In fact, the Grail itself has G as the initial (see Chrétien, *Perceval*, pp. 130 ff). In *Perlesvaus*, Gawain, in order to see the Grail, must bring the sword that beheaded Saint John the Baptist, which was now in the possession of the worst king, called Gurgaran (*La légende arthurienne*, pp. 171-172).

[3] Guénon, *Aperçus sur l'initiation*, pp. 207-208.

David"; it also has to do with the initiatory symbolism of the "youngest." In fairy tales and other initiatory stories the hero is not only very young; he is "the youngest." There is a special reason to present the "elected" one not only as a child, but also as "the youngest."

Jesus states that he is the emblem of God, but his emblem is the child.[1] It is not only a child, but also "the least" among all, and in fairy tales, the youngest brother (or sister) is "elected" to be the solar hero. The laws of symbols act without error: what is the greatest in corporeal order is the smallest in spiritual order; what is the least in corporeal order is the greatest from the divine point of view. The kernel or the seed is the smallest thing, but it is the greatest spiritual entity. David is the youngest child of Jesse, and like Cinderella, he is away when Samuel comes into Jesse's house to find the "elected" child. The eldest of Jesse's sons stands in front of Samuel, who "said: Surely the Lord's anointed is before him. But the Lord said unto Samuel: Look not on his countenance, or on the height of his stature; because I have refused him: for the Lord sees not as man sees; for man looks on the outward appearance, but the Lord looks on the heart."[2] The heart is the sacred kernel, the smallest; the outward appearance is the profane skin, the biggest, and David, the youngest, is actually the Lord's anointed.[3]

Perceval is also the "youngest"[4] and his childhood is similar to that of David[5]; the Biblical David killed and beheaded the

---

[1] "And Jesus, perceiving the thought of their heart, took a child, and set him by him, and said unto them: Whosoever shall receive this child in my name receives me; and whosoever shall receive me receives Him that sent me: for he that is least among you all, the same shall be the greatest" (*Luke* 9:47-8).

[2] *1 Samuel* 16:7.

[3] In the Celtic tradition, Peredur is a child, the youngest of seven brothers (*Mabinogion* 152). See our *The Everlasting Sacred Kernel*, pp. 43-44.

[4] He has two older brothers (Chrétien, *Perceval*, pp. 15-16). But Perceval is also the "Widow's son" (p. 5).

[5] "And Samuel said unto Jesse, Are here all thy children? And he said, There remaineth yet the youngest, and, behold, he keepeth the sheep" (*1 Samuel* 16:11). Even though Perceval is not a shepherd, he is as ignorant as a shepherd: "all Welshmen are inherently more dumb than grazing beasts could be: this one [Perceval] is simple as a sheep" (Chrétien, *Perceval*, p. 10). Tristan,

dragon Goliath[1] and, correspondingly, Perceval killed the Red Knight.[2] There are three visible stages in David's sacred life; in the story of Perceval, there are three well marked initiatory degrees.[3] Each stage in David's case is represented by a symbolic "replacement": first, David takes Goliath's place (he assimilates Goliath's "powers" by taking his armour and, later, his sword[4]); second, he takes Jonathan's place[5]; third, he takes Uriah's place.

Perceval, even though "chosen" (he is the Widow's son[6]), is first presented as a profane ignorant, a situation characterized by two main elements: he does not know his name and he asks question after question[7]; his weapon is the javelin, which was

---

under the name of Drystan, was a guardian of pigs (Jacques Bonnet, *Le Mythe de Tristan et Yseut*, Études Traditionnelles, 1986, no. 493, p. 154; for Bonnet, Tristan was an equivalent of the boar).

[1] Goliath "had a helmet of brass upon his head, and he was armed with a coat of mail" (*1 Samuel* 17:5). His scale-armour is the dragon's skin.

[2] Both David and Perceval are very young; both use "un-chivalric" weapons (David uses the sling, Perceval the javelin); both keep their old garments, but take possession of the dragon's skin (*1 Samuel* 17:54, Chrétien, *Perceval*, p. 36); both illustrate the *Dao De Jing*'s description of the neophyte: "*Nor wear armour and shields in battle* [our italics]; The rhinoceros finds no place in them for its horn, The tiger no place for its claw, The soldier no place for a weapon, For death finds no place in them" (L). We should add that Tristan played the harp like King David (Strassburg 89, Bédier 9).

[3] There is an allusion to these three degrees at the beginning of the story, when Perceval, ready to leave his mother, wants to take with him three javelins and the mother let him have just one ("his mother, though, took two away, because he seemed too Welsh to her," Chrétien, *Perceval*, p. 19); the one left represents the mother.

[4] "And the priest said, The sword of Goliath the Philistine, whom thou slewest in the valley of Elah, behold, it is here wrapped in a cloth behind the ephod: if thou wilt take that, take it: for there is no other save that here. And David said, There is none like that; give it me" (*1 Samuel* 21:9).

[5] "And Jonathan stripped himself of the robe that was upon him, and gave it to David, and his garments, even to his sword, and to his bow, and to his girdle" (*1 Samuel* 18:4).

[6] Tristan also is the "Widow's son" (Bédier 4).

[7] This is not about a super-individual anonymity, but an infra-individual one. Perceval is part of *Prakriti*, like an amorphous substance. About his ignorance and the numerous questions see Chrétien, *Perceval*, pp. 6-11. Wolfram von Eschenbach presented Perceval, in his *Parzival* (*Parzival and Titurel*, Oxford

prohibited by Chivalry.[1] His first main initiatory degree is governed by his mother,[2] and the transition to the second degree occurs when Perceval, after he kills the Red Knight,[3] agrees to wear the Knight's red armour but only over the

---

Univ. Press, 2006), as the Widow's son and living with his mother (Queen Herzeloyde of Waleis) in the forest, away from the world, in a paradise-like place (pp. 50-51). We mentioned before the paradise-like center built by Mayasura; as well, we mentioned already the garden of Irem.

[1] Eschenbach 66. Iwanet, Queen Guinevere's squire, confiscated Perceval's javelin; it is an important episode related not only to the rules of Chivalry, but to the very existence of the medieval traditional society. Another rule: "In those days it was the custom and practice that in an attack two knights should not join against one" (Chrétien, *Arthurian Romances*, p. 37). These rules were an illustration of the initiatory dictum "Ordo ab Chao." If we compare Chivalric war with modern war, we understand how advanced is the decadence of our world (see also Guénon, *Autorité spirituelle*, p. 88).

[2] We should observe the importance of the "kiss," stressed by the mother's teaching (Chrétien, *Perceval*, pp. 17, 21-22). Also, Perceval still does not have a name, his mother calling him "dear son." There is an "initiatory secret" of the mother, which Dante and the Templars knew, and Perceval is about to learn. This secret is one of the main differences between exotericism and esotericism. The one who effectively realizes this secret instantly achieves the center.

[3] Another dragon-like character, Aguynguerran the Red, tried to take Tristan's place by beheading the dragon that the hero had just killed (Bédier 24). Two elements of importance: first, the "Act of Truth," illustrated by the fact that Tristan had cut the dragon's tongue (the difference between cutting the tongue and the head could be interesting to elaborate); second, the colour red, which became the mark of the dragon (like the red donkey, the Egyptian Set's symbol; see Guénon, *Symboles fondamentaux*, p. 161); in *The Story of White Arab* the Red Emperor is presented as a dragon; and the hero's father warns the White Arab to avoid the "red man" and the "bald man." We should add that as Tristan brought Iseult for his master, King Mark, so the White Arab had to bring the Red Emperor's daughter for his master (but in the fairy tale, the master, who is an evil bald man, is killed and the White Arab marries the maiden; therefore, Mark is an aspect of the dragon). However, the colour red also marks spiritual Love (the highest of the theological virtues) and the pinnacle of the Great Work (*rubedo*), and therefore Grison considered that, if the Red Knight was a messenger of the Other World (and red was an infernal colour), Perceval with the red armour represented Love and the Holy Spirit (*Notes*, ET, no. 442, p. 67).

garments made by his mother.[1] The second main initiatory degree is guided by the knight Gornemant of Gohort[2]; now Perceval accepts to abandon the garments made by his mother and her guidance,[3] and to follow an "oath of silence,"[4] which could be found in various traditions as an initiatory stage.[5] During this second degree, Perceval starts the quest of his mother,[6] which means in a way to err, to go astray, to try to go back into the profane world, and also, since his mother died, to

---

[1] Chrétien, *Perceval*, pp. 34-36. Eschenbach's story follows Chrétien's closely (pp. 52-66). In Boron's *Perceval*, the red armour is also present, but here Elainne, Gawain's sister, gives Perceval this red armour; later on we see another red knight (*Merlin*, pp. 117-118, 121-122). In *The Story of White Arab*, the Red Emperor rules the *Greater Mysteries*, while the Green Emperor presides over the *Lesser Mysteries*.

[2] Gurnemanz de Graharz for Eschenbach (p. 69); we notice the letter G. Aurell is right to state that Perceval's initiation has three masters: his mother, Gornemant, and the hermit (pp. 353-354); see Chrétien, *Perceval*, pp. 171-173, where the hermit (who is the Fisher King's brother) and his teachings are presented (he advises Perceval to help the widows and the orphans, and we know that the Templars had a similar duty).

[3] Chrétien, *Perceval*, p. 47.

[4] See also Eschenbach 73-74. In Tristan's tale, the hero taught his dog to remain silent (Bédier 71).

[5] Chrétien, *Perceval*, pp. 48-50. "The wise man's saying's always been that, 'Too much talking is a sin.'" For the Ancient Egyptians, the seers were those who were silent; Plutarch said that the crocodile has received honour because "it is said to be the only tongueless creature and thus a likeness of God" (*De Iside et Osiride*, Univ. of Wales Press, 1970, p. 237). In Boron's *Perceval*, Perceval does not ask the question because "his mother had told him not to talk too much or to ask too many questions" (*Merlin*, p. 141). However, we should stress that, in fact, Perceval, as an excellent neophyte, abandoned any "free will" and obeyed completely his advisers, which makes the episode with not asking the question a success for Perceval's initiation. About this episode see Waite, *The Holy Grail*, p. 439, who considered that only in the Grail stories (and not in any other Mysteries) is there such a thing as asking the question; we should say that Waite is hardly trustworthy: he talks about the "secret" of the Grail (like all current New-Age authors), and considers the Grail to be an "appeal against the Church" and Vatican (pp. 479, 510-511, 520).

[6] "He was eager to get started, to find his mother" (Chrétien, *Perceval*, p. 50). Eschenbach says that the mother died immediately after Perceval left her (p. 55); similarly, Râma's father died after the hero went to the forest. Tristan's mother, Blanchefleur, also died when he was a child, and Tristan became an "orphan" (Bédier 5).

look for something forever lost; on the other hand, this quest of the mother is actually the exhaustion of the possibilities related chiefly to the corporeal world. There are two centers that Perceval reaches, both of them illustrating the end of the world (or of a cycle) and both of them being an opportunity for him to prove his "oath of silence."

The first center is a castle, where Blancheflor, Gornemant's niece, lives, and Perceval finds out that "the fields were barren, empty ground, within there was impoverishment; he found, no matter where he went, the streets were empty in the town. He saw the houses tumbled down without a man or woman there… the town was wholly desolate."[1] Blancheflor is the only real "citizen," she is the center of this modality reached by Perceval through initiatory effort, she is the "sole consciousness,"[2] and the "kiss"[3] liberates her or makes the hero take possession of this state[4]; at the same time, Perceval "refrained from conversation and remained completely silent," and did not ask any questions.[5]

The second center Perceval reaches in his quest for his mother is the Grail castle, but, obviously, he is not spiritually ready for such a realization (he tries to find his mother, not the

---

[1] Chrétien, *Perceval*, pp. 51-52. In Eschenbach, the castle is called Pelrapeire, and its people are starving to death. Here, the lady of the castle is Queen Condwiramurs.

[2] Coomaraswamy, *The Bugbear of Literacy*, p. 101.

[3] In Eschenbach, there is more than a "kiss," since Perceval considers Condwiramurs his wife (pp. 77, 86, 90). Eschenbach is, as usually, more explicit and "naturalistic."

[4] About this symbolism, including the *Fier Baiser*, see Coomaraswamy, *On the Loathly Bride*. A sacred union is suggested, when Perceval said to Blancheflor: "Come lie beside me in this bed; it's wide enough for you to stay… The knight kissed her; within his arms he held her clasped, and gently, tenderly, he grasped and wrapped them in the coverlet, and what is more, the maiden let the knight kiss her… So they lay the night together, side by side and mouth to mouth till morning tide" (Chrétien, *Perceval*, p. 59). There is also, of course, a description of the hero's efforts to liberate the maiden: he defeats Anguingueron, who wanted the girl and was besieging the castle, and then overcomes Clamadeu, Anguingueron's master (see the similarity with Eschenbach 84-85, 87, 90-91).

[5] Chrétien, *Perceval*, p. 54.

Holy Grail)[1] and he is still under the "oath of silence."[2] Therefore, he is a silent witness of the Grail procession[3] and again we find a double meaning: on the one hand, by not asking the question, Perceval loses the Grail[4]; on the other hand, by

---

[1] In Eschenbach, after the episode regarding Queen Condwiramurs, Perceval decided to go and look for his mother (p. 94), which stresses the level of his initiation and the impossibility of reaching the Grail, at this stage.

[2] We may stress that the second center also illustrates the end of the cycle, as proved by the Fisher King's description: "he is a king, you may be sure, but in a battle he was lamed, so badly wounded, he was maimed. He cannot move and must have aid, hurt by a wound a javelin made between his thighs" (Chrétien, *Perceval*, p. 97); the javelin is Perceval's weapon and we could assume, based on the symbolism of the fairy tales, that he was the one who wounded the king (in a similar way Kronos wounded his father, Uranus). The Ugly Maiden also depicted the end of the cycle, when she accused Perceval of not asking the question: "Do you know what we must withstand, if the king cannot hold his land and for his wounds obtains no cure? The married women will endure their husband's deaths [they will be widows, without *Purusha*], lands will be wrecked, and orphaned maids will live abject, with many deaths among the knights, calamities and other plights" (Chrétien, *Perceval*, p. 128). The Ugly Maiden, of course, illustrates the end; at the same time, with the birth of a new cycle she becomes the Beautiful Maiden. In *Perlesvaus*, the end of the cycle is symbolized by Arthur's melancholy, his paralyzed will, the incessant wars, and the dispersion of the Round Table's Knights; even after Arthur gathers back the Knights, a bald girl, who arrives at his Court, illustrates the end, since that is the meaning of baldness (in the Hindu tradition, the hair represents the universal manifestation), and the maid declares that she will get her hair back when Perceval asks the question (see also Eschenbach 107, 132-134); it is curious that Perceval, because he did not ask the question, is considered responsible for this situation (*La légende arthurienne*, pp. 125, 134, 144); it is an upside down view.

[3] Chrétien, *Perceval*, pp. 87-91. In Malory's story, we see the knights sitting around the table and "there was no knight might speak one word a great while, and so they looked every man on other as they had been dumb. ... And when the Holy Grail had been borne through the hall, then the holy vessel departed suddenly, that they wist not where it became; then had they all breath to speak" (*Le Morte D'Arthur*, II, pp. 247-248). Let us make note of the sudden disappearance of the Grail.

[4] A most beautiful damsel admonished Perceval: "Perceval the wretched! You were at the house of your grandfather the rich Fisher King, and saw pass before you the vessel that contains Our Lord's blood, which is called Grail. Three times you saw it pass, but still you didn't have the wit to ask about it! ... you've lost all this" (Boron, *Merlin*, pp. 142-143).

interrupting his silence, Perceval would have lost the Grail forever, since this vision of the Grail is also a temptation, and Perceval must follow a spiritual realization to truly attain the Holy Grail.[1]

The third main initiatory degree begins with Perceval finding the Fisher King's secret (which is related to the end of the world and how a new cycle can start); he also discovers that his mother died (the "outer world"), and he "guesses" his name (an initiatory realization).[2] Eventually, he recovers the head of the white hart,[3] a preview of the supreme deed, when he gains back the Grail.[4]

---

[1] In parallel with Perceval's quest for his mother, Chrétien presents Gawain's quest, which leads to his mother, even though Gawain did not look for her. Gawain arrives at a castle that symbolizes the center: "Across the water [we notice the "other world"] was a grand, strong castle, well designed and planned. I won't allow myself to lie: no living man has laid an eye on any fortress so extensive, so grandiose, and so expensive, built on a cliff, on living rocks" (*Perceval*, pp. 193-194). The castle, which is a substitute for the Earthly Paradise ("by some enchantment or device no traitor, coward can survive; no perjurer can stay alive; inside that palace, cheats die fast," p. 202), is populated with many maids and ladies, and we recall that in Râvana's center lived his many wives, "women of royal sages, Brâhmanas and Daityas, and of Gandharvas, of Râkshasas – all those unmarried girls surrendered from lust to Râvana." Gawain crosses the river, enters the castle ruled by two queens, and reaches the center of the center, which is again a bed, the Wondrous Bed. Gawain is presented as "prisoner in Paradise" (pp. 220-221), and he cannot stand it and leaves the center, even though the queen advised him not to, "please God you never leave this palace for goals so futile to achieve." After he left the castle, Gawain meets Guiromelant, who revealed that one queen is Arthur's mother and the other one is Gawain's mother. We see the other facet of this symbolic quest: if in Perceval's quest the mother represents the outside world, in Gawain's case the mother indicates, the contrary, the center.
[2] "Not knowing his real name at all, he guessed his name was Perceval" (Chrétien, *Perceval*, p. 99). In Boron's *Perceval*, it is stated that Perceval is Alain li Gros' son and Bron, the Fisher King, is his grandfather (*Merlin*, pp. 115, 119). Eschenbach, whose story is more explanatory and open to the public, makes Sigurne (Herzeloyde's niece) reveal to Perceval his name at the beginning of the initiatory endeavour (p. 60).
[3] For Grison, the quest of the white hart is comparable to Erec's quest for Enide (*Notes*, ET, no. 439, pp. 207-208).
[4] Boron, *Merlin*, pp. 143, 154-156. In *Perlesvaus*, the Fisher King dies and the Grail castle is now in the hands of the worst king. Eventually, Perceval (after

These last two phases are fundamental for a *Kshatriya* initiation, and we already elaborated about it when Râma's initiatory path was presented, which is a spiritual journey from the first Adam to the second Adam,[1] from the primordial state before the "fall" to the primordial state after the "redemption," from the virtual Universal Man to the effectively realized Universal Man.[2] As we said before, the decline of the *Manvantara* starts with the cycle itself, at the very moment the wheel commences to turn,[3] and four *avatâras* of Vishnu are needed to restore the "Golden Age" again and again; at the same time, the "revolt" has already begun in the *Satya-yuga*, after the second *avatâra*, but this "revolt" is rather universal and at the *principial* level,[4] concerned with the passing from non-manifestation to manifestation and not so much with humankind, for which reason René Guénon suggested that the counter-initiatory forces in our world have their roots in Atlantis (the "Atlantis Year" begins with the second half of the

---

he found his widowed mother) conquers the castle and the Grail. In this story, Gawain also arrived at the castle, met the Fisher King and witnessed three times the Grail procession, yet, lost in his thoughts, he did not ask the question. The third knight arriving at the Grail castle was Lancelot, who could not see the Holy Grail since "he was guilty of loving the Queen" (*La légende arthurienne*, pp. 187-195, 211-215, 235, 246-251). The quest for the Grail is here an ordinary episode and many things are mixed up, which suggest an individual intervention.

[1] "And so it is written, The first man Adam was made a living soul; the second Adam was made a life-giving spirit" (*1 Corinthians* 15:45).

[2] Guénon, *Le symbolisme de la croix*, p. 23. The Knights Templar's initiation seems to have contained a "fall" and "redemption."

[3] As Guénon said, the founding of the first secondary centers already represented a degree of decline with respect to the Primordial Tradition, because the supreme Center was no longer in direct contact with the outside, but only made contact through the secondary centers (*Symboles fondamentaux*, p. 61). Also, between the beginning and the end of the cycle (marked in the Christian tradition by the Earthly Paradise and Heavenly Jerusalem, which are timeless exterior manifestations of the Center of the World), during the evolvement of the cycle, the center is concealed, and as the cycle evolves, the center becomes more and more hidden (Guénon, *Le règne*, pp. 218-219).

[4] This "revolt" is a projection into our world of Râvana's universal oppressive "rebellion."

"Age of Silver").[1] It was a *Kshatriya* "deviation" and "revolt," which in the end produced a "counter-tradition" and established "counter-initiatory" forces that today are in full development in our world, having as models and masters the "fallen angels."[2] Yet the existence of the "counter-initiation" implies the existence of an "initiation,"[3] which became necessary when the center was lost, and we could consider for the present human cycle the examples we gave regarding Vishnu's *avatâras* that show how, because of the "counter-initiatory" forces and the loss of the center, an initiatory endeavour was needed to destroy those forces and recover the center.

Therefore, in the *Kshatriya* initiatory tales, the hero starts out in an imitation or false paradise and must accomplish a spiritual realization to restore the real center.[4] The feminine aspect, as we know, plays an important role in a *Kshatriya* initiation,[5] and in the Grail stories, it becomes fundamental in explaining the need for initiation. A woman has caused the loss of the center, and a woman will be the spiritual guide in restoring the center (often, this woman is an equivalent of the center). The feminine role has many facets, only one goal: to initiate an initiation.

---

[1] See Guénon, *Le règne*, pp. 351-352.

[2] Guénon, *Le règne*, p. 352.

[3] As Guénon said, the "'counter-initiation' derived from the unique source to which every initiation is attached, and, generally speaking, everything that manifests in our world has a 'non-human' element."

[4] Guénon described how, at the beginning, man spontaneously had an effective consciousness of his possibilities; later on, he lost this conscience (which corresponds to the state of unconsciousness, characterizing the false paradise), and therefore the initiation became necessary to permit the recovery of this conscience and the primordial state (René Guénon, *Mélanges*, Gallimard, 1976, p. 77). See also his work, *Initiation et réalisation spirituelle*, p. 52, where Guénon said that, "for the human beings of the primordial times, the initiation would have been useless and even inconceivable, because the spiritual development, at all levels, was natural and spontaneous, considering their proximity to the Principle."

[5] See Guénon, *Autorité spirituelle*, p. 74, and *Initiation et réalisation spirituelle*, p. 148 (where Guénon relates the *Bhakti-mârga* to the *Kshatriyas* and indicates that the *Kshatriyas'* functions correspond to the collectivity's "psychism," which emphasize the feminine aspect).

Even the fact that Eve instigated the "fall" means that she was ultimately the source of the initiatory quest for the lost center.[1] With her abduction, Sîtâ activated Râma's initiatory journey[2] and at the end there still was a doubt in the hero's mind about her role, since he thought she was impure and Sîtâ had to be purified by fire.[3] On the other hand, Sîtâ is the goal of Râma's initiatory expedition; she is the "way to redemption," and she represents the center. In a similar mode, Helen of Troy's abduction caused the initiatory journey described as the Trojan War, and she is the goal as well, but here, in comparison to Sîtâ, she is not sinless, because of her miraculous love for Paris (Aphrodite's gift).[4] In the Grail stories, a maiden is usually the Grail bearer, and the initiatory adventures are marked by many other maidens and queens. The feminine character either tries to keep the hero from leaving (like Perceval's mother) or pushes him to leave (like in Enide's case); but as contradictory as it seems, in both cases the woman triggers the initiation.

There is another element, which is fundamental in understanding this symbolism related to the *Kshatriya* initiation. All the episodes of the Grail tales or of Râma's way occur mainly and primarily inside the neophyte's being, even though the historic events have their own reality.[5] The sinful Eve, the

---

[1] In fact, as Guénon said, anything could be the occasion and the starting point for a spiritual development, in accord with one's nature; in the case of the *Kshatriyas*, usually this "anything" is a "terrestrial love" or a woman (*Aperçus sur l'ésotérisme chrétien*, p. 89).

[2] However, another woman, the stepmother Kaikeyî, was the one who made Râma leave for the forest.

[3] Agni says: "Râma! This is your Jânakî. She is stainless. She has not committed any sin by word, action, or thought... Her heart is pure and she is absolutely sinless" (*Râmâyana*, p. 552).

[4] The ancient Greek sources are elliptical and contradicting, for the simple reason that, as in fairy tales, the maiden often appears as the dragon's wife, similar to Queen Guinevere.

[5] History and geography are symbols of a higher reality and because of that they have their own relative reality (see Guénon, *La Grande Triade*, p. 196); therefore, the prehistorical facts are not simple "legends" and "myths" (Guénon, *Autorité spirituelle*, p. 21). Yet this inner journey is an initiatory process and not at all mystic or psychological; it is a process much more

Loathly Bride, the ugly maiden, the beautiful maidens, the Grail bearer, Sîtâ, the kiss, the silence and the question are all elements of an inner process. We must not forget for a moment that all the "adventures" are initiatory steps correlated with various modalities, different from the corporeal modality, which are part of an intimate and continuous series of efforts leading to a final transmutation that is in fact a virtual transformation allowing the realization of the second Adam and the consummation of the real wedding in the center of the conditions that limit our world, i.e. in the center of time and space, where the knight fully becomes a Grail Knight, or a Rose-Cross, or a Templar, mastering an unutterable freedom. [1]

---

profound and based on a clear knowledge and precise technique, not something about which we cannot say where it comes from or what it is (Guénon, *Symboles fondamentaux*, p. 60).

[1] In order to really understand the Grail stories, we have to understand first that the corporeal modality is just a tiny part of human individuality and that many of the "adventures" refer to the subtle domain. For example, in the tale of Yvain, the lion, the dwarf and the giant are subtle forces, therefore it is said that the lion fought in Yvain's place; also, the castle with the 300 maidens in the power of the "two hideous, black sons of the devil," is another subtle center (Yvain liberates the maidens; it is interesting to mention that the king of the Isle of Damsels – another name for the center – had to send 30 maidens every year to the two devils, and these maidens are similar to Hindu *ushas* and symbolize the abducted light or dawns) (see Chrétien, *Arthurian Romances*, pp. 233-239, 247-254). Communication with the superior states needs the subtle modalities and their centers as intermediary, and the first step of the initiatory journey has as an objective to restrain the corporeal senses, because otherwise it would be impossible to "centre" the "conscience" on the superior realities. The multiple activities of the corporeal world represent a "distraction," and, as Guénon said, we should consider the etymology of this word (the word comes from Latin *distraho*, signifying "to be pulled in all directions, to tear to pieces, to split, to pull apart"), its significance indicating a "dispersion" in the multiplicity. But even when the corporeal "temptations" are surpassed, the "dangers" in the subtle domain are greater, not only because of the possibility of a higher "distraction," but also because during the initiatory process subtle "powers" are acquired and the journey could fail, either because the neophyte stops happily there, or because he will be diverted on a reverse path leading to disaster (like in the Râvana's case) (see Guénon, *Aperçus sur l'initiation*, pp. 109, 153-155).

René Guénon affirmed that, in accord with the sayings of some *mutaçawwufîn*, "Paradise is still a prison,"[1] referring to the completion of the *Lesser Mysteries* and to the fact that absolute Liberation and the absolute spiritual realization are achieved only after the super-individual states are taken into possession (as part of the initiation into the *Greater Mysteries*) and the Heavenly Paradise is reached. This affirmation could be extended at various levels, applying its symbolism in an analogical mode. For example, even Heavenly Paradise is a "prison," since the most complete spiritual realization involves not only an ascendant process but also a "return," a descent, which means to be liberated from the supreme center and through a sacrifice to reintegrate the non-manifestation and the manifestation. Also, each center hierarchically lower than the Earthly Paradise is a "prison" and needs to be left behind by "liberation," because otherwise it would keep the neophyte in a fake paradise and the initiation would fail; so much the more, the beginning point is a "prison," as it was for Perceval.[2]

The tale of Yvain illustrates what we attempt to clarify. The center here is described with the habitual symbols: the "spring (fountain) which boils, though the water is colder than marble,"[3] the evergreen tree, the rock (made of emerald, like the Holy Grail, with four rubies "more radiant and red than is the morning sun"[4]), and a chapel (temple); and the center is guarded by wild bulls, a boar,[5] a black monster, and a knight.[6] Yvain reaches this center, after he has mortally wounded the

---

[1] *Aperçus sur l'ésotérisme chrétien*, p. 40.

[2] Eschenbach 54, Chrétien, *Perceval*, p. 14.

[3] *Coincidentia oppositorum*. Grison also considered the fountain a "very neat image of the Center of the world" (*Notes*, ET, no. 442, 1974, p. 63).

[4] We see the similarity with the Islamic tradition.

[5] The boar was an important Celtic symbol (see Guénon, *Symboles fondamentaux*, p. 177); it is mentioned more than once in Tristan's story (Tristan was wounded by a boar, Bédier 55, Beroul 63-64; "Iseult dreamt this dream: that she held in her lap a boar's head," Bédier 149). In *Kulhwch and Olwen*, a Welsh tale, Arthur hunting the boar (*Twrch Trwyth*) is an essential element (Aurell 55); Arthur is the bear, and fighting the boar suggests the *Kshatriyas'* revolt.

[6] Chrétien, *Arthurian Romances*, pp. 180-187, 190.

knight and (almost like in Christian Rosenkreutz's case[1]) he will take his place. This center is the one that separates the "holy land" from the "outside darkness"; when Yvain passes the gate, "like a hellish devil the gate dropped down, catching the saddle and the horse's haunches, which it cut off clean," thus the profane part is separated from the sacred one.[2] Yvain not only takes the knight's place as a guardian of the center, but he also marries his wife, who represents the center and the immutable tradition transmitted from knight to knight.[3] But this center and

---

[1] See the Seventh Day of the *Wedding*, where Christian, because he contemplated the nude Venus, must take the Doorkeeper's place.

[2] Chrétien, *Arthurian Romances*, p. 192. The gate is analogous but not identical to the "Sun Door." See also Coomaraswamy, *Traditional Art*, pp. 534-535. Later on, when he helps the lion and kills the serpent, Yvain will cut off the lion's tail (to which the serpent was attached); we could say that the pair lion-serpent is the *jîvâtmâ* and Yvain cuts off *jîvâ* liberating *âtmâ*. There is a similar episode in the Second Day of Christian Rosenkreutz's journey: "Under this gate lay a terrible grim lion chained, who as soon as he saw me arose and made at me with great roaring; where upon the second Doorkeeper who lay upon a stone of marble woke up, and asked me not to be troubled or afraid, and then drove back the lion... I was just about to enter into discourse with him, when it began to ring in the castle, whereupon the Doorkeeper counselled me to run, or else all the pains and labour I had hitherto undergone would serve to no purpose, for the lights above were already beginning to be extinguished. Whereupon I went with such haste that I did not heed the Doorkeeper, I was in such anguish; and truly it was necessary, for I could not run so fast but that the Virgin, after whom all the lights were put out, was at my heels, and I should never have found the way, had she not given me some light with her torch. I was moreover constrained to enter right next to her, and the gate was suddenly clapped to, so that a part of my coat was locked out, which I was verily forced to leave behind me. For neither I, nor they who stood ready without and called at the gate, could prevail with the Doorkeeper to open it again, but he delivered the keys to the Virgin, who took them with her into the court." We may notice the haste, which is specifically initiatory, and here it is suggested that if you linger or yearn after what is behind, you will be cut off entirely from any spiritual realization.

[3] Chrétien, *Arthurian Romances*, pp. 207-208. We notice the same theme of the "forbidden" love. As David provoked Uriah's death, so Yvain killed the lady's husband, and then married her; but there is no moral issue here, since the meaning, which is completely beyond the profane mentality, regards the conquest ("con-quest") of something impossible or very difficult to reach.

this marriage are a "prison" for Yvain, which would make fail his initiation, and here Gawain is the one who influences Yvain to break the chains.[1] The wife agrees to let Yvain go for one year (until "a week after St. John's day"),[2] and, obviously, Yvain forgets to return in time.[3] Consequently, he loses his wife and the center, this forgetfulness characterizing well the end of the cycle (year). Only now is Yvain ready to accomplish the actual spiritual realization of the second Adam and after many adventures he genuinely obtains this wife and the center.[4]

The "forbidden" love is also present in Chrétien's *Cligés*, where the hero is in love with his uncle's wife, Fenice; and in *Tristan and Iseult*.

[1] He asks Yvain: "Will you be one of those who degenerate after marriage? Cursed be he by Saint Mary who marries and then degenerates!" (Chrétien, *Arthurian Romances*, p. 212); the invocation of Saint Mary is significant. This episode also appears in Chrétien's *Erec et Enide*, where the hero reaches a center called "The Joy of the Court" and the king of the castle brings him to the center of a garden (the center of the center of the center), marked by a silver bed with a maiden and defended by a red knight who was "chained" to the girl and could be liberated only if defeated by another knight who would take then his place (in fact the knight and the maiden are *alter-egos* of Erec and Enide; in Tristan's story there are two Iseult, projections of the same character, as Bonnet also noticed in his *Le mythe de Tristan*, ET, no. 493, p. 159). Grison considered The Joy of the Court a prefiguration of the Grail castle; also, he rightly remarked that the knight, defeated and liberated by Erec, is Erec himself (*Notes*, ET, no. 439, pp. 209-210).

[2] In a similar way, Ulysses left Penelope. Also, Christian Rosenkreutz was allowed to leave his post (as a guardian).

[3] One year symbolizes the duration of a specific cycle.

[4] Likewise, Perceval loses the Grail after an initiatory stage, and Râma, after a period of time spent in the forest, loses Sîtâ (after Ayodhyâ, the forest was now imitating paradise, and Râma is shown unconsciously happy; he said: "I feel great delight in this beautiful hill abounding in fruits and flowers and in tuneful birds. ... My forefathers have assigned forest-life as best suited for the attainment of salvation. ... So I feel myself immensely happy"). This situation (the "loss") could be compared to Adam's "fall," when he loses the Grail, but from an initiatory point of view it represents an intermediary phase, when the neophyte becomes acutely conscious of what is lost and what he has to recover (in fact, in the stories, both Perceval and Yvain were repeatedly accused of being silent and forgetting, an initiatory ritual that will illuminate their inner chaos and destroy their ignorance). If Adam's Paradise was genuine, Râma, Yvain, and Perceval lived in a paradisiacal imitation characterized by unconsciousness, and their first initiatory stage represents the

There is another tale transmitted by Chrétien, *Erec et Enide*, where the same symbolism is envisioned. Again, the first Adam is simulated by the wedding of Erec and Enide,[1] and the loss of this status is provoked by Enide herself, who tells Erec that he spends the whole time in a *dolce far niente*.[2] It is not difficult to recognize the Biblical theme: Enide, like Eve, induces the "fall" from paradise; moreover, for this action, Erec forces her to observe an "oath of silence" as punishment, but Enide, like

---

exhaustion of the past and inferior states and could be considered a descent to "hell." Râma's contentment, Yvain's forgetfulness (followed by his life in the forest as a madman and a savage, Chrétien, *Arthurian Romances*, p. 217), and Perceval's silence are three different ways to characterize the same decisive initiatory moment. Dante starts his *Divine Comedy* with: "Nel mezzo del cammin di nostra vita,/ Mi ritrovai per una selva oscura,/ Chè la diritta via era smarrita./ Ah! quanto, a dir qual era, è cosa dura,/ Questa selva selvaggia e aspra e forte,/ Che, nel pensier, rinnova la paura!"; he is already in the forest and acknowledges that he has lost (*smarrita*) the way (and Beatrice), which means that he needs an initiatory journey comprising a descent to hell, and cannot climb directly to Paradise ("the short road up the hill," *bel monte*, is barred, *Inferno*, II, 120). We should stress in the end that only the real Paradise could bring authentic joy and contentment ("il dilettoso monte,/ Ch'è principio e cagion di tutta gioia," *Inf.* I, 77-78), metaphysical silence and a spiritual forgetfulness (which is the oblivion of the ephemeral world and a full awareness of God), since Paradise is their principle.

[1] Only now did Enide reveal her name. Another element worthy to be mentioned is the symbolism of the "kiss" (King Arthur kisses Enide, because he killed the White Hart and the one who did such a deed had to kiss the most beautiful maiden; we see that the "kiss" suggests a spiritual transmission) (Chrétien, *Arthurian Romances*, pp. 23-24, 27).

[2] "He [Erec] devoted all his heart and mind to fondling and kissing her [Enide]... he rarely left her society." Enide told him: "In this land they all say – the dark, the fair, and the ruddy – that it is a great pity that you should renounce your arms... I am blamed for it ... You must choose another course" (Chrétien, *Arthurian Romances*, pp. 32-34). As we see, Enide kindles the initiatory journey, but she also is its reward. In fairy tales and in the Grail stories, there are always various and even contradictory characters (ugly maiden, beautiful maiden, etc.), but also circumstances that would initiate the initiatory journey. We can envision them as activities of the spiritual influence; when the neophyte receives the spiritual influence at the very beginning of his path (this is the actual "initiation"), he must carry on with a personal, continuous and inner effort supported and "provoked" by that spiritual influence (and the means the spiritual influence uses are innumerable and in accord with the different modalities of the being).

Eve, will violate the oath three times.[1] Yet, from an initiatory point of view, Erec would complete a trial each time Enide broke the silence.[2] While the hero suffers an initiatory death, his

---

[1] On the contrary, Perceval keeps his oath faithfully.

[2] We cannot elaborate here about the initiatory trials symbolically described in the Grail stories, but we would like to give an example. Erec abandons the simulated paradise and his first initiatory step is a purification stage composed of various trials that would purify his "soul" and "mind" (it is about emptying, and so, preparing the heart to receive illumination; in the end, absolute purification would occur when the ignorance is completely destroyed). This stage must be covered in a very alert rhythm (in a rush, as Dante did), without hesitations and looking back over the shoulder, without stalling, since the adverse forces, more and more nervous (and so, more aggressive), will try to stop the liberation process. Queen Guinevere, for instance, punished Lancelot because he hesitated (even though just for a second) in climbing into the cart (Chrétien, *Arthurian Romances*, pp. 319-320, 327-329; we may notice in the same story Lancelot's rush). Erec's journey is, therefore, described as a run away, and because he is not allowed to look back towards the profane world, his wife will be the one who, apparently violating her "oath of silence," will inform him about the adverse forces coming after them. These forces, represented by knights, are divided into three groups and described as brigands. The first group is composed of three knights, the second of five. What should be stressed is that all these trials obey a specific symbolism and initiatory rules, including a complex gradation. Erec defeats the first three knights progressively: he kills the first one, wounds the second one and throws to earth the third knight (Chrétien, *Arthurian Romances*, pp. 37-38). This gradation describes symbolically how the adverse forces are not only destroyed but converted and reintegrated into the center; this reintegration is an "act of mercy" that in the Grail stories is symbolized by the gathering of the defeated or liberated knights at Arthur's center; that is what Perceval did (Boron, *Merlin*, pp. 124, 134; Chrétien, *Perceval*, pp. 65, 109; Eschenbach 85, 91) and also Erec (he sent to Arthur the knight he liberated from the giants' hands, Chrétien, *Arthurian Romances*, pp. 56-59). The reintegration in Erec's story is underlined by the fact that he strives to gather all the horses of the defeated knights, first three and then the other five (he also defeated the second group of five knights) (pp. 38, 40); the horse symbolizes the subtle elements (mainly *prâna* and *manas*). We may add that the three horses of the first group represent three degrees marked by colour: white as milk, black, and dappled (about the symbolism of black and white see Guénon, *Symboles fondamentaux*, pp. 134, 306; see also Gawain's horse half white half black, Chrétien, *Perceval*, pp. 183-185, and Eschenbach's Feirefiz, p. 25; or the black and white sheep on the two sides of the river, met by Peredur, *The Mabinogion*, p. 175; and see the Templars' banner).

wife will be abducted,[1] which means that now, with the "loss of the Grail," Erec is ready for the actual spiritual realization; indeed, he is resurrected, kills the dragon, liberates Enide and, right after that, the real wedding takes place.[2]

At the end of the tale, Erec, like the White Arab, returns to Arthur and is crowned king. This last episode is noteworthy for two reasons: first, the spiritual authority is the one that accomplished the crowning[3]; second, Erec's robe is described. Regarding the second element, we should remember that, symbolically, a spiritual realization is a journey from Loathly Bride to Beautiful Maiden, from frog or Cinderella to princess, from serpent to solar maiden. Therefore, Perceval is depicted at the beginning of his voyage poorly dressed,[4] while Erec, at the end, will appear as a projection of the Lord of the World[5]; the

---

[1] Chrétien, *Arthurian Romances*, pp. 61-64. Before that, he had to fight the giants and liberate a knight (who is, in fact, a subtle modality of Erec). Tristan also had to fight a giant on an island (center); and the giant is Iseult's father! (Bédier 14-16). Enide becomes the dragon's wife (a count plays the role of the dragon). It is interesting that, if in David's case he provokes Uriah's death, here Enide saves Erec's life accepting to become the count's lover (another example of how the symbols cannot be limited and constrained in systems and schemes).

[2] Chrétien, *Arthurian Romances*, p. 68. The same end for *Cligés*: the uncle dies; Cligés marries Fenice and becomes emperor (Chrétien, *Arthurian Romances*, pp. 176-178).

[3] "The Bishop of Nantes himself, who was a very worthy and saintly man, anointed the new King in a very holy and becoming manner, and placed the crown upon his head." And "when they [Erec and Enide] came to the cathedral, the procession came out from the church with relics and treasures to meet them. Crosses and prayer-books and censers and reliquaries, with all the holy relics, of which there were many in the church, were all brought out to meet them" (Chrétien, *Arthurian Romances*, p. 89) (the spiritual influence that participated at the coronation was transmitted through the ritual by the bishop himself and by the relics).

[4] "His mother, as befitted him, attired and outfitted him, in a course hempen shirt and breeches made in the Welsh style, ... a hood and coat of buckskin leather" (Chrétien, *Perceval*, p. 16).

[5] "Four fairies had made it [Erec's robe] with great skill and mastery [we notice the number 4]. One represented there geometry, how it estimates and measures the extent of the heaven and the earth, so that nothing is lacking there; and then the depth and the height, and the width, and the length [the

horse, which plays a fundamental role in Chivalry (and initiation),[1] also illustrates this symbolism.[2]

---

tri-dimensional cross]. Such was the work of the first fairy. And the second devoted her effort to the portrayal of arithmetic, and she strove hard to represent clearly how it wisely enumerates the days and the hours of time, and the water of the sea drop by drop, and then all the sand, and the stars one by one, knowing well how to tell the truth, and how many leaves there are in the woods... The third design was that of music, with which all merriment finds itself in accord, songs and harmonies... The fourth ... the best of arts she there portrayed. She understood astronomy, which accomplishes so many marvels and draws inspiration form the stars, the moon, and the sun... Concerning whatever inquiry it makes of them, whether in the past or in the future, they give it information without falsehood and without deception. The work was portrayed on the stuff of which Erec's robe was made, all worked and woven with thread of gold" (Chrétien, *Arthurian Romances*, pp. 87-88) (the four fairies represent the *Quadrivium*, and these four arts could symbolize the higher initiatory degrees, as it is in Masonry; see Guénon, *Mélanges*, pp. 102-103).

[1] Erec, we recall, strove to gather the eight horses. Yvain's horse lost its backside passing the gate. Lancelot, during his journey, lost two horses (they died) and so is somehow forced to climb into the cart (Chrétien, *Arthurian Romances*, pp. 271-275). The horse plays a major role in Gawain's story (see Chrétien, *Perceval*, pp. 180-185, 190-191).

[2] Gawain's horse "was ridiculous in gait. The nag was ugly and ill fed, with a lank neck and outsized head, long dangling ears, and all the flaws and blemishes old age can cause" (Chrétien, *Perceval*, p. 192). The nag has to be in accord with the "ugly maiden," therefore, when Perceval found a horse that "was so forlorn, so miserable and travel worn, so starved and lean, so gaunt and tired," this horse belonged to the "ugly maiden" ("no maid more miserable was seen") (Chrétien, *Perceval*, pp. 102-103). Even more interesting is Perceval's case, because he had a nag when he departed from home: "[Perceval] repeatedly asked his mother for a horse... She thought: 'I don't want to deny him anything, but it'll have to be a most miserable nag'" (Eschenbach 54). An echo of this symbolism appears in Dumas' *Les trois mousquetaires*, where D'Artagnan, when he left his home to go to Paris, received a crock horse from his father. However, in fairy tales, the jade, after eating fire, changed into a beautiful and miraculous horse (see for example *The Story of White Arab*).

X

THE LOST CENTER

In a traditional society, every element was a symbolic support and had a sacred meaning, which is why in Chivalry, for example, the clothes, the arms, the shield, the armour and the horse's robe all bore hermetic and spiritual significances. In *Erec et Enide*, the sceptre Erec received at his coronation was "of one solid emerald, fully as large as your fist. I dare to tell you in very truth that in all the world there is no manner of fish, or of wild beast, or of man, or of flying bird that was not worked and chiselled upon it with its proper figure."[1] However, this Art was transmitted uninterrupted from a "non-human" source and it would be a serious error to think that it was the product of an individual mind; we find the same Art in Homer's *Iliad*, when Hephaestus made Achilles' shield.[2]

---

[1] Chrétien, *Arthurian Romances*, p. 89.

[2] "First he shaped the shield so great and strong, adorning it all over and binding it round with a gleaming circuit in three layers; and the baldric was made of silver. He made the shield in five thicknesses, and with many a wonder did his cunning hand enrich it. He wrought the earth, the heavens, and the sea; the moon also at her full and the untiring sun, with all the signs that glorify the face of heaven... He wrought also two cities, fair to see and busy with the hum of men. In the one were weddings and wedding-feasts... About the other city there lay encamped two hosts in gleaming armour, and they were divided whether to sack it, or to spare it and accept the half of what it contained. But the men of the city would not yet consent, and armed themselves for a surprise; their wives and little children kept guard upon the walls, and with them were the men who were past fighting through age... He wrought also a fair fallow field, large and thrice ploughed already... He wrought also a field of harvest corn, and the reapers were reaping with sharp sickles in their hands... He wrought also a vineyard, golden and fair to see,

The above examples, from the *Iliad* and the Grail stories, are not just something "theoretical" or belonging to "legends" and "myths"; in accord with the precise laws of symbolism, they are to be found on a historical level as well, bearing the same esoteric significance.[1] Therefore, King Roger II of Sicily had a robe similar to that of Erec, depicting the cosmos[2]; and Geoffrey Plantagenet's shield could symbolize the center.[3] However, it would be a mistake to consider that the Angevins (mainly Geoffrey, Henry II, and Richard the Lionheart) simply copied the Grail stories or that, on the contrary, the Grail stories illustrated the historical Angevins, the Templars and others; in fact, the esoteric and initiatory realm has the highest

---

and the vines were loaded with grapes... He wrought also a herd of horned cattle. He made the cows of gold and tin... Along with the cattle there went four shepherds, all of them in gold, and their nine fleet dogs went with them. Two terrible lions had fastened on a bellowing bull that was with the foremost cows, and bellow as he might they haled him, while the dogs and men gave chase: the lions tore through the bull's thick hide... Furthermore he wrought a green, like that which Daedalus once made in Cnossus for lovely Ariadne. Hereon there danced youths and maidens whom all would woo, with their hands on one another's wrists... There was a bard also to sing to them and play his lyre, while two tumblers went about performing in the midst of them when the man struck up with his tune. All round the outermost rim of the shield he set the mighty stream of the river Oceanus" (XVIII, 508 ff).

[1] History, properly viewed, has its place in the realm of integral knowledge, but its real value is represented by the possibility of ascending, using the historical (and, therefore, ephemeral) events, beyond these very contingencies. See Guénon, *Autorité spirituelle*, pp. 21, 23.

[2] See Aurell's illustration and comment, and also Robert Viel, *Les origines symboliques du blason*, Bert, 1992, pp. 73 ff. about the "cosmic robe" of the emperors and kings. Viel, even though he quoted Guénon, uses mixed sources and should be read with caution; his viewpoint is more profane than traditional (his expression "vital universal force" is really disturbing).

[3] See Viel's viewpoint (pp. 31-40). Geoffrey Plantagenet (called the Handsome), count of Anjou, and later duke of Normandy, was the son of Fulk V of Anjou, who became in 1131 king of Jerusalem and was very close to the Knights Templar. Viel suggested a mystic connection between the Angevins, Grail stories and Jerusalem, and Eschenbach was the one who wrote about it (Viel 41, Aurell 395-396).

reality, and only by referring to this reality we can understand the historical data.[1] There is no doubt that the Angevins and the Templars were close to the Grail stories, but chiefly because of the initiatory lore concealed there, and from this perspective we should understand Arthur's archetypal function for Henry II and Richard the Lionheart, even though, in their case, the royal position also has to be taken into account.[2] Similarly, the importance of Glastonbury in relation to Arthur's tomb is primarily an illustration of the symbolism of the center and its reality, rather than an "invention." It was said that at the beginning of Richard the Lionheart's reign, the tomb of Arthur at Glastonbury was invented, yet others believed that Henry II was the one who ordered the excavations in search of Arthur's remains.[3] However, apart from these "historical" elements, René Guénon considered Glastonbury, with its "Temple of the Stars," as an image of the primordial center where the tradition was conserved and transmitted from the ancient times to the druids and then to the Christian monks. He also assumed that the Templars had to have a role in this conservation, which would be in accord with their supposed connection to the "Knights of the Round Table" and their alleged role as "guardians of the Grail."[4]

Waite presented various hypotheses that considered either the Grail legend as a source for the Order of the Temple, or the Knights Templar as models for the Grail Knights,[5] but Guénon

[1] Ponsoye specified that probably Eschenbach, when he referred to the Angevins, had in mind a "spiritual race" rather than the historic dynasty (Pierre Ponsoye, *L'Islam et le Graal*, Denoël, 1958, pp. 46-47). On the other hand, René Mutel did not agree with Ponsoye, and for him Anjou was a real spiritual center ("*L'Islam et le Graal,*" *Vérités, ambiguities et erreurs*, Études Traditionnelles, 1959, no. 352, pp. 53-55), but this is not the point. See also Mutel (pp. 55-58) about the historic Angevins.
[2] Aurell presented the scholars' opinions about how much Henry II took advantage of the Grail legend to make Arthur his ancestor (pp. 166. 168, 186).
[3] See Aurell 195-202.
[4] *Symboles fondamentaux*, pp. 114-116.
[5] *The Holy Grail*, pp. 383-395. Waite, who considered the Grail legend a purely Christian tradition, rejected the Templar influence or association. Regarding

judged that Waite had treated this subject too superficially; also, the German version of the Grail legend, Guénon added, deserves more consideration,[1] and we know that saying this he had in mind the Islamic influence[2] and the Templars of Munsalvaesche, mentioned by Eschenbach.[3] Yet, Eschenbach's open remarks regarding these elements are also a "sign of the times," because the end of the Christian traditional society was near[4] and, faithful to the meaning of the center's name

the Templars and the Grail, see also Evola pp. 183 ff.; for Evola, the fight against the Order of the Temple could be qualified as a *crusade against the Grail* (it is the title of Otto Rahn's well known book).

[1] *Symboles fondamentaux*, p. 61.

[2] However, it does not mean that, as Geay thought, Guénon's work was of Islamic inspiration, which would drastically limit it (*Mystères et sign. du Temple maç.*, pp. 14, 174).

[3] "It is well known to me that many a valorous hand resides by the Grail at Munsalvaesche. In search of adventure they constantly ride many a journey. Those same templars – wherever they meet with grief or fame, they count it against their sins. A combative company dwells there … A noble brotherhood resides there. By their combative hands they have kept people from all lands in ignorance of Grail, except for those who are summoned there, to Munsalvaesche, to the Grail's company"; and the Templar's battle-cry was suggested: "'Amor!' was his battle-cry" (Eschenbach, *Parzival*, pp. 197-201). Grison suggested a connection between the Templars and the *Cours d'Amour* (*Notes*, ET, no. 437-438, p. 165); and Guénon showed the similarity between the "palais de l'Amour" of Andreas Capellanus, who lived in the 12th Century, the Temple of Solomon and the *Cour d'Amour*, all representing the center (*Aperçus sur l'ésotérisme chrétien*, pp. 92-93). It seems that Eschenbach was part of the Order of the Temple (Ponsoye 42). We also should mention how Joseph of Arimathea made a red cross (with his blood) on a white shield (Malory, II, pp. 255-256), but there is no direct reference to the Templars' colours; however, it is very probable that the Knights Templar's initiatory teachings and the Grail legend come from a common source. We note that Pope Eugene III granted to the Templars, in 1147, the right to wear a red cross on their white robe.

[4] The signs were already present in Charlemagne's times. It is said that Charlemagne "grieved because this scholarship was not reaching the high standards of the early fathers, and in his dissatisfaction he exclaimed: 'If only I could have a dozen [like the Knights of the Round Table] churchmen as wise and as well taught in all human knowledge as were Jerome and Augustine!' The learned Alcuin answered: 'The Maker of heaven and earth Himself has very few scholars worth comparing with these men, and yet you expect to find a dozen!'" and the author added: "I prefer to rely upon the chance of our

(Munsalvaesche), Eschenbach tried to save and preserve in his work parts of a "secret history."[1]

A special interest raised Eschenbach's narrative about an Islamic influence. As René Guénon irrefutably showed, the Islamic civilization strongly influenced the development of Western Christian society[2]; we also tackled this subject, describing, in addition, how the Near West (the Byzantine Empire) had its own contribution to Islam and Western Europe.[3] Nevertheless, with regard to the esoteric domain, Islamic influence and collaboration were essential as Eschenbach's story or Christian Rosenkreutz's legend indubitably revealed.[4] Following Guénon, Pierre Ponsoye tried

---

ancestors being truthful rather than upon the lazy inaccuracy of men of our own period" (Einhard and Notker the Stammerer, *Two Lives of Charlemagne*, Penguin Books, 1969, p. 102).

[1] Eschenbach presented the symbolism of the Grail in a more explicit manner. He stressed the connection between the Grail and Paradise and he indicated that the Grail is a heavenly stone.

[2] Guénon, *Aperçus sur l'ésotérisme islamique*, pp. 76 ff.

[3] See our article *The Near West* in Sophia, Oakton, Volume 9, No. 1, 2003. In *Cligés*, Chrétien assumed that Chivalry came from the Byzantine Empire (*Arthurian Romances*, pp. 91-93); Grison's interpretation that the Byzantine princes came looking for light in the West, at Arthur's court, should be partially revised (*Notes*, ET, no. 439, p. 211). René Mutel agrees with Ponsoye regarding the Islamic influence, but he also acknowledges the "Byzantine imprint" and "the immense influence of the Oriental Christianity" (ET, no. 351, pp. 23-25, no. 357, 1960, p. 28) (the Byzantine influence upon Masonry would be, among others, an interesting subject to pursue; see, for example, Jean Tourniac, *Lumière d'Orient*, Dervy, 1979).

[4] Guénon wrote many times about this subject. See *Aperçus sur l'ésotérisme islamique*, pp. 86-87, *L'ésotérisme de Dante*, pp.42-43 (where, besides the relations between the Orders of Chivalry and Islam, and the Islamic influence upon Rosicrucianism, he mentioned the Islamic influence upon Dante), *Aperçus sur initiation*, p. 243, *Orient et Occident*, p. 164. There is no doubt that the Templars, for example, had special relations with their Muslim counterpart; but also Richard the Lionheart and other knights, even though they fought the Saracens, had enthused relations with them. Therefore Chrétien mentions three Saracens as examples of excellent knights: "Do you see that knight yonder with a golden band across the middle of his red shield? That is Governauz of Roberdic. And do you see that other one, who has an eagle and a dragon painted side by side upon his shield? That is the son of the King of Aragon, who has come to this land in search of glory and renown. And do

to prove that the Grail legend was profusely in debt to the Islamic influence, Eschenbach's message in *Parzival* being that Islam was a "predestinated agent" of the divine Work.[1]

A rivalry between orthodox traditions and a discussion about which is the only true one do not help; similarly, a competition between the Christian and Islamic influences with regard to the Grail legend leads us astray from the essential point, which is, and it should not be forgotten, that the Grail tale uses history as a cover and pretext to transmit fundamental initiatory truths, chiefly for the benefit of the *Kshatriyas*. For this reason a comparison with fairy tales is always valuable, since the fairy tales clearly are beyond history. No doubt, the Grail stories had

---

you see that one beside him, who thrusts and jousts so well, bearing a shield with a leopard painted on a green ground on one part, and the other half is azure blue? That is Ignaures the well-beloved, a lover himself and jovial. And he who bears the shield with the pheasants portrayed beak to beak is Coguillanz of Mautirec. Do you see those two side by side, with their dappled steeds, and golden shields showing black lions? One is named Semiramis, and the other is his companion; their shields are painted alike. And do you see the one who has a shield with a gate painted on it, through which a stag appears to be passing out? That is King Ider, in truth... That shield was made at Limoges, whence it was brought by Pilades, who is very ardent and keen to be always in the fight. That shield, bridle, and breast-strap were made at Toulouse, and were brought here by Kay of Estraus. The other came from Lyons on the Rhone, and there is no better under heaven; for his great merit it was presented to Taulas of the Desert, who bears it well and protects himself with it skilfully. Yonder shield is of English workmanship and was made at London; you see on it two swallows which appear as if about to fly; yet they do not move, but receive many blows from the Poitevin lances of steel; he who has it is poor Thoas" (*Arthurian Romances*, pp. 343, 364); we quoted the whole text to illustrate the science of heraldry at work. The "language (or gesture) of the shield" is composed not only of what is on the shield, but also of the shield's position; in *Parzival*, a profound distress is illustrated by carrying inverted shields (Eschenbach 43).

[1] Ponsoye 99. Of course, the idea of an "Islamic influence" was not too agreeable to the Christian "traditionalists"; after René Guénon disappearance, Jean Reyor, his collaborator, shifted Études Traditionnelles towards Christianity (see ET, no. 354, p. 189) and Ponsoye's ideas were fervently refuted by René Mutel in that journal. Even today such a battle continues. If some, like Gilis or Geay, try to limit Guénon to an "Islamic inspiration," others (Catholics) accuse him of destroying Christianity, or, even worse (like the antitraditional people), of fuelling extremism.

their roots in various traditions, including the Celtic and Islamic ones, and in the times of the Crusades they became completely Christian; yet, their essence belonged to the universal symbolism and it was primarily a support for the Royal Art (that is why they flourished during Chivalry's reign and, of course, they reflected outwardly that epoch with the Chivalric Orders, the Templars, the subtle *concordia* with Islam, etc.).

Eschenbach's *Parzival* is, though, important to our work for its references to the symbolism of the center. First, Toledo, where Kyot[1] found "lying neglected, in heathen script, this adventure's fundament," appears as a spiritual center, not because it was externally an important city, where Jews, Christians and Muslims lived together during a so called "golden age" (*La Convivencia*), but because here was kept the Grail story, written by "a heathen, Flegetanis," who "was born of Solomon's line."[2] Second, Baldac (Baghdad) is described as the Center of the World, but again, even though Baghdad was called the "City of Peace" (*Madînat as-Salâm*) by the Abbasids, it was only a substitute for the real center.[3] The

---

[1] Guénon assumed that "Kyot de Provence" was in fact the Benedictine Guyot de Provins; he mentioned Eschenbach as a "Suabian Templar" (*L'ésotérisme de Dante*, p. 35).

[2] Eschenbach 191. Toledo was the ancient Roman city Toletum, and later became the Arabic Tulaytulah, and it is easy to see the homophonous relation with the name of the primordial center Tula (Tolosa, the ancient name of Toulouse, also deserves attention). Eschenbach described how Perceval invocated God: "If God's skill possesses such help, let it direct this Castilian of mine along the best road for my journey," and "he laid the reins over the charger's ears." Something similar occurred to Muhammad the Prophet when he was riding his camel without reins. Toledo was the capital city of Castile, and it could be suggested that Perceval's Castilian horse belonged to this center, and was directing him to another center, the "Fontane la Salvatsche," where the chaste Trevrizent resided (who was the son of Frimutel, the Grail King, and brother of Herzeloyde, Repanse de Schoye, Schoysiane, and Anfortas, the Fisher King). See also Ponsoye 22-24, 38; he suggested that Flegetanis could be *Felek-Thâni*, "the second sphere," which was the circle of Mercury with Jesus (Seyidnâ Aïssa) as Pole (pp. 26-27).

[3] Gahmuret, the young Angevin, went to this center, where Baruch, representing the Lord of the World, ruled (Eschenbach 7-8). Ponsoye specified that Baruch is not a man's name but designates a function (ET, no.

allusion to the real center is made in a curious way: Gahmuret marries Belacane, the black queen of Zazamanc, and then[1] Herzeloyde, the white queen of Waleis[2]; and Feirefiz Angevin, the son of Gahmuret and Belacane, is a miraculous child, "both black and white was his appearance."[3]

With respect to the traditional Christian society (which prospered between the reign of Charlemagne and the end of the Order of the Temple), we have to acknowledge the existence of various substitutes and secondary spiritual centers, sometimes difficult to identify or "localize," but its prime center should be placed, symbolically and not only, in the East (*Oriens*).[4] Obviously, the Grail Castle or Temple,[5] Corbenic,[6] and the Round Table represent such secondary centers,[7] but we should

359, 1960, p. 140). Baruch means "the blessed one" in Hebrew. See Ponsoye 51-53. See also Mutel (ET, no. 351, p. 37), where he considered Baghdad not the supreme center but symbolizing this center.

[1] Gahmuret went to Toledo (Eschenbach 26).

[2] "Lady Herzeloyde cast such radiance that even if all the candles had been extinguished, she alone would have supplied light enough." We see here two traditions, the Grail tradition (Herzeloyde, the Fisher King's sister) and the Islamic one (the Muslim Belacane), converging into Gahmuret. It is interesting to notice the similarity with the fairy tales: "The Queen of Waleis … was a maiden, unmarried, and offered two countries as well as her person to whoever won the prize there" (Eschenbach 27).

[3] Eschenbach 25. The hero of *The Story of White Arab* also is black and white. As Guénon explained, the center is black within (because it is the "place" of non-manifestation) and white on the outside (because from the center the light radiates) (*Symboles fondamentaux*, p. 136). See also Ponsoye 96-97.

[4] This center was a direct projection of the Center of the World, and the Grail Knights, as well as the Knights Templar, had the main function of ensuring communication between the Orient and the Occident. "This center was always described, at least in the 'historical' times, as situated at the Oriental side" (Guénon, *Le Roi*, p. 70, and *Aperçus sur l'initiation*, p. 246, about the Rose-Cross as liaison between East and West).

[5] See Mutel, ET, no. 355, pp. 221-222, where he comments on Titurel's Grail Temple.

[6] Lacy 44-45.

[7] As Guénon said, the real "secret of the Holy Grail" has to be correlated with the very "positive" founding of the spiritual centers; in the Islamic tradition, the word *es-sirr*, the "secret," refers to what is the most central in the being,

not forget the analogy that exists between the supreme center and the secondary ones, which implies similar descriptions and makes it more difficult to identify which is which.[1] Another center was Glastonbury, which Guénon considered to be one of the images of Tula, the Hyperborean center, established as residence for the spiritual powers derived from it; yet to identify Glastonbury with Avalon, as some scholars did, would mean to identify the image with the original center, which is evidently a mistake, since Avalon is another name for the supreme center.[2] We could add other, more exterior, centers, like Toledo or the Anjou province, and many others mentioned in the Grail stories (as we presented them above), but which should be regarded, first and foremost, from the perspective of an inner spiritual realization.

Besides Baldac, there was another Oriental center mentioned in the Grail legend: Sarras, located between Babylon and Salamander, where Joseph of Arimathea brought the Holy Grail sheltered in an ark (as Christ told him to do). Sarras was the center of the Saracens (hence their name) and the Temple of the Sun was there, the most beautiful temple in the city, where Joseph entered with the Holy Grail[3]; Joseph was lodged in a palace called the Spiritual Palace.[4] And Christ, Malory reported,

---

and has a direct relation to the supreme Center, since it is something that cannot be communicated (*Symboles fondamentaux*, pp. 61, 271).

[1] See Guénon, *Symboles fondamentaux*, p. 41.

[2] Guénon, *Symboles fondamentaux*, pp. 116-117. As Guénon said, Avalon was inaccessible (from a historical or external point of view).

[3] Lacy 16-19, *The Quest of the Holy Grail*, pp. 58-60. See also Mutel, ET, no. 355, pp. 225-6. The Temple of the Sun corresponds to the supreme center, called Syria (not the historical one), Avalon or Heliopolis (Guénon, *Symboles fondamentaux*, pp. 116-118); Guénon also mentioned the "solar citadel" of the Rose-Cross (p. 69). We should mention the existence in Sarras of an altar dedicated to Apollo, whom the Saracens called the god of wisdom (Lacy 31) (the word "Avalon" is the equivalent of "Apollo").

[4] The Spiritual Palace is another name for the center. It seems obvious that, in this narrative, the Islamic influence is openly admitted, but the symbolism could be more complicated. Evalach, the ruler of Sarras, is called Evalach the Unknown, because no man knew in what country he was born; Joseph encouraged Evalach to destroy the idols. It appears that we have here a

told Galahad: "This is the holy dish wherein I ate the lamb on Sher-Thursday. And now hast thou seen that thou most desired to see, but yet hast thou not seen it so openly as thou shalt see it in the city of Sarras in the spiritual place."[1] Indeed, the Holy Grail was so elusive: "And when the Holy Grail had been borne through the hall, then the holy vessel departed suddenly, that they wist not where it became."[2]

What we learn from these symbolic episodes is that the secondary centers of the Occidental tradition became more and more unstable, that less and less persons were qualified to find and see the Holy Grail, and that the final quest leading to the spiritual center Sarras, represented, from a deeper perspective, a withdrawal into the supreme center, which was another way of saying that, for the Western world, the center became a "lost center" and the Grail was lost forever.[3] Christ ordered Galahad to leave the "kingdom of Logres"[4] and escort the sacred Vessel to Sarras,[5] where Galahad became the new king; yet after his death, a hand came down from heaven that took the Holy Grail and the lance, "and carried them up to heaven, to the end that no man since has ever dared to say he saw the Holy Grail."[6]

The Holy Grail, when recovered, instead of finding its peace and stability in the center of the Round Table, was escorted to Sarras, to *Oriens*. Robert de Boron told a similar story: Merlin

---

Nestorian influence (whoever these Nestorians would be; see Guénon, *Franc-Maçonnerie*, I, p. 169).

[1] Malory, II, p. 366, *The Quest of the Holy Grail*, pp. 274-276.

[2] Malory, II, p. 248.

[3] As Guénon said, the disappearance of a secondary center meant that it was reabsorbed into the supreme Center, since this one was its origin and the secondary center was an emanation of it. However, there are degrees to discern, since the secondary center could become more hidden rather than lost forever, and the same symbolism could be used for all these situations, as it happened in the case of the Grail (it was raised to heaven or it was transported to the Realm of the Prester John) (*Symboles fondamentaux*, p. 61).

[4] This was another name for an Occidental center; Guénon assumed that the name Logres came from that of the Celtic god Lug (*Symboles fondamentaux*, p. 117).

[5] *The Quest of the Holy Grail*, p. 276.

[6] *The Quest of the Holy Grail*, pp. 282-284. Ponsoye 144-146.

informed King Arthur, who was sitting at the Round Table, that Perceval found the Grail, and so Arthur's "reign has seen the fulfilling of the greatest prophecy of all time. For the Fisher King is healed, and the enchantments of the land of Britain are cast out."[1] Yet the Holy Grail did not come back to the Round Table, "and squires and knights of the Round Table said they would stay with King Arthur no longer, but would cross the sea and seek out knightly deeds." Boron also described how Arthur attacked and conquered France, becoming its king; and then he fought against Rome (which was allied with the Muslims); and finally he battled Mordred, his nephew, who stole the throne, and in this war Arthur died. Arthur told his knights that he will live eternally in Avalon: "I shall not die. I shall be carried to Avalon." Merlin told all these events to Blaise, who wrote down everything: "how Arthur had been carried off to Avalon ... and how the knights of the Round Table had ended their days."[2]

The dispersion of the Grail Knights and Arthur's withdrawal to the inaccessible island of Avalon symbolize nothing else but the end of the Occidental tradition and the loss of its center (and the communication with the supreme center). Wolfram von Eschenbach's *Parzival and Titurel* ended with the same conclusion. After Perceval fought and made peace with his brother Feirefiz Angevin, they left Arthur's center together to acquire the Holy Grail. But only Repanse de Schoye could carry the Grail; she married Feirefiz and left the Occident, travelling to India, to the Realm of Prester John, which, as we know, represents the supreme center, *Oriens*, "near Paradise"; Munsalvaesche also left the West and was transported to the same *Oriens*.[3]

---

[1] Boron, *Merlin*, p. 156.

[2] Boron, *Merlin*, p. 171.

[3] Eschenbach 309-344; Evola 199-200; Ponsoye 55, 135. See also Albrecht's *Jüngere Titurel*. As Guénon said, the Nestorians (or those who used to be called by this name) constituted an important part of the external cover for Prester John's center (*Le Roi*, p. 16). See also Guénon, *L'ésotérisme de Dante*, pp. 35-36.

A traditional society lives only if it is supported and nourished by a spiritual center,[1] and the connection with the center is assured and guarded by a few "chosen" persons that participated in esotericism, which means that esotericism is an intermediary between the center and the exotericism.[2] For the Christian traditional civilization, after the Templars disappeared, after the Holy Grail disappeared, and after the Rose-Cross disappeared, this connection with the center was forever broken and the center was lost (or, from another viewpoint, became hidden).[3] The Church, as a traditional organization, continued to exist, apparently unchanged,[4] but now it became more and more vulnerable and it has visibly declined, which made the chances for redemption decrease; the Church became more and more hostile with regard to any esotericism, and if, in the beginning, it was right to banish some heterodox sects (among

---

[1] Therefore the Holy Grail had this function to heal and nourish. Guénon gave another example: the stone that produced water to the Jews (*Symboles fondamentaux*, p. 294). We could add a similar function for the head (and in particular for the mouth); therefore, it is more than an aesthetic element the head carved in stone, having an open mouth, from which a spring comes out.

[2] It is true that normally initiatory organizations, like Masonry and Chivalry, aimed at the Earthly Paradise (supporting an initiation that corresponded to the *Lesser Mysteries*), which also was the goal of religious "salvation," but esotericism implicitly helped the realization of "salvation," not to say that because of the fundamental differences between the esoteric and exoteric techniques, the "chosen" ones, that is, the "qualified" ones, could effectively complete their spiritual realization and, therefore, they would become support and secret inspiration for the people at large. They were, as "adepts," the genuine messengers of the center. Esotericism and the initiatory organizations were the ones capable of surpassing sectarianism and, even though based on a specific traditional form, they could surpass it and enter the domain of Unity.

[3] Another loss was that of the Sacerdotal Art, to which belonged Operative Masonry (the art of the builders of the medieval cathedrals was indeed "sacerdotal," and the Church should take this into account). Guénon said that around the year 1459 this Art was lost for Masonry, and the expression "royal art" used today in Masonry is just a feeble substitute, which also has lost its real meaning (see Guénon, *Autorité spirituelle*, pp. 36-37). It is known that in the year 1459 (on Easter day) the new Masonic statutes were approved in Regensburg, and then in Strasburg; we see the role played by Germany in recovering, but also in distorting and revealing the esoteric data.

[4] See Guénon, *Symboles fondamentaux*, p. 62.

which there were sects that had some initiatory data but did not
know what to do with them), later the Church banished
everything and with such an ardour that it ended fighting
against itself.[1]

---

[1] From the Year's perspective, the decadence of the Church is only natural.
There is a mysterious episode, a "problem event," which scholars could not
solve in an adequate way: "Moses striking the rock," and this episode
illustrates the mentioned decadence, even though the Christians theologians
considered it a representation of Christ's crucifixion. In the *Exodus*, it is said:
"And the people thirsted there for water; and the people murmured
against Moses, and said, Wherefore is this that thou hast brought us up out
of Egypt, to kill us and our children and our cattle with thirst? And Moses
cried unto the Lord, saying, What shall I do unto this people? They be almost
ready to stone me. And the Lord said unto Moses, Go on before the people,
and take with thee of the elders of Israel; and thy rod, wherewith thou smotest
the river, take in thine hand, and go. Behold, I will stand before thee there
upon the rock in Horeb; and thou shalt smite the rock, and there shall come
water out of it, that the people may drink. And Moses did so in the sight of
the elders of Israel" (17:3-6). Here we witness an esoteric episode, meant only
for the "elders of Israel" (the "elite"), the "rock in Horeb" representing the
spiritual center and for this reason Saint Paul could compare Christ with this
rock: "and all drank the same spiritual drink. For they drank from the spiritual
Rock that followed them, and the Rock was Christ" (*1 Corinthians* 10:4) [The
real everlasting Rock is Christ and not Peter]. In a subsequent episode, the
"striking the rock" becomes an exoteric event, unfolding in front of all people
and where Moses [the Church] shows his human arrogance: "And the people
chode with Moses, and spake, saying, Would God that we had died when our
brethren   died   before   the   Lord! And   why   have   ye   brought   up
the congregation of the Lord into this wilderness, that we and our cattle
should die there? And wherefore have ye made us to come up out of Egypt,
to bring us in unto this evil place? it is no place of seed, or of figs, or of vines,
or of pomegranates; neither is there any water to drink. And Moses and Aaron
went from the presence of the assembly unto the door of the tabernacle of
the congregation, and they fell upon their faces: and the glory of the Lord
appeared unto them. And the Lord spake unto Moses, saying, Take the rod,
and gather thou the assembly together, thou, and Aaron thy brother, and
speak ye unto the rock before their eyes; and it shall give forth his water, and
thou shalt bring forth to them water out of the rock: so thou shalt give
the congregation and their beasts drink. And Moses took the rod from before
the   Lord,   as   he   commanded   him. And Moses and Aaron gathered   the
congregation together before the rock, and he said unto them, Hear now, ye
rebels; must we fetch you water out of this rock? And Moses lifted up his
hand, and with his rod he smote the rock twice: and the water came out

As René Guénon affirmed, "in Europe, any tie consciously established with the center through the regular organizations is broken today,[1] and it has been like this for some centuries."[2] This interruption, Guénon added, did not happen suddenly, but in a sequence of phases, starting with the destruction of the Order of the Temple.[3] After this event, the ties with the center became hidden, but still active through various organizations, heirs of the Templars, like *Fede Santa*, *Fedeli d'Amore*, the *Massenie du Saint-Graal*, and probably others, about which we do not know anything. The Rose-Cross played an essential role for a while, but in the end, they also withdrew to the Realm of Prester John (Guénon said about them that they "withdrew to Asia, somehow reabsorbed towards the supreme Center, for which they were its emanation"),[4] and therefore, today, for the

---

abundantly, and the congregation drank, and their beasts also. And the Lord spake unto Moses and Aaron, Because ye believed me not, to sanctify me in the eyes of the children of Israel, therefore ye shall not bring this congregation into the land which I have given them" (*Numbers* 20:3-12). While in the esoteric episode the main request is "water" and the need stems from [spiritual] "thirst," in the exoteric episode people ask for many things and only at the end do they ask for water; and Moses strikes the rock in front of all the people, unveiling an esoteric mystery and disobeying Lord's command to use words, not the rod; not to mention that Moses brought the water in his name and not in the name of the Lord. Similarly, the Church has changed and declined.

[1] We must insist that the spiritual center is the one that inspires and supports any regular initiatory organization and its withdrawal means ceasing any activity. However, even if an initiatory organization does not understand anymore what this tie means and it is not conscious anymore of the spiritual influence that it shelters, it is possible to continue transmitting this influence; and, because this transmission is uninterrupted, someone among those who have received the spiritual influence (through initiation) could become conscious of this connection with the center (Guénon, *Aperçus sur l'initiation*, p. 66). Guénon alluded here to Masonry.

[2] *Le Roi*, p. 70.

[3] *Le Roi*, pp. 70-71, *Symboles fondamentaux*, p. 113. It was predicted that six centuries must pass after this event before some hidden teachings could be revealed, and this prediction should be connected to René Guénon's function (see Guénon, *Aperçus sur l'ésotérisme chrétien*, p. 70, where Guénon applied this prediction to Dante's work).

[4] See also Guénon, *Aperçus sur l'initiation*, p. 243.

Occidental world there is no more "holy land" to guard. And René Guénon asked instead of a conclusion: "how long this situation would last, and could we hope that the ties will be restored?"[1]

What does a "lost center" or the withdrawal to *Oriens* mean? In Nicholas of Cusa's words it would be a reabsorbing of the explication into complication, which means that the "lost center" will hide as an essential possibility in the supreme Center, which "is a 'place' not in a topographical or literal sense, but in a transcendental and *principial* sense"[2]; therefore, because the Center "realizes itself in any 'center' that is consecrated and established in a regular way," these centers will withdraw into the Center, not *in corpus* but *in spiritus*, when the corresponding traditions are exhausted and invaded by the "outside darkness." This means that the spiritual influences will be reabsorbed into the Center, but there were cases when also the *corpus* disappeared, being reabsorbed as essential possibility. When it is said that acquiring the Holy Grail means to obtain the "sense of eternity,"[3] this does not allude to a topographic "place" but to a *principial* one, representing the primordial state, the center of time and space, and simultaneously the center of the integral being. Therefore, "it is useless," Guénon said, "to look for a 'geographical' place where the Rose-Cross retreated," and the most convenient appellation would be the "Realm of Prester John," which is a representation of the supreme spiritual Center and where all the traditional forms are guarded and preserved in a latent state, until the end of the present cycle, namely, all the

---

[1] *Symboles fondamentaux*, pp. 62, 113. It is on this hope that Michel Vâlsan based his opinion about the foundation, in 1908, of the *Ordre du Temple rénové* with René Guénon as commander. Immediately after René Guénon's death, in the special issue of the *Études Traditionnelles* (no. 293-294-295, 1951), he wrote an article called *La fonction de René Guénon et le sort de l'Occident*, in which he suggested that the birth of the *Ordre du Temple rénové* could be a result of the activity of the ancient retired center of Western tradition, aiming at the restoration of a Western elite, with Guénon as initiatory pivot (p. 250).

[2] Guénon, *Aperçus sur l'initiation*, p. 265.

[3] Guénon, *Symboles fondamentaux*, p. 40.

traditional forms that, for one reason or another, ceased to manifest externally, that is, ceased as explication.[1]

Beyond any limitations, the "lost center" could at will appear again, and disappear again, which is what happened to the Grail Castle or to the Temple of the Rose-Cross, for example. And as the *dwîpas* of the Hindu tradition subsist in an "invisible" mode and appear successively to the exterior with the various *Manvantaras*,[2] so the "lost center" will appear again with a new secondary or principal cycle.

The reapparition of the "lost center" would mean the manifestation in the corporeal world of the spiritual influences (as "activity of presence"[3]) and of some extraordinary "messengers" charged with a special "mission."[4] There is though one condition: the world should be ready to receive them or, at least, to have a "desire" for them and be conscious of the current disastrous situation; and even though the entire world could not be conscious, at least an "elite" must be, and this "elite" must act, not in its name, as Moses wrongly did, but in the name of God.[5]

For where two or three are gathered together in my name, there am I in the midst of them.[6]

[1] Guénon, *Aperçus sur l'initiation*, p. 243.
[2] Guénon, *Aperçus sur l'initiation*, p. 270.
[3] Guénon, *Aperçus sur l'ésotérisme islamique*, p. 125.
[4] It means that the Occident, to become again traditional, needs to have representatives in the Center of the World (Guénon, *Orient et Occident*, p. 202).
[5] As René Guénon explained, "the work of an initiatory organization must always be accomplished "in the name" of the spiritual principle from which it proceeds (*Initiation et realisation spirituelle*, Éd. Trad., 1980, p. 185).
[6] *Matthew* 18:20.

www.ingramcontent.com/pod-product-compliance
Lightning Source LLC
Chambersburg PA
CBHW061737270326
41928CB00011B/2267